The
Baby
on the
Fire
Escape

ALSO BY JULIE PHILLIPS

James Tiptree Jr.: The Double Life of Alice B. Sheldon

The
Baby
on the
Fire
Escape

CREATIVITY, MOTHERHOOD,
AND THE MIND-BABY PROBLEM

Julie Phillips

W. W. NORTON & COMPANY
Independent Publishers Since 1923

For information about permission to reproduce selections from this book,
write to Permissions, W. W. Norton & Company, Inc.,
500 Fifth Avenue, New York, NY 10110

For information about special discounts for bulk purchases, please contact
W. W. Norton Special Sales at specialsales@wwnorton.com or 800-233-4830

Manufacturing by Lakeside Book Company
Book design by Ellen Cipriano
Production manager: Lauren Abbate

ISBN: 978-0-393-08859-5

W. W. Norton & Company, Inc., 500 Fifth Avenue, New York, N.Y. 10110
www.wwnorton.com

W. W. Norton & Company Ltd., 15 Carlisle Street, London W1D 3BS

1 2 3 4 5 6 7 8 9 0

To Kit, Jan, Eise, and Jooske
My mother, my husband, my children

Contents

The Mind-Baby Problem   *1*

"The Presiding Genius of Her Own Body"   *21*

Outlaw Mothering: *Alice Neel (1900–1984)*   *27*

All the Time: *Art Monsters and Maintenance Work*   *57*

The Discomfort Zone: *Sex and Love*   *65*

Incompatible Pleasures: *Doris Lessing (1919–2013)*   *73*

The Discomfort Zone: *The Unavailable Muse*   *103*

"Poems Are Housework": *Books versus Babies*   *111*

All Happy Families: *Ursula K. Le Guin (1929–2018)*   *121*

The Discomfort Zone: *Ghosts*   *149*

The Discomfort Zone: *Late Success*   *159*

Mother, Poet, Warrior: *Audre Lorde (1934–1992)*   *165*

The Discomfort Zone: *Not Being All There*   *195*

Freedom: *Alice Walker (1944–)*   *211*

The Baby on the Writing Desk; *or, Two Things at Once*   *239*

Her Own Version: *Angela Carter (1940–1992)*   *245*

Time and the Story   *273*

ACKNOWLEDGMENTS   *279*
NOTES   *281*
BIBLIOGRAPHY   *308*
TEXT CREDITS   *311*
ILLUSTRATION CREDITS   *312*

The Mind-Baby Problem

The maternal subject [is] a figure that disrupts or interrupts our notions of subjectivity. (LISA BARAITSER)

I insist . . . that motherhood is an undiscovered country in the literary sense, one we must venture into lest our experience [go] unrecorded. (SARAH RUHL)

PICTURE AN ARTIST OR WRITER at work, and you probably imagine sustained, solitary concentration. Proust, scribbling in bed in his cork-lined room. Yeats, descending from his tower, encountering his two children, and asking, "Who are they?" Wittgenstein, who is said to have eaten nothing but Swiss cheese sandwiches for weeks on end because even changes in the flavor of his food disturbed his thoughts.

The artist may be in the midst of family life but obsessively at work, like Henri Matisse, whose painting pulled him in like a "vortex." "He could think of nothing else," his daughter said. The creator may be an "art monster," Jenny Offill's term for the creator who lives only for the work.

The great writer may be a detached observer, a flâneur soaking up scenes of city life. If natural beauty is his subject he may write alone in a cabin in the woods or wander "lonely as a cloud," enjoying "the bliss of solitude." She may agree with the poet Mary Oliver that "creative work needs solitude. It needs concentration. . . . It needs the whole sky to fly in, and no eye watching," or with Gertrude Stein, who warned, "It takes a lot of time to be a genius, you have to sit around so much doing nothing, really doing nothing."

A typical picture of a woman with children is of someone whose children are constantly breaking in. Perhaps she has shut herself into a room to write. Her kids have promised not to knock or to make noise. But she knows they are there because they are lying down and *breathing* under the door. Adrienne Rich longed in vain, amid "the discontinuity of female life with its attention to small chores," for the "freedom to press on, to enter the currents of thought like a glider pilot, knowing that your motion can be sustained, that the buoyancy of your attention will not be suddenly snatched away." Alice Walker saw her daughter in her mind's eye as she worked, "the lonely sucking of her thumb / a giant stopper in my throat."

In place of the solitary flâneur, imagine Naomi Mitchison in a London park, writing on a board balanced on her pram. Think of Shirley Jackson making plot notes in the kitchen while dinner was on the stove; Toni Morrison driving to work with a pad of paper in the car so that she could write whenever the traffic slowed. Here the act of writing is not continuous but provisional, contingent, subject to disruption—and yet the words are still coming and the work is getting done.

THE DIVISION BETWEEN mothering and creative work once seemed (more or less) absolute. Sylvia Plath feared that a woman must "sacrifice all claims to femininity and family to be a writer." Tillie Olsen wrote: "In the twenty years I bore and reared my children . . . the simplest circumstances for creation did not exist." It was a physical problem, a time problem; it was also a question of selfhood. "The obligation to be physically attractive and patient and nurturing and docile and sensitive and deferential . . . contradicts and *must* collide with the egocentricity and aggressiveness and the indifference to self that a large creative gift requires in order to flourish," Susan Sontag said, overstating things as usual, but the expectation that women (more than men, even now) should be ever present for their children does compete with creative selfhood.

Sometimes mothers had trouble giving themselves permission. Alice Neel said that until she received a major retrospective in her seventies, "I had always felt in a sense that I didn't have a right to paint because I had two sons and I had so many things I should be doing and here I was painting." Sometimes the judgment came from others: Neel's in-laws claimed, on no evidence, that she had once left her baby on the fire escape of her New York apartment when she was trying to finish a painting. It's a vivid image of the dangers, in their mind, of trying to do two things at once.

Maternal bliss conspires with maternal guilt to erode creative work. Margaret Mead: "[It's] not because the baby cries, but because the baby smiles so much," that the hours get lost. Jenny Offill: "The love you feel for your child has a way of obliterating whatever you used to think you loved."

In 1962 Olsen could still state that almost no mothers, or any other "part-time, part-self persons," had written books that would endure. But in or about that same year, the careers of women with children were beginning to flourish, not just in ones and twos but in numbers big enough to matter. Mothers found ways to do their work, and were recognized for it: Doris Lessing won the Nobel Prize; Ursula K. Le Guin was awarded the National Book Medal, America's highest literary honor. Alice Walker won a Pulitzer and sold millions; Audre Lorde opened a conversation around intersectionality. Angela Carter was acknowledged as one of the defining literary voices of twentieth-century Britain, and Susan Sontag as one of the great English-language critics. Alice Neel saw her art accepted into the canon.

I've tried in this book to trace the course of that change. I've tried to find out what mothering plus creativity looks like, not just in the first few years, but as part of a life story. What does it mean to create, not alone in "a room of one's own," but in a shared space? What kinds of work have come out of that space? What is the shape of a creative mother's life?

THIS WAS MY PLAN: to explore the blank spot on the map where mothering and creativity converge. I had never been able to convey the full power of my own life as a mother: I remember how empty even the simple sentence "I have two children" felt in comparison to the experience, as though I was recounting a dream that made no sense in daylight. Because I didn't have words, I wanted others to speak for me. In investigating the lives of great women, I hoped to see my own experience with new eyes.

That blank spot should have told me something. The more I read and wrote, the more the place where mothering and creative work come together seemed not to be an intersection of identities, but a negative space, an impossible position. I read brilliant first-person accounts of mothering but couldn't see patterns or a path. The stories of my subjects' lives as mothers wouldn't hang together. When I looked at the work, the mothering vanished, and vice versa. When I read essays, memoirs, and stories, I found contradictions, fragments, anecdotes, scraps of enlightenment. I encountered what psychoanalytic theorist Lisa Baraitser calls the "intractable problem of how . . . intellectual and maternal labor appear to cancel one another out."

Parenting affects, and is affected by, each person's circumstances, and is affected too by race, resources, sexuality, family relationships, (dis)ability. Not all mothers have given birth; not all end up raising their children. The women I wanted to write about came to mothering by different paths, did or didn't have a partner, were older or younger, had more or less money and support. They became pregnant by accident or by choice, fostered a teenager, confronted infertility, lost a child. They admitted anger and pain, rejected stereotypes ("superwoman," "angel in the house"), explored maternal ambivalence.

But where is mothers' creative self? Do mothers have inner lives? What is the subjective experience of being a mother, and why, despite a steadily growing body of writing on the phenomenology of mothering, does it still seem, on a deeper level, so unnarratable, undramatic, everywhere in practice, but in theory nowhere?

I started saying I was "exploring maternal subjectivity." That got some people's attention, especially academics', or at least it didn't make their eyes glaze over the way "I'm writing about mothers" did. Proposing "mother" as a subject position surprises people, and it also, on the evidence, baffles them. Over and over again my friends forgot the subject of my book, until I started to wonder if my "blank space on the map" was unthinkable, beyond memory.

Searching for a theory of motherhood that might make my narratives hang together, I investigated psychoanalysis. It was like looking at the Brueghel painting of the Fall of Icarus. In the foreground, children grow and develop, while off in the distance the mother as a person with a narrative of her own disappears from view.

Psychoanalysis focuses so intently on the child's development that the mother, in her paradoxical state—created by the child but existing apart from it—can never be the central character. The psychoanalytic insistence on the Oedipal drama as the origin of both creativity and the self relegates the mother not only to a supporting role but to a predetermined one. "Both essentialism and normativity loom large" in thinking about mother love, Baraitser writes, "and our need to maintain a fantasy of maternal love as a 'given' suffuses a huge variety of psychological discourses."

The Freudian view (as Susan Sontag observed, to her annoyance, while she was ghostwriting her husband's book on Freud's influence) was that mothering was the end of growth and achievement for a woman. As a mother she merely assumed her natural role. By the time a woman is thirty, Freud claimed, her psyche "has taken up its final positions, and . . . there are no paths open to her for further development." If anything, she relinquishes her independent self entirely. The early analyst Alice Bálint wrote in 1939 that the ideal situation was one in which "the interests of mother and child are identical."

More reassuring to creative women is the idea that one can be a "good enough mother." This was the term the psychiatrist D. W. Winnicott used in describing a mother-child relationship that is healthy and nurturing despite the mother's less-than-complete attention to the baby. "Good enough" is useful in dismissing the demands of "attachment parenting" and other attempts to move the goalposts of maternal devotion. But good enough for whom? In this model it's still the child's needs, not the mother's, that are being met and the mother remains, in Baraitser's words, "the impossible subject, par excellence . . . a shadowy figure who seems to disappear from the many discourses that explicitly try to account for her."

My sexuality and gender can be theorized as social and historical constructs. My vocation as a writer may originate in my childhood experience. But what about my relationship to my child, and to myself as a mother? Am I supposed to put a fence around that and call it a theory-free zone? Is it true that the mother is, as the French feminists have suggested, unspeakable in a phallocentric tongue? Maggie Nelson writes that she rejects the "quarantining of the feminine or the maternal from the realm of intellectual profundity." But she also quotes the poet Alice Notley on her new baby: "He is born and I am undone—feel as if I will / never be, was never born."

Playwright Sarah Ruhl, looking at the lack of mothers as protagonists, wonders if "the experience of motherhood is unstageable—beyond narrative and language." Then she worries that "the experience is tellable, but no one wants to see it. Mothers aren't meant to have points of view."

In her memoir *A Life's Work*, Rachel Cusk comments that "the experience of motherhood loses nearly everything in its translation to the outside world. In motherhood a woman exchanges her public significance for a range of private meanings, and like sounds outside a certain range they can be very difficult for other people to identify." In queer theory mothers are too "heteronormative," while African American writing emphasizes the primacy of mothers, but often in a context of community-building rather than individual creative agency.

You might think that the parenting of infants is simply too low in status, too abject, too deep in what Plath called "the stink of fat and baby crap," for theoretical interest. But that can't be the real problem, since even bodily waste has been a site of critical thought—though when I page through the French theorist Dominique Laporte's tongue-in-cheek *Histoire de la merde*, I find that even he has left out the most poop-stained of all human relationships, the parent-infant bond.

Nonetheless, diapers challenge drama. When my kids were small I went out in the evening to see the conclusion of the Lord of the Rings *trilogy in a movie theater. Wiping a bottom the next morning, I felt my elated identification with the future ruler of Middle-earth ebbing away. I'd been banished from epic into low comedy. I wasn't the hero of the story; I was one of Monty Python's peasants, saying, "'ow do you know he's the king?" "e 'asn't got shit all over 'im."*

Many writers almost reflexively protect the mother-child space, conspiring to keep it unexamined. This might be a question of the child's privacy ("Mom, you're embarrassing me!") or one's own inadmissible feelings. It might be lack of distance: Sarah Manguso asks, "Is it possible to truly observe one's own child, as a writer must, while also simultaneously loving him? Does a mother have something like writer's block—*perceiver's block?*"

Feminist psychoanalyst Julia Kristeva sees mother love as an "escape from representation" and its unrepresentability as its subversive power. In her famous essay "Stabat Mater" she calls mothering "a catastrophe of identity" that casts the self into "that 'unnameable' that somehow involves our imaginary representations of femininity, non-language, or the body." This relegation to the "unnameable" feels not far removed from Le Guin's cynical observation that to become a wife and mother is to turn into "a nobody." I find that unsatisfying, another mythification. I can't believe that mothering is beyond representation. I think making mothers mysterious is another way of keeping them unacknowledged. *It also sounds like one of my kids complaining that they can't find their favorite shirt. Where have you looked? Have you tried looking harder?*

WHEN WRITERS AND ARTISTS describe their experience of mothering, they often use the word "divided." Louise Erdrich muses that parents "live and work with a divided consciousness" that is "uncomfortably close to self-erasure." Rachel Cusk describes being torn away from a conversation to console a crying baby as being "split in two. . . . Like a divided stream, the person and the mother pay each other no heed, although moments earlier they were indistinguishable: they tumble forwards, each with its separate life."

Sometimes it feels more like disintegration. When Offill became a mother she felt "like a bomb had gone off" in her life. Devoted to the needs of a small baby, Gwendolyn Brooks couldn't "call my soul my own." Baraitser writes that mothering is complicated by "the constant attack on narrative that the child performs: literally breaking into maternal speech . . . as well as [the mother's] own self-narrative which is punctured at the level of constant interruptions to thinking, reflecting, sleeping, moving, and completing tasks. What is left is a series of unconnected experiences that remain fundamentally unable to cohere."

In *Maternal Encounters: The Ethics of Interruption*, Baraitser speculates that to be a parent is to have a subjectivity that is shared, impinged on, that has to "budge up" to make room for a radically unpredictable other. When she became a mother she "felt chained to her child, unable to finish a sentence, think, or sleep, lost her sense of being agile, capable, quick, self-reflective." As she explored this new state, new ways of seeing emerged. "The child's relentlessly unpredictable and extreme presence forced her into an appreciation of experiences she had skimmed over before." She felt "heightened sentience, a renewed awareness of objects, of one's own emotional range and emotional robustness, . . . a renewed encounter with oneself as a speaking subject."

Instead of wishing for more coherence, Baraitser looks at what could be gained from embracing a shared self. Against the solitary writer in the tower she places a subjectivity that, itself interrupted, is alert to the questions that interruption asks of "normal" life. Against the figure of the flâneur she offers the mother engaged in parental parkour, practicing the extreme sport of getting a fully loaded stroller over curbs and up and down flights of stairs. She invites us to look at whether this struggle with maternal "stuff," in an "environment that [the mother] rediscovers through perpetual navigation," might in its own way be generative.

In fact, Baraitser argues, psychoanalytic theory has been saying for some time now that the unified self is an illusion. To recognize that well-boundaried self as a retrospective fantasy, rather than an indispensable writing aid, might help writers and artists cope with the "attack on narrative" that they suffer in caring for a child.

Like Offill, who sought to "capture this new fractured consciousness on the page," Manguso wrote her memoir of motherhood as "an assemblage of already exploded bits that cohere anyway, a reminder that what seems a violent interruption seldom is."

Sarah Ruhl writes:

There was a time, when I first found out I was pregnant with twins, that I saw only a state of conflict. When I looked at theater and parenthood, I saw only war, competing loyalties, and I thought my writing life was over. There were times when it felt as though my children were annihilating me . . . , and finally I came to the thought, All right then, annihilate me; that other self was a fiction anyhow. And then I could breathe. I could investigate the pauses.

In accepting interruption, she was able to recollect herself and recover her artistic agency.

I'M DRAWN TO this image of interruption in part because of my own sense, as I've worked on this book, that I can't get it together. The stories of the artist and the mother exist side by side, occasionally breaking into or commenting on each other, but more often stubbornly refusing to be one thing. Writing and mothering seem to turn away from each other, thematically speaking, and the practical, real-life divisions between work and parenting run right down the middle of my text.

But maybe the stories aren't meant to come together. If it's so hard to move beyond anecdote and discord onto some higher plane of maternal theorizing, maybe it's because the interruptions are what I'm meant to be noticing. Perhaps interruption and disruption are not what keep me from seeing mothering clearly, but are the conditions of maternal creativity.

The second-wave feminists hoped that gender equality would resolve all the practical and emotional contradictions of writing and mothering. This is Lessing's dream of a "golden notebook," the one that would join the separate narrative strands of a woman's life. It is Hélène Cixous's image of women writing in the "white ink" of the maternal body, as if nursing an idea and a baby were the same and not two different acts done sequentially or simultaneously by the same body and mind. It is Adrienne Rich writing wistfully, "There must be ways . . . in which the energy of creation and the energy of relation can be united."

In this narrative, the problem is interruption (whether by children, guilt, or self-doubt) and the resolution is harmony. But as I look at mothers' lives, I think these visions may not do justice to the actual maternal creative process, which alongside periods of harmony seems to involve foregrounding disruptions, leaping across gaps, piecing together careers, and other provisional and drastic measures. The frustration—and pleasure— that writer-mothers experience seems better expressed with images of

improvisation and compromise than of multiple selves in amicable con-
cord. If Rich's energies of "creation" and "relation" can't be united, parents can still hold them in a sometimes frustrating, sometimes generative
balance. Ruhl compares the balance to a heartbeat, the "great systole and
diastole of work and children."

This is the baby on the fire escape—not the slanderous story but the
reality that it stands for, the precarious situation in which the child is just
far enough out of sight and mind for the mother to have a talk with her
muse. It's the mental and temporal distance that an artist or writer needs
to place between herself and her children, so she can have the presence,
the permission, the "little sips of selfhood" (Natasha Randall) that sustain
creativity. It's keeping and letting go. It's art and care going on at once, for
a moment, a day, a lifetime.

*INTERRUPTION WAS A CLUE. But still I felt like the more I read about moth-
ering, the less I knew. Maternity often seems to be all description and no
story.* For many parental sensations there aren't even words. My thesau-
rus lists dozens of synonyms for "depression," "love," and even "tedium"
but has no word for the state of boredom, alienation, and adoration
induced by playing a game with a one-year-old, or the after-hours cock-
tail of exhaustion, fury, and addled romance served up by night waking.
(The term "maternal ambivalence" doesn't evoke the full flavor, though
Sianne Ngai's term "stuplimity," for what is both sublime and stupefy-
ing, might come close.) Fragment and anecdote appear to be the default
modes of speaking, partly because, as Baraitser observes, they are what
survives children's interruptions, their "attack on narrative," partly
because they allow vital information to be disassembled and smuggled
out from behind the barrier of love that—ideally—shields kids from
the world.

Ursula Le Guin corresponded with a childless friend who asked her
regularly what mothering was like. Ursula would answer that she had cried

during her eldest daughter's cello recital, or mention that with Christmas coming and her son home sick, she planned to spend the day cutting out paper ornaments and getting glitter in the rug. It's all maternal praxis, raw material for a phenomenology of mothering.

It was this quality of lived experience that I wanted to get at when I first thought of writing about mothering biographically. I wanted to describe whole lives in which mothering was a part. And in writing about my subjects' lives I've tried to honor that anecdotal quality and to keep an eye on the role that interruption plays. But interruption didn't give me a story; it lacks the dimension of time, the biographer's thread through the labyrinth. Freud thought a woman who became a mother had come to the end of her story. Anne Enright thought that after the birth of her child she had "found a place before stories start." I realized that if I wanted to put up a counter-image to the solitary writer, it would have to allow not only interruption but change.

Twentieth-century mothers' stories were shaped—and constrained—by a common narrative I thought of as "the motherhood plot." As feminist biographers, including Phyllis Rose and Carolyn Heilbrun, have pointed out, most people live their lives according to the stories they are offered by history and convention. For women, getting married and having children has been that story. In the motherhood plot, a traditional marriage and children are a woman's achievement, the aim of her life's adventure, her means of economic survival and promise of emotional sustenance.

It was astonishingly difficult for the women I wrote about not to follow the motherhood plot: their reasons were individual, but the outcome kept being the same. They married for love, like Alice Neel, or to get out of the house, like Angela Carter. They were looking for financial support or creative collaboration, so they wouldn't feel so artistically alone. They married, like Doris Lessing, to fill the empty space where their fate should be.

They had children because that was what married women did, or because a pregnancy made their choice for them. Middle-class parents felt stifled by the work of maintenance, while poor women and women of color struggled to keep their children fed and safe in a world that didn't welcome their coming. The African American motherhood plot emphasized strength, ingenuity, and financial independence, but also selflessness, suffering, and endurance. Black mothering under white supremacy—which has often involved the additional work of caring for white mothers' children—has brought with it an extra burden of resistance, Dani McClain writes: "If we merely accepted the status quo and failed to challenge the forces that have kept Black people and women oppressed, then we participated in our own and our children's destruction."

For almost all women, the motherhood plot was what happened if you were not living your life with intention, or if you didn't know what your options were. In *Lesbian Nation*, Jill Johnston called her marriage and two children "the illusory solution to a problem I didn't know was much bigger than me. . . . I didn't know what else to do and [marriage] was always a thing to do in fact a basic thing to do, it was all around you." In her great exploration of motherhood, *Of Woman Born*, Adrienne Rich said of herself in the "family-centered" 1950s: "I had no idea of what *I* wanted, what *I* could or could not choose. I only knew that to have a child was to assume adult womanhood to the full, to prove myself, to be 'like other women.'"

The motherhood plot is compelling partly because, in the right circumstances, love of partner and children can be a powerful source of joy, support, freedom, and strength. Toni Morrison said that becoming a mother was "the most liberating thing that ever happened to me. . . . I could not only be me—whatever that was—but somebody actually needed me to be that." Ursula Le Guin found in marriage and children a stability that allowed her to work.

Mother love can be revolutionary, particularly for poor and marginalized women fighting for time and space to care for their children. Alexis Pauline Gumbs writes, "The radical potential of the word 'mother' comes after the 'm.' It is the space that 'other' takes in our mouths when we say it.

We are something else. We know it from how fearfully institutions wield social norms and try to shut us down." Poet Christy NaMee Eriksen adds, "A brown mother's love is her biggest protest."

But the motherhood plot makes no provision for the creative self. If anything, it insists on selflessness, not only toward babies and children, but toward husbands, partners, and others. For a while, divorced with two small children, Morrison lost herself: "I was somebody's parent, somebody's this, somebody's that, but there was no me in this world."

Enright writes:

> Babies demand your entire self, but it is a funny kind of self. It is a mixture of the "all" a factory worker gives to the conveyor belt and the "all" a lover offers to the one he adores. It involves, on both counts, a fair degree of self-abnegation.
>
> This is why people who mind children suffer from despair; it happens all of a sudden—they realise, all of a sudden, that they still exist.

Most of the women in this book started out following the motherhood plot, all of them contended with it, all of them left it. When they ran off the cliff and found themselves in midair, when they felt knocked sideways by love, relegated to the margins of their own lives, when they found themselves storyless, they had to improvise. At some point they had to think very clearly about who they were and what they wanted and have the courage to break with expectations—and lack of expectations—in order to make that happen. Working and mothering against the grain, they learned, fought, suffered, and grew.

TWENTIETH-CENTURY CREATIVE WOMEN fought against the expectation that they would be selfless, not only toward their children, but toward husbands and lovers. Mothering within traditional marriages drained them emotionally, leaving them without the energy or independence of mind necessary to creation. Again and again women ran up against the impossibility of working, not only because they didn't have time but because their partner, family, or community demanded too much of them or seduced them into setting aside their vocation. Erdrich comments that women writers "must often hold their mates and families at arm's length or be devoured."

To get their work done, some mothers took steps to limit their emotional availability to husbands and lovers. Several lived in open relationships, like Alice Neel, who said of one partner that he "was always *enamorado*—always chasing the girls," but "this didn't bother me so much because I wanted freedom to paint." Some acted in ways that seem illogical or self-denying: taking up with partners who were unavailable or unwilling to nurture them, rejecting supportive men, refusing anything that looked like domesticity. These acts of emotional sabotage let them set boundaries without feeling hard-hearted. If it meant not getting their own needs met, for some creative mothers it seemed like the only way to break their addiction to nurturance. Sontag felt that the creative self requires ego to thrive, but really what it requires is not being too generous with one's emotional labor.

Communities around motherhood—family, friends, fellow parents—can be supportive or oppressive. The essayist Ellen Willis remarked that having a child at forty-two challenged her sense of herself as a countercultural rebel, plunging her and her partner into "the pit of urban middle-class Nuclear Familydom" and "a daily life overwhelmed with domestic detail. . . . My life as a mother did have a dimension of transcendence, marked by intense passion and sensual delight; yet while I'd always insisted that real passion was inherently subversive, my love for my daughter bound me more and more tightly to the social order."

Parenthood can also feel chaotic in all its self-loss and self-discovery.

You may lose your way, feel vulnerable or pushed out of the center of your life. You may find yourself, experience a new authority. You may contend with depression, disappointment, or "overwhelming, unacceptable anger" (Rich). For Anne Lamott, the hardest part of becoming a parent was "being face-to-face with one's secret insanity and brokenness and rage."

My early motherhood asked more of me emotionally than any experience ever has, sometimes insisting on my capacity for bliss and tenderness, sometimes leaving me despairing at my limitations. Motherhood challenged me and revealed me to myself; in that sense it was like writing, only more so, but it also, for long stretches, made my work nearly impossible. I felt more myself in one way, lost to myself in another. To regain my footing, I had to learn about this new place; I had to undergo a psychic transformation.

"Motherhood is an identity, and the passage to motherhood is one of the most significant shifts in identity that transpires in adulthood." Andrew Solomon, author of *Far from the Tree*, writes in his 2013 doctoral thesis in psychology that a woman who becomes a parent has to deal with two new relationships: one with her child, one with herself as a mother. Building these relationships—and for a creative mother, rebuilding her relationship to her vocation—involves redefining herself as a person, both in relation to her child and in relation to what she expects from motherhood. In effect, she comes of age all over again. New parents are oblivious and self-centered, not only because they're busy, sleepless, depressed, and/or drunk on love, but because they're looking inward, reassessing everything.

Baraitser again: "It is to moments of undoing, I argue, that we need to apply ourselves theoretically, if we are to try to glimpse something we may term maternal subjectivity."

Undoing is a clue. Even under the best circumstances—if you have access to child care, if you aren't criticized for doing your work, if you have the financial and emotional support you need—all the stress and bliss of mothering can push you out of the center of your life, leaving you to recollect yourself and to approach your work anew. A person in the act of mothering is someone who contends with her child, with motherhood as an institution, and with a self that is changing in response to those two powerful influences. Ideally she is also someone who goes on developing in response to her work, her children, and the other events in her life, who gains self-knowledge, who gains or regains her agency. She is not only transformed, as a person and artist, when she becomes a mother, she is transformed over and over by it, throughout her life. Her acts of self-creation and self-revision are her story.

If psychology can't lead to a theory of maternal subjectivity, maybe narrative can. Feminist philosopher Adriana Cavarero takes up Hannah Arendt's suggestion that subjectivity is a product of narrative, and that it's fundamentally biographical. A life story, she writes, invites the reader to recognize herself as having the potential for agency—as being her own protagonist. Subjectivity is a hero's tale, with each person the hero(ine) of a "unique and unrepeatable" story.

Say "mother" and "hero" and most people will default to visions of self-sacrifice. But creative motherhood is not that kind of story; it's not about fighting, or rescue either. It's the story of a central figure who goes on a journey of self-discovery. Someone who follows a trail of breadcrumbs (and anecdotes, and incoherent moments). Someone who descends into the underworld and comes back. A protagonist who gets lost in the forest and finds her way.

When I started looking for mother-heroes, I saw that they'd been in women's stories all along. Their subjectivity was in their losing and finding of themselves, first in adolescence, then in maternity, then in maturity, confronting their "annihilation" and regaining their power.

So in a spirit of rebellion, a refusal of erasure, a smack to young Oedipus who failed to recognize his mother, I have tried to write my mothers' stories as hero-tales. I've tried to look at the crises of self, the moments when their maternal or creative understanding of themselves falls apart, when they get lost in the woods and come out—if they do come out—with new insight, and with themselves changed.

DISCLAIMER

The notion of a universality of human experience is a confidence trick and the notion of a universality of female experience is a clever confidence trick. (ANGELA CARTER)

On the subject of motherhood there are no experts. (ADRIENNE RICH)

Advice. Opinions. Judgment. Mothers' choices are endlessly scrutinized and censured. "The institution of motherhood finds all mothers more or less guilty," Adrienne Rich writes. Not only that, she observes, it judges all women and finds them wanting, whether they have children or not. "Mothering and nonmothering have been such charged concepts for us, precisely because *whichever we did has been turned against us*."

"Any woman who has ever had children will tell you it is no picnic of affirmation," Karen Joy Fowler writes. "Any woman who has not had children can tell you that that, too, is a controversial place to be." Psychotherapist Rozsika Parker observes that from guilty women to disappointed children, "the fantasy of the maternal ideal . . . dispenses feelings of inadequacy right across the board."

The work of raising children is central to human existence—which is why, Ellen Willis writes, it is so relentlessly policed. "It's because families, and mothers, serve primal needs that the institution has been such a powerful vehicle of social control." While all mothers are liable to be judged, white supremacy casts Black maternity in particular, Jennifer C. Nash observes, as "pathological, excessive, and marked by aberrant performances of gender and heterosexuality that threaten both the nuclear family and the heterosexual state."

I've (mostly) tried not to pass judgment on anyone's choices. I don't believe that one kind of mothering is better than another, or that women should be mothers, or that mothers should be women, or that women who have given birth must care for their children, or that mothers must give birth. I've tried to let my own narrative be interrupted, to make room for more than one set of experiences, and for multiple points of view.

When I thought about who to write about, I looked for people born early in the tumultuous twentieth century: young enough to have experienced the changes that came with feminism, old enough to have mothered for a lifetime. I looked for people who had had a wide variety of experiences, though I'm aware it isn't wide enough. I looked for parents who had chosen, in their art or their writing, to make their stories public. I looked for men who fit these qualifications but didn't find any. With regret, I limited myself to British and North American writers and artists for purposes of practicality.

This book takes as its inspiration the words of Frieda Lawrence's daughter, who defended her mother for abandoning her family: "I believe she was right to act as she did; all the boring women who have told me 'I could never leave my children' have helped to convince me." It is also inspired by Toni Morrison's answer to the question of how she wrote her first novel: "I wrote a list of the things I had to do. I found sixty-three. Then I wrote another list of things I wanted to do. I found two—write and mother my children."

Above all I hope that you will take the advice of Alice Walker, who in commenting on her essay "*One* Child of One's Own" urged her readers to "listen to what [is] useful and ignore the rest."

"The Presiding Genius of Her Own Body"

I simply could not have existed, as I am, in any other preceding time or place. . . . I could have been a professional writer at any period since the seventeenth century in Britain or in France. But I could *not* have combined this latter with a life as a sexually active woman until the introduction of contraception. (ANGELA CARTER)

We need to imagine a world in which every woman is the presiding genius of her own body. In such a world . . . sexuality, politics, intelligence, power, motherhood, work, community, intimacy, will develop new meanings; thinking itself will be transformed. (ADRIENNE RICH)

To PARAPHRASE JENNY OFFILL, there is no writing apart from the body that writes. Creativity thrives on physical sensations and strong feelings. Mothering, too, begins, if not in pregnancy or childbirth—neither one a requirement or a given—then in the sensuous or comforting touch of parent and child. The experiences of parental bodies are very different from one another, and the dangers of essentialist thinking, of reducing mothers to their bodies, are real.

But there's one story that is common to all my mother-artists and mother-writers: the hero's journey of gaining control over one's fertility. Reproductive rights—including access to abortion, contraception, fertility treatment, and health care—are a necessary part of creative mothering.

I was surprised—though I shouldn't have been—to discover that a book on mothering was also about not-mothering. Yet the disaster of an unplanned pregnancy—and, to a lesser extent, the struggle to conceive—is a story that runs throughout this book. Almost all the women I write about had problems accessing birth control. Almost all had at least one accidental pregnancy, almost all—Neel and Le Guin, Carter and Lorde, Sontag and Walker—had an abortion. All of them saw control over the timing and material circumstances of their pregnancies, whether they were able to achieve it or not, as essential to the practice of their art.

Before the twentieth century most contraception was ineffective—sponges, withdrawal—not to mention awkward and gross. (A typical method was douching with a household cleaner such as Lysol.) Condoms were expensive: when D. H. Lawrence lost his virginity in 1910, one packet cost him five shillings from his forty-shilling weekly salary as a teacher. (A person earning $800 a week would pay $100 now.) They were also taboo: a man could be expelled from university in England if condoms were found in his rooms. Even the rhythm method only became an option in 1929, when scientists finally discovered when ovulation occurs.

Yet for most women, sexual abstinence was not an option either. Twentieth-century women sought emotional and financial support in marriage. They had affairs for the pleasure of it, or to prove that they were just as tough and daring as their male counterparts, or to prove to someone else or themselves that they weren't queer. They had sex because it fired their creativity. Naomi Mitchison thought sex was "utterly important, it is fuel for the imagination, it puts brilliance and vigor into one's vision." Discovering the pleasure of being made love to by a woman, Susan Sontag wrote in her diary, "The orgasm focuses. I lust to write."

Not coincidentally, the careers of mother-writers began to flourish in the 1920s, when the first effective birth control for women, the diaphragm and cervical cap, became more available, affordable, and legal in Britain and the US. The invention of latex condoms made prices drop. Mitchison publicly advocated the diaphragm for polyamorous relationships, saying it made love possible both in and outside of marriage.

But that didn't mean birth control was easy to get. When Alice Neel married in 1925, the diaphragm was a distant rumor emanating from New York, and it was still illegal to send contraceptives, or even information on contraception, through the US mail. In her novel *The Group*, set in the 1930s, Mary McCarthy famously described the problems even for a wealthy young American of using a "pessary" even if you could get one: the expense, the invasive fitting, and most of all, the shame and lack of privacy that made it impossible to think of actually using it.

In her memoir *Under My Skin* Doris Lessing describes meeting a young white couple in Cape Town, South Africa, who had come to the city with their three small children so the wife could get fitted for a diaphragm.

> She took out her new Dutch cap from its film of silky powder and said, "But look at it, just look, I can't use that thing." "But sweetheart, we've got to." "Oh, heck, sweetheart, you mean I've got to." "But when I use a french letter you just get pregnant." "*When* you use a french letter, you mean." And they fell into each other's arms, laughing. . . .
>
> She was pregnant before she went home to Windhoek.

Angela Carter, as a married woman of twenty, used a cervical cap but complained in her diary about the greasiness and sticky hands that came from using the "plug."

All forms of contraception were illegal in France when Ursula Le Guin got married there in 1953. The new couple's most valued wedding gift was a gross of US military-issue condoms, sent by a friend in the armed forces in Germany, with suggestive comments written all over the box. When Doris Lessing had a tubal ligation in 1948, securing for herself the sexual freedom she celebrated in *The Golden Notebook*, she was undergoing a new and controversial procedure.

Some men and women saw contraception as a barrier to the true expression of love. Elizabeth Smart and her poet lover believed that sex was "two-dimensional" without the chance that "Eternity [might] enter the bed." They had four children together, but raising them was Elizabeth's task alone.

Illegal abortion remained an essential though dangerous and frightening recourse. Le Guin's college boyfriend assured her she wouldn't get pregnant without a condom, and she believed him. Audre Lorde, living on her own at seventeen, had breakup sex with a boyfriend so she wouldn't feel so lonely. A pregnancy scare frightened Sontag so much she ran out of the room while her husband took the doctor's call. Walker chose an illegal abortion because her alternative was suicide.

A common view among doctors was that women could not be trusted with their fertility. When Adrienne Rich decided to have a tubal ligation in 1958, after having an unplanned third child, she had to present a letter, countersigned by her husband, to a committee of physicians, all of them male, tasked with judging her fitness for the procedure. In the letter she grudgingly cited her rheumatoid arthritis, hating to have to use disability as a reason for what should have been normal care.

In 1960, the British critic and writer Lorna Sage, having gotten pregnant at sixteen, asked her family's doctor after the birth about contraception. He answered, "Now that you're married your husband will take care of that," though the teenage father of her baby had no more information than she did. "In any case, [the doctor] must have thought, I was now in all probability going to revert to white-trash type and have more babies, and in a way decorum demanded that I should; I was some sort of nymphomaniac, and mustn't be allowed to have my cake and eat it."

Some physicians believed that contraception would thwart the deeper workings of maternal instinct, preventing a woman from having the children for which she unconsciously longed. In 1964, after Le Guin had given birth to an unplanned third baby, she consulted her doctor about more reliable contraception. In surprised condescension, he asked,

"What do you want, 100 percent certainty?"
I looked at him and said, "Of course." I didn't say, "you asshole."

By then the Pill had been approved in the US (1960) and Great Britain (1961) and was already in widespread use. Abortion became legal in Great Britain in 1967 and the US in 1972. For Angela Carter, a legal abortion as a single woman of thirty-four was a matter-of-fact decision. For the writer Fay Weldon, a thirty-nine-year-old, married mother of three, a legal abortion was a necessary choice when she discovered she was pregnant in 1971, "six months after the last birth, an immediate family of six largely dependent upon my earnings, the new baby due to be born on my sister's birthday, her death still new in my head, her three orphaned children also my responsibility—my mother as well . . ." For Lorde, Walker, and Sontag, an illegal abortion was an act of bravery that felt like a desperate reclamation of their lives.

Beyond access to birth control, there are broader questions in women's lives of reproductive justice. This concept, originally developed by African American feminists, includes access to medical care for mothers and children: Alice Neel's infant daughter died partly because Alice and her husband had no money for a doctor. It includes children's safety: Audre Lorde had to give her son "the Talk" that Black parents give to their children, telling them how to de-escalate unsafe encounters with the police.

It includes the right to parent a child: in 1962, after Sontag's ex-husband discovered that she was in a relationship with a woman, he tried to use her sexuality to win custody of their son. It includes questioning the myth of the "undeserving" mother of color and addressing "time poverty," the market-driven, capitalist lack of paid leave, affordable day care, and fair working hours that constrains the choices of many creative women.

One of the stories of this book is about how motherhood went from being an accident and an obligation to being a choice, and how profound that effect has been on women's lives. In reading about women writers' careers it's essential to remember how little choice some of them had. As Alice Neel said of her first marriage: "In the beginning I didn't want children. I just got them."

Alice Neel with her sons Richard and Hartley, New York, 1943.

Outlaw Mothering

ALICE NEEL (1900–1984)

◆

Be nobody's darling; / Be an outcast. (ALICE WALKER)

You have to have a certain sense of defiance in you [as an artist] so you don't self-destruct. (CAMILLE BILLOPS)

IMAGES OF MOTHERHOOD, art, and success all trouble one another. Bring them together and they yield unexpected conjunctions: painter, grandmother, art-world celebrity. In 1977, seventy-seven-year-old Alice Neel could be seen pirouetting on the red carpet at a black-tie arts benefit, wearing gray suede space shoes, her silver lamé jacket swinging while her "eyes underneath the mink hat twinkled with delight." A *New York Times* photographer caught her in conversation with the sculptor Louise Nevelson while her son Richard proudly looked on.

To become both painter and mother, Alice had had to spend a lifetime refusing others' expectations. She was the matriarch of a close-knit, affectionate family. She was also an artist who had stubbornly followed her personal vision and had had to live with the discomfort of her genius. At times she had been an art monster, tenacious and difficult, known for both her skilled and original use of paint and the edgy, unsettling drama of her portraits. One critic called her painting's "auntie-hero."

To find out about the selfhood of a mother-artist, in all its complexity, look at works like Alice's early painting *Well Baby Clinic*. In 1928, in New York City, overwhelmed after her daughter Isabetta was born, she portrayed her own situation with unsettling honesty. She was wondering what she and her husband would do for money, how she would find time to paint, and how much arguing their marriage could stand. She was worried about the baby, and even more about herself: what if she didn't have enough talent, nerve, or hours in the day to keep making her work?

The painting shows a hospital ward where rows of women are changing infants. A white nurse in a spotless uniform holds a newborn confidently in her arms while the new mothers, white and brown, struggle to follow her example. At one edge of the painting, Alice looks down, her face ghostly, her gaze a blank. At her elbow a woman glances up from her task with a look of maniacal joy. ("I wondered how that woman could be so happy, with that little bit of hamburger she's fixing the diaper for," Alice later commented.) Another mother shows her baby to the doctor. Her breasts are bare, her mouth open in a wail of distress. The nurse models contentment and maternal care, but the women portray some of the other emotions new mothers feel: unease, grief, helplessness. Alice is alienated from the women around her, who can offer her no support. They're either deluded or in too much pain themselves to be on her side.

Years later, after she had lost her child, recovered her art, and become a portrait painter—what she called a "collector of souls"—Alice returned to the subject of motherhood. Under her sensitive eye, her pregnant daughter-in-law doesn't look beatific but clumsy and anxious. Mothers and children stand awkwardly apart from each other; parents hold infants who try to squirm away. The impressionist Mary Cassatt was famous for portraying women and infants in states of mutual bliss; Alice added in the other part, the ambivalence and conflict.

Her own motherhood had taught her how much friction there could be, especially between artistic vocation and maternal care. When Alice was nearly eighty a younger artist observed her "in a polka-dot dress . . .

her hair pinned up in a limp, grandmotherly twist," wondered at the steely determination underneath, and asked, "How in the world did a bosom in patterned rayon ever become the heart of a soldier-at-arms?"

PAINTING BEGAN FOR ALICE as a refuge and a claim to selfhood. Born on January 28, 1900—beginning with the century, she liked to say— Alice Hartley Neel grew up in Colwyn, Pennsylvania, a lower-middle-class suburb of Philadelphia, the fourth of five children of a clerk for the Pennsylvania Railroad. Her mother, also named Alice, was intelligent and dissatisfied and gave off a sense that life "really wasn't what one expected and hoped for." This was understating the distress of a woman who felt trapped in her own life and more than once told her children she wanted to kill herself.

Not surprisingly, Alice told an interviewer, Eleanor Munro, that she had been a susceptible and fearful child. "Other people loomed too large. Everybody could knock me off base. . . . I'd make such an effort to be what they wanted, a pretty little girl, that I wouldn't be myself at all." Alice didn't dare disturb her mother with her own feelings. "She was so superior, so sensitive, she couldn't bear anything. . . . I had to keep her happy all the time." Only when Alice painted could she be her own person: "The minute I sat in front of a canvas, I was happy. Because it was a world, and I could do as I liked in it." Painting, she once said, "was my only real life."

In a series of interviews Alice gave in her eighties to the art historian Patricia Hills, she spoke of feeling storyless in her "benighted" little town. Her street, which had once been an orchard, still had a few rows of pear trees, and the gardens were filled with flowers. "It was utterly beautiful in the spring, but there was no artist to paint it. And once a man exposed himself at a window, but there was no writer to write it. The grocer's wife committed suicide after the grocer died, but there was no writer to write that. There was no culture there. I hated that little town. . . .

And in the summer I used to sit on the porch and try to keep my blood from circulating."

But instead of studying art she went to secretarial school, out of fearfulness and a guilty wish to help her family. In any case there was no money for her education: her parents were saving to send her younger brother to college instead. She lived at home, worked as a typist, and took art classes at night until one day, at twenty-one, she realized that if she went on living that way it would become her life. She took her savings and applied to art school—not the elite Pennsylvania Academy of the Fine Arts but the Philadelphia School of Design for Women, where, unusually for the time, women were educated for a trade. Stubborn and anti-elitist, she didn't trust the idea of painting pretty pictures. "I didn't see life as [Manet's] *Picnic on the Grass*. I wasn't happy like Renoir."

In 1921 the school's dress code was skirts, gloves, and hats, but Alice was part of the first generation of women permitted to paint nude male models. Getting access to the body as a subject was a victory for women artists; later, when she began painting pregnant nudes, Alice was aware of a kind of defiant taking possession. The students were inspired by Robert Henri, a leader of the Ashcan school, who encouraged them to record scenes they witnessed in bars, at construction sites, and on the street. As critical fashions changed, Alice would remain loyal to Henri's philosophy: "Paint what you feel. Paint what you see. Paint what is real to you."

In a society structured to keep them financially dependent, single women in the 1920s looked for ways to get men's affection, attention, and money without compromising their autonomy. For a while in art school Alice strung along a boyfriend she didn't care for because he helped her financially. "He used to give me dollars for art's sake. . . . I'd fold them up and put them in my shoe. The little square would press my heel, it made me feel powerful. Nobody could make me stop the school as long as I had dollars."

It was thirty of those dollars that first set up, for Alice, the impossible conflict between love and art. In 1924, that money paid her tuition for a summer art course outside the city, where she met Carlos Enríquez, her great love. He was the romantic, rebellious, artistically gifted son of a family of Cuban sugar planters, with sleek black hair and a sexual sophistication that she desired and aspired to. He made pretty, pink-cheeked Alice feel like "the most repressed creature that ever lived."

Carlos returned to Havana, but a year and many (passionate, illustrated) love letters later, he came back to Pennsylvania and walked down the aisle with Alice in June 1925, a few days before her graduation. "Well I couldn't help it—I married him," she later said, not the only woman in this book to feel that her marriage hadn't really been a choice. But when it came down to actually going away with him, she panicked and balked, apparently with an inarticulate fear that she was losing control. For one thing, she wasn't ready for children, but she had no access to contraception. Even if she could have obtained a diaphragm, they planned to live with Carlos's parents, where she would have no privacy. The most common form of birth control at the time wouldn't be available: Carlos's father, a doctor, was "100 percent against abortion."

All she could think of to do was refuse to leave home. Every day she went to her studio to paint while Carlos waited at her parents' house. Eventually he gave up and left, and only when he came back in February, eight months after the wedding, did she finally go with him. She became pregnant within a few weeks of arriving in Cuba.

WHEN ALICE FIRST MOVED to Havana, her marriage didn't seem like such a danger to her autonomy after all. Though the Enríquez family didn't think much of Carlos's painter wife, Alice ambivalently enjoyed her privileged life in their marble-floored mansion, with servants, peacocks in the garden, and afternoon drives in the Rolls-Royce. She was delighted by the tropical light and color, liked Cuba's language and culture, and enjoyed the lively, welcoming artistic community she found among Carlos's bohemian friends. She and Carlos often painted together, and in two important group shows, their work was singled out for acclaim.

Unfortunately, a good life-work balance between partners doesn't always survive the birth of a child, and the arrival of their daughter Santillana, on December 26, 1926—after "eight hours of agony" without anesthesia, for which Alice never forgave the Cuban hospital—ended their equal marriage. It's not entirely clear what happened, but it seems likely that her parents-in-law pressured her to give up painting so she could care for the baby. Carlos started going out with other women, leaving Alice at home with his jealous, disapproving sisters, who took his side and made fun of her distress. In May 1927 she fled her gilded cage, taking Santillana back to her parents' house in Colwyn. A few months later Carlos contritely came after her and the three of them moved to New York.

No matter where they lived, it was too early in the world's history for household equality. Carlos apparently helped with the baby but not the housework: a man might claim to respect a woman's talent, but seldom to the point of cooking meals or washing his own underwear. With no money, they argued over who got to paint, who had to take a day job, who would watch the baby. In December, Alice and Santillana got sick. Alice, ill and frightened, put off calling the doctor. Santillana died of diphtheria just before her first birthday.

Her daughter's death filled Alice with grief and confusion. That she hadn't wanted a child only made her feel guiltier. She blamed herself for not calling the doctor, for not buying a five-dollar oil stove to keep the apartment warm. "After Santillana's death I was just frantic. Then I was already in a trap. All I could do was get pregnant again," she later said. When she did get pregnant, she felt worse. The prospect of a baby to replace Santillana didn't ease the pain—or change anything between her and Carlos.

Later, after she'd lost two daughters, Alice read a news story about an infant who had been strangled between the bars of a crib, then painted a picture of a baby lying dead in its bed. She called it *Futility of Effort*. "Into went the amount of effort you put into having a child. Pregnancy. All the rest. Then the tragedy of losing it. Everything. Everything."

As her due date for her second pregnancy came closer, Alice could no longer hold off her depression. She seldom doubted her gifts, but two weeks before the birth she wrote in her journal that she felt "consumed by an actual fire of jealousy" toward Carlos. Was she good enough, did she deserve to go on painting at the cost of his work? "When his work is awfully clever, I feel selfish and wrong to insist on painting and so hold him back—but think of a long bleak life of stupidity and yet I am so nervous perhaps I will never do anything."

A few days later, after a visit from a childless writer friend, Fanya Foss, she had an anxiety attack: "I lay in bed just screaming inside—sick and destroyed—the room squeezing in close to me in a black circle, then widening—all my dreams and desires clear canvas and new wooden stretchers all the pictures in my brain that I've been saving—and the work to do in this house—the terrible foolishness and failure of our lives."

The new baby, Isabetta, was born in November 1928, eleven months after Santillana's death. A poem Alice wrote in the months that followed tells of postpartum self-loss and her inability to be happy with her new daughter:

> My house is beside a river of lead
> I build a snow woman
>
> . . . .
>
>
> I burn my snow woman's
> Black coal eyes and still I am
> Not warm
>
> . . . .

my tropical soul

frozen in ice

molded with pain

A year later, she made a sketch of her friend Fanya holding forth obliviously while Alice, with a distracted look and three arms to represent extra work, struggles to cope with Isabetta's interruptions. The situation will be familiar to any new parent with a tactless friend, but Alice's frustration is obvious under the comic surface.

Having heard from Alice that Carlos's sisters had been jealous of her, her daughter-in-law Ginny Neel suspects that it was the Enríquez family who later told Isabetta that her mother had once forgotten her on the fire escape when she was concentrating on her painting. Alice's younger children dismiss the story as a fabrication. What is certain is that she and Carlos were looking for a work-baby balance in time and space, and that without resources—childcare, help, money—she could hardly get a moment to herself. Yet it seemed to her that she, not the world, was divided. "I always had this awful dichotomy," she later said. "I loved Isabetta, of course I did. But I wanted to paint."

Alice would have gone on making the daily choices that hold care and art together, but Carlos, also depressed and still mourning Santillana's death, wanted a change. When Isabetta was one and a half, he made a plan. He would give Alice a break by taking Isabetta to Havana. Alice would join him there and the three of them would go to Paris to live. Thrilled to have a few weeks of freedom, Alice worked day and night. Then she got word that Carlos had gone on to Paris alone, leaving Isabetta with his two sisters in Cuba.

In shock at Carlos's desertion, Alice froze. She didn't think the Enríquez family would give Isabetta back without a fight. Her mother, burdened for years with her own five children, declined to help. Though she didn't judge Alice's choices, she may have thought Isabetta would be better cared for where she was. Alice painted frantically, trying to lose herself in her art. "The nights were horrible," she wrote in her journal.

> I dreamed Isabetta died and we buried her right beside Santillana. Well then I was crying alone in a room and someone came and said they were moving the cemetery and that when they dug up those two baby coffins they could see them moving inside. . . .
>
> Isabetta was alright—just like now. . . . But her hands and arms were like mummies all cracked and dried. I had to save her from breaking them off. She was tall—as old as she must be by now—and the hands you could see them getting better, coming back to life. If only dreams were life.

Then she broke down. For weeks she lay in bed, convinced she was dying. In October her parents committed her to a hospital in Philadelphia, but when the doctors there wouldn't let her paint—they blamed her condition on her "bohemian life"—she got worse. Years later she told Ginny, "Don't ever think it's romantic to lose your mind. It's the most horrific thing that can happen to you."

Alice's married older sister Lily sent Carlos money to come back from Paris, and in January 1931 he showed up full of remorse and promises. It was too late. After he brought her back with him to her parents' house, she put her head in the oven. (When her brother found her unconscious in the kitchen the next morning, he thought at first she was their own mother, finally carrying out her suicide plan.) After she was sent back to the hospital, she tried to eat glass. It wasn't until a nurse gave her paper and let her draw again that she at last began to fight for herself and to get well.

She was eventually sent to a sanatorium, where she was allowed to work while she convalesced. There she wrote despairingly:

> now is the great renunciation
> now I know I'll never be strong enough mentally or physically

to put the things I see and feel in any concrete form
. . . .
oh I was full of theories
of grand experiments
to live a normal woman's life
to have children—to be the painting and the painter
but now I have no strength
. . . .
I've lost my child my love my life and all the god damn business
     that makes life worth living

To get well she would have to make the choice she'd been dreading. When she finally left the sanatorium in September 1931, she had decided that her therapists were right: an artist couldn't be a mother. Carlos stayed in Paris, Isabetta stayed in Cuba, and Alice moved to bohemian Greenwich Village to build a life around her vocation.

EVERYONE IN THIS BOOK had periods of depression and failure. They left a marriage; they lost a child or a partner or their way; something in them died. After the bleak days and the hard choices, they had to find their way back to the land of the living, and for some it was a slow, painful road. When Alice went to New York she was still grieving. And though she had chosen for her art, she still felt confined within the narrow limits of what was possible for a woman artist. "I'm not sure I was ever myself," she once said. "I was myself, but myself in our social systems."

But the Village was full of other storyless people, and by portraying them she discovered that she could convey something of what it was like to be her. The shock of the Depression was visible everywhere, and Alice, still in shock herself, made social unease a lifelong subject: New Yorkers struggling with poverty and exclusion. Through the faces and bodies of fellow sufferers she sought to express her own "hypersensitivity" to "the life that comes crashing about you." Other people still "loomed large" for her, but when she painted them she could encounter them on her own terms.

She had come to New York to live with Kenneth Doolittle, a sailor and committed socialist she had met through friends. Drawn through him into overlapping activist and artistic circles, she began painting union organizers, socialists, and poets. She made portraits of gay men, depicting them with sympathy for their self-presentation and what it concealed. "Orphans of the avant-garde," the critic Anatole Broyard called the residents of the Village, people whose sexuality, sensibility, circumstances, or convictions had put them at odds with traditional society. Alice recorded their oddities in paint. When she did a legendary nude of the Village character Joe Gould, an impoverished intellectual with, Alice thought, a secret exhibitionistic side, she portrayed him with a satyr's mad grin and three sets of genitals, one in the usual spot, one in the middle of his belly, and one dangling below his chair.

An artist needs to work out not only a creative but a public self, a persona to interact with the world. It was here that Alice put a chip on her shoulder and refused to care what other people thought. The view expressed ad nauseam by Alice's male colleagues was that women were too cautious and domestic to make *real* art. To be granted any kind of credibility as an artist, a young woman had to live like one, that is, wildly, with a male artist's creative bravado. Alice proved her credentials by acting tough and not wearing her heart on her sleeve.

She had to armor herself against tenderness, too. Most men in the Village were looking for a woman whose kindness they could depend on, and if you didn't want to be exploited, it was best not to be kind. Convention, duty, and self-sacrifice were all weeds that sprouted up and had to be cut down, and rudeness was a well-established way to do it. The poet Edna St. Vincent Millay and her sister Norma, renowned free spirits of the 1910s, used to practice swearing while darning their socks until they could curse without shocking themselves. ("Needle in, shit. Needle out, piss. Needle in, fuck. Needle out, cunt. Until we were easy with the words.") Alice seldom used bad language, but in the Village she developed a sharp tongue and forthright manner that contradicted her fresh, innocent "dairy maid" looks—and, later on, her grandmotherly face and figure.

Artist Sally Eckhoff recalls hearing Alice lecture on her work when she was in her eighties, softening her language but not her frankness:

> She showed a series of her nude portraits from the 1960s and talked about getting a visit from an electrician when she was working. The man stopped in front of a painting. "That's her pussy, isn't it?" he had asked. "Did he really use that word?" came a voice from the back of the lecture hall. Alice responded, "No, I did."

In private she painted more truths about bodies, including her own. A watercolor sketch of Kenneth shows him slouched in a chair, his legs spread wide, fixing the viewer with an attractively devilish grin. When she began her long sexual relationship with her friend John Rothschild, she celebrated it in a series of humorous erotic drawings.

Witnessing the poverty and suffering of the Depression deepened her socialist sympathies. She wasn't a dedicated activist and meetings weren't her thing, but the *Daily Worker* reviewed her shows and she briefly joined the Communist Party. Influenced by social realism, a movement that strove to depict poverty and injustice in art, she recorded street scenes, demonstrations, and political meetings—what she called her "revolutionary paintings."

If her way of life made it impossible for her to have her daughter with her, that had partly to do with another tribe she now had to deal with: other mothers, who like any community can be chosen or uninvited, supportive or censorious. Carlos's two sisters, who were now raising Isabetta in Havana, were judgmental, and so was Alice's older sister Lily, who lived with her family in suburban New Jersey and disapproved of Alice's way of life. With them against her, Alice had little hope of reuniting with her daughter, even after she started earning a steady income.

Socialism is kinder to mothers than capitalism, and for a decade, Alice's money problem was solved by the "socialist" New Deal. In 1933 the Works Progress Administration, the government agency tasked with creating jobs during the Depression, set up a program to employ artists. The Federal Art Project ultimately paid a living wage to several thousand Americans, who designed murals for public buildings, took photographs, or, like Alice, simply turned in a painting once every six weeks. Greenwich Village social realists, Harlem Renaissance luminaries, future superstars of abstraction such as Mark Rothko and Jackson Pollock—all of them were on the Art Project. New York's postwar artistic fame, when it became the art capital of the world, was due in part to the Art Project's steady support for artists early in their careers.

Alice was paid just over $100 a month when she started, $90 a month when the Art Project ended ten years later. Her $1,200 a year was just enough to live on, and didn't come near Virginia Woolf's 1928 demand of £500 a year (which represented a solidly middle-class family income, about $2,500). But for the first time Alice had money of her own, time to paint, and the validation that comes with actually earning a living. In 1938 her first solo show was judged by the *New York Times* an "excellent" debut.

Having an income made her even more free to seek love without male ownership. All full-time artists and writers have to find a satisfying mix of solitude and companionship, and being in a committed partnership doesn't necessarily make it easier. Though Alice said of herself that she was never "promiscuous," she didn't ask the same fidelity of the men in her life. An open partnership was a way for her to set boundaries on what she was willing to give a man—to define herself in relation to her own desires and capacity for love, not in relation to men's needs. Alice knew how easy it was for a woman to get drawn into the role of nurturing a man's career.

What Alice wanted was not only freedom but the kind of reckless love that rearranges one's perspective and feeds one's art. She had these loves, but they made her unsafe, too, and it's sometimes hard to tell the difference in her romantic life between self-realization and self-harm. The first year she was on the Art Project, 1934, her partnership with Kenneth ended in violence. He had started using drugs. Alice had started seeing John Rothschild, a businessman who took an interest in her work. In the fall of 1934 she got pregnant and he gave her money for an abortion. When Kenneth found out that Alice was involved with John, he flew into a jealous rage and attacked Alice's work, taking a knife to about sixty of her paintings and destroying many of the watercolors and drawings Alice kept as a diary of her daily life.

Alice fled to John's apartment, but when he offered to marry her she got a place of her own instead. Shortly afterward she fell in love with a Puerto Rican nightclub singer, José Santiago Negrón, who reminded her of Carlos. He was ten years younger than Alice and was married, though his pregnant wife kicked him out when she realized he was running around. Together they threw parties, went dancing, stayed out late. At thirty-seven Alice got pregnant by José and decided to keep the baby, but she miscarried at six months while José asked his wife to take him back, like "a rat who scuttles off the ship that's going down."

Improbably, they got back together. She had her own man on the side, John, who settled with her into a sexual friendship that endured through all their changes of partners. She sometimes claimed she cared only about his money, but that was bravado: she also relied on his confidence in her talent, his steady presence, his willingness to help her career.

The ambivalence of her years with José may have been a reaction to an unsettling event that happened when she was still with Kenneth Doolittle: a visit, in the summer of 1934, from her daughter. That spring Carlos came back from Europe and, from Havana, let Alice know that he wanted to renew their relationship. Alice, who still loved him despite everything, was torn. Shortly afterward, possibly in hopes of persuading her, he arranged for Isabetta to come stay with Alice and her parents in a rented house on the New Jersey shore.

Isabetta had barely been walking when Alice last saw her. Now she was a beautiful five-year-old with olive skin and her mother's blue eyes. In the picture Alice made of her that summer she faces the viewer, nude, with her feet planted, her hands on her hips, her gaze assured, her pose confident. Alice was taking pride in her daughter's strong, young body, the same maternal pleasure she would later explore in depictions of her sons. But there seems to be an element of wishful thinking here too. Children in her paintings often look fragile, astonished, curious, restless, but this is a portrait of an independent, almost invulnerable child—a daughter who doesn't need her mother.

Alice didn't take Carlos back, but she was confused and hurt by his offer of love. That fall, after Isabetta went home, Kenneth ripped up Alice's canvases (including the one of Isabetta, which she later repainted) and her life blew up, as if she were externalizing her doubt and pain at her lost marriage and motherhood. Maybe it was Carlos's doing, or maybe Alice's sister Lily, who kept in touch with the Enríquez family, put in a bad word for her about her troubles, but Isabetta didn't come back the next year, or the next.

Though Carlos was now living in Havana, he wasn't a strong presence in his daughter's life. He settled into a house and studio on the outskirts of the city, where he painted, wrote, and had legendary parties that brought together all of artistic and literary Cuba. He collaborated with poets and composers; he ran off with the wife of his best friend, the novelist Alejo Carpentier. Isabetta was allowed to visit one afternoon a week. The man Isabetta called "Papi" was Carlos's unmarried brother Antonio, who died suddenly of a tetanus infection when she was about nine years old.

Shortly after losing her uncle, in the summer of 1939, Isabetta was again sent to stay with her American mother. This time when she came home she announced that she was never going back.

Alice didn't talk much about her visits from Isabetta, and what happened isn't clear. Maybe Isabetta resented Alice's new pregnancy—she was again expecting a baby with José. Maybe Alice didn't have the gifts of tact and patience she needed to mend her relationship with her daughter, or didn't want to have to cope with her needs. Alice was not always a protective mother, particularly if it involved standing up to a lover, and a childhood friend believed that Isabetta was sexually molested, possibly by José.

Two years later, Isabetta sent Alice a sad Christmas card: "Dear mother, why don't you ever write. I've written and written and never get an answer. I'm waiting to hear from you. With love, Isabetta." Alice did write, Ginny Neel says, but her letters were never given to Isabetta. Mother and daughter would meet again only once, and their relationship would never be repaired. Though there are many possible readings of this story, Isabetta understood herself to be a casualty of her mother's selfish pursuit of her career.

In September 1939, Alice's son Richard Neel was born. A few months later José ran off with an underage sales clerk at a department store. Alice was angry but her heart wasn't broken; she wasn't even really surprised. She soon fell in love with another man, and with him she had another child.

It was family-making at the last minute: she was thirty-nine and forty-one when her sons were born. Unlike her first, these two babies were intentional and very much wanted, and they gave her a sense of family that she lacked in her partnerships. Having found her footing as an artist, gained an income, and thoroughly put behind her the temptation to live a comfortable, conventional woman's life, Alice was ready to commit to the kind of self-created household that Adrienne Rich called "outlaws from the institution of motherhood."

In 1943, Alice made a portrait of her second son that is also a self-portrait of her motherhood. This time she isn't frantic, the way she was with Isabetta, but in control of the situation and her work. In *Hartley on the Rocking Horse* she places her two-year-old son in the foreground as he plays in their apartment. His wide eyes seem fixed on the viewer, but the one he sees is Alice, who is revealed in a dresser mirror as she paints and watches over her child—artist and mother in a moment of unity.

More sure of her path now as she entered her forties, Alice was able to be both herself and a mother. She enjoyed her children's company and loved being able to give them love. Her home life kept her out of the Village with its culture of late nights and impulsive behavior, though it also isolated her in ways that hurt her career.

She worked less but never stopped working. "If you decide you are going to have children and give up painting during the time you have them, you give it up forever. Or if you don't, you just become a dilettante. It must be a continuous thing," she said. A family friend observed that Alice had "worked out her own code of behavior, whose cornerstones are two: 1) her freedom to paint; 2) the well-being of her two boys. For 1, she will surrender everything else. . . . The second . . . comes lower—but higher than anything else but the first."

She was poor—after the Art Project ended in 1942 she lived on public assistance—and eccentric, the kind of mother who pauses on Thanksgiving morning to paint a picture of the turkey in the sink. Throughout the prosperous and conformist Fifties she wore shabby clothes, lived in a slum, and spent all her money on art supplies. She did make sure her sons got an elite education. When they were in nursery school she traded art teaching for their fees; later they had scholarships to a private school on the Upper East Side. Her socialist friends judged her for that, and she didn't care. She arranged piano lessons for Richard, dance lessons for Hartley, tickets to concerts and the ballet. Part of her agency and satisfaction as a mother came from giving them the culture she'd longed for as a child. When they were in college, she summoned her old secretarial skills and typed their papers.

When the boys were older she was a sympathetic, resourceful, and exciting parent, and her house was the place where their friends liked to gather. But when they were small they sometimes felt underparented or unsafe. People came and went in Alice's apartment, wandering at all hours through the boys' bedroom on the way to and from the living room. Once when Alice left her sons home alone, at ages five and three, they flung her record collection out the window.

If people who become mothers must renegotiate their vocation, their children must also form a relationship to their progenitor's art. Alice respected her sons' life choices, and in turn they respected her devotion to painting. Looking back, Hartley Neel said he was proud of Alice's achievements. "If she had been satisfied with the paradigm of what women were supposed to be in her era," he pointed out, "she would have accomplished nothing." Richard said, "Every single one of us has to deal with what we're dealt, and the people we are exposed to. And it was a gift to have her as a mother."

Alice's new motherhood started with a step away from the art world. While she was pregnant with Richard, she and José left the Village and moved one hundred blocks uptown to the neighborhood known as Spanish Harlem. (*Flight into Egypt* was her title for a painting of herself with her pregnant belly and José with his guitar, moving north.) She settled into an apartment on 108th Street, just off Central Park, where the front room doubled as her studio. The rent was low, and José's mother and sisters lived nearby and occasionally helped care for Richard. She would live there for the next twenty years. She felt at home—and relatively safe from judgment—among the Puerto Rican immigrants who were the neighborhood's largest group. She often asked her neighbors to pose for her and was one of the few white artists of her time to portray people of color not as symbolic figures but as individuals viewed with interest and empathy.

The father of Alice's fourth and youngest child was Sam Brody, a photographer, filmmaker, and socialist she'd met at a WPA meeting. Like José he already had a partner when they got together, but he left his wife and two children and moved in with Alice (not in that order). Except for John Rothschild, Sam was the man who stayed in her life longest. He shared her politics and her conviction that the artist has a responsibility to society. As abstraction came in and figurative painting went out of fashion, he encouraged Alice to go on doing her own work. They sometimes worked together on art projects or pottery. He didn't mind her tenement apartment or her cheap clothes. He made her feel less isolated in her motherhood.

Painting was draining work for Alice, who said that when she finished a portrait she sometimes felt "like an untenanted house, utterly alone." Hartley recalled that after she painted she would often lie down in her bedroom, needing to rest and be by herself. But when she wasn't working, she loved being in the midst of a family. She especially enjoyed intelligent talk, and she and Sam were at their happiest listening to music and discussing books, politics, and art.

Yet as sympathetic as Sam could be, their relationship was also full of conflict, including screaming fights. Ginny suspected he was manic-depressive, and he was competitive and easy to anger. The target of his negative feelings was often his stepson, Richard. "He would terrorize me," Richard recalled of his stepfather's verbal abuse. "When I was learning how to read he said, 'If you learn how to read I'll kill you.'"

Alice and her sons all suffered from the conflicts between Sam and Richard. In a 1940 canvas called *Minotaur*, Alice portrayed Sam as a horned, black-hearted demon, with her infant son Richard screaming behind his back. Three years later, in *Alice and Richard*, she painted herself distraught, her eyes black circles, holding her son protectively against her.

Yet she never threw Sam out, partly because he took her and her work seriously. Before feminism, it was a rare man who could appreciate what a woman artist was trying to do, and Alice valued his support. "Of course I stayed with Sam," Alice later told a friend. "There I was in Spanish Harlem and nobody knew what I was doing and Sam understood."

It's also possible, given the taboo on mothers' anger and unhappiness, that Alice may have let Sam be the "monstrous" parent so she didn't have to stop being the loving one. By all accounts she was a willing participant in her scenes and arguments with Sam. Long after he left her, there was still a good chance a family get-together would end in a fight, or that a museum gala would see Alice offending some rich patron. "If things were going too smoothly, she'd throw a monkey wrench into it," Richard recalled. His daughter Olivia said that even at family dinners she still liked to provoke people. "Alice was of the belief that you should find out what people don't like and *give plenty of it.*"

"She enjoyed the give-and-take of a relationship that was not on the sort of 'bourgeois,' middle-class, stupid level," her son Hartley said. "Out of the chaos of the emotional situation, Alice somehow teased out some higher reality for herself. I don't know how to say it exactly, but she got energy from the emotional stress and intellectual jousting."

If Alice's sons respected her vocation, the one who couldn't was Isabetta. By the time she saw her mother again, she was nineteen and carrying a powerful load of resentment. She had been brought up to believe that Alice had abandoned her, and that her career was proof that she hadn't cared enough about her daughter.

Lonely and longing for love, she had become engaged at seventeen to a young man from a wealthy Havana family. Two weeks before the wedding he called it off, apparently because his mother had objected to her background. Isabetta was crushed. On the rebound, she married an agricultural engineer named Pablo Lancella. On their honeymoon they came to visit her aunt Lily in New Jersey and arranged to meet Alice at a New York hotel.

Though Alice was excited to see Isabetta and introduce her sons to the sister they'd never met, the meeting ended in disaster. Alice's daughter-in-law Nancy Neel, who heard about it from Alice years later, believed that Isabetta had made it clear she was ashamed of her mother: her clothes, how she looked, how she lived. If Isabetta said this, or blamed Alice for abandoning her, it might have wounded Alice deeply. Another relative claimed that a few days before that meeting, Alice had gone to Lily's house hoping to see Isabetta but that her daughter had angrily refused to speak to her.

Neither mother nor daughter ever got over her disappointment. Isabetta's husband later told Alice's biographer, Phoebe Hoban, that she couldn't understand why her mother had left her. It wasn't Alice Neel, the painter, who mattered to her, he explained. "It was just another mother, but she needed her." But if Isabetta needed a mother who wasn't a painter, that was the one thing Alice couldn't be.

A HAZARD OF MOTHERHOOD in any creative life is that the momentum of success that carries you through the first years of childhood may start to fade, and isolation and discouragement set in. Artists' careers often grow slowly and mature late. A painter needs to produce a whole body of work, into which she may invest years without ever knowing whether she will succeed. Making art is glorious when you're young, but if you're middle-aged and unsuccessful, where's the glamour in that? Living slightly apart from New York's artistic community, neither a fresh face nor an established figure, in her forties Alice saw her career begin to stall.

A warning sign came in 1944, when *Life* magazine reported that the federal government was selling paintings acquired by the Art Project as scrap canvas for four cents a pound. The *Life* article was illustrated with several discarded works, one of which was Alice's. She managed to buy a few of her canvases back from a Canal Street junk dealer, but the bulk of the Art Project paintings—which would have been worth millions on today's market—were lost or destroyed.

Social realism was on its way out, partly because, in the conservative postwar era, anything connected to Communism was suspect in America. In 1951 Alice had two one-woman exhibitions, but the important event of that year was the one she wasn't in. The Ninth Street Show, including work by Pollock, Willem and Elaine de Kooning, Franz Kline, Joan Mitchell, and other artists of what became known as abstract expressionism, swept New York off its feet and figurative painting out the door. Between then and 1960 Alice had only one more show.

Nonetheless, she stayed committed to portraiture, her chosen work. One way for a woman to achieve prominence in any discipline is to pick an unpopular field and make it her own. Otherwise she may lose too much energy competing with others; or, if she's truly innovative, she may find herself at the margins instead of in the lead. The low status of the portrait in the 1950s gave Alice an extraordinary freedom to explore and master the genre—and that in turn gave her room for her gifts and originality.

Her portraits also let Alice go on being critical in paint, showing the marks left on her subjects by poverty and exclusion, insisting on the human and aesthetic value of their lives, seeing each one as the hero of their unique and unrepeatable story. More direct political statements weren't safe. Some of Alice's left-wing friends were persecuted by the House Un-American Activities Committee, and even Alice was being watched. In the 1950s, Richard and Hartley once answered the door to two Feds in trench coats. Alice got rid of them fast, Hartley remembered. "She said, 'The only thing I don't have in my collection are FBI agents. Would you please step in the other room? I can paint you . . .' They just got red in the face and left." But she understood their visit to be a warning.

In 1953, Alice's frail, elderly mother came to live with her. The same year Richard, at fourteen, left home for a progressive boarding school in New Hampshire. "I hate like the devil to see [Richard] go and I know I'll miss him like mad," Alice wrote a friend, Phillip Bonosky. But "right now with mother sick most of the time things get so complicated and also as I said before that raging wolf 'Sam.'"

The next year her mother died, leaving Alice feeling both liberated—"I doubt I was really myself until my mother died," she later said—and bereft. At the same time her children were leaving home. When Hartley followed Richard to boarding school Alice wrote Bonosky that she missed not only her sons but her role as mother: "At first one resists children, tries to keep on with one's life, etc., however as time goes on more and more one becomes that normal thing—'a parent' and relates with it. Then suddenly . . . life yawns in front of you, that same big black terrifying hole you've always been afraid of."

Even creative mothers may lose themselves after their children leave home, falling for a while from the busy present tense of daily responsibilities into an eddying, backward-flowing time of nostalgia and stuckness. Alice was adrift for a while, not as an artist—she was doing excellent work—but in her emotional life. Sam started seeing another woman and Alice mourned, feeling her age. By 1958, though the two remained friends, he had moved out and they were no longer lovers.

In 1957 Carlos, at fifty-six, died after a period of alcoholic decline. What if Alice too had died in middle age, instead of living into her eighties, making some of her best paintings in her final two decades? Does the quality of the work make a difference in how we judge artist-mothers' careers? In a documentary on Alice's life, Ginny Neel commented that Alice "became famous, . . . so it was worth it. Just the slightest twist and she could have never been much heard of. And then what, it wouldn't have been worth it?"

But Alice didn't die in the creative wilderness; instead, as she approached sixty, she regained her momentum. The year Sam left, Alice began seeing a therapist, a young man who advised her to believe in herself and show her work. She started giving lectures, showing slides of her paintings while telling stories about the sitters and explaining her artistic choices. They were a success, bringing in money and, more important, creating an audience for Alice's art and persona. With her children grown, she confronted her fears and made the move that all successful artists must, from the domestic to the public sphere.

She'd always gone down to the Village for meetings of the Club, the artists' organization all the painters belonged to, and in 1959 two artist acquaintances, Alfred Leslie and Robert Frank, asked her to be in their short film *Pull My Daisy*, along with the stoned poets Gregory Corso, Allen Ginsberg, and Jack Kerouac. Playing den mother to the young gay men of the Beat generation was a role that suited Alice, while the film itself was a goofy, campy harbinger of change. Where the Fifties had been narrow, conformist, and wary, in the Sixties all of a sudden anything went—including women, and including the work of Alice Neel.

In 1962, Alice was profiled in the influential magazine *ARTnews*—her critical breakthrough at sixty-two. That same year in London, Doris Lessing published *The Golden Notebook*, a bold literary statement made by a fierce, fortyish mother of three. In Portland, Oregon, Ursula Le Guin sold her first science fiction story; in Bristol, England, Angela Carter, a "wide-eyed provincial beatnik" of twenty-two, had her first story in a magazine. In New York, Susan Sontag published her first essay and finished her first novel, while her ten-year-old son David stood by to light her cigarettes for her as she typed.

African American women had more battles to fight and were on a different trajectory. Gwendolyn Brooks was already a well-established poet but was denied teaching jobs because of her race until she finally gained that financial security in 1963. Alice Walker was in college, reading Lessing and marching with the civil rights movement. She would publish her first book of poetry in 1968, as would Audre Lorde. Artist Faith Ringgold, inspired by the Black Arts Movement, got her first show in 1967 (and ten years later would sit for a portrait by Alice). In 1969, Alice joined a picket line at the Met protesting the exclusion of Black artists, and in the watershed year 1970 Walker and Toni Morrison published their first novels, while Toni Cade Bambara edited *The Black Woman*, a groundbreaking feminist anthology whose contributors included mother-writers Walker, Lorde, Nikki Giovanni, Paule Marshall, and herself.

Women's luck was starting to change, and when it did, Alice was ready.

AN UNCOMPROMISING EYE is less threatening in an older woman than a young one. In the 1960s, under the influence of pop art (Roy Lichtenstein's comic-strip paintings, Andy Warhol's silk screens) Alice adopted brighter colors, a more fluid, self-assured line, and an approach to her subjects that was less outraged and more outrageous. "I try to paint the scene," she said in 1968. "The swirl of the era is what you're in and what you paint." Artists, curators, and collectors all came to pose as if taking a dare: Were you brave enough to sit for Alice Neel? Even Warhol rose to the challenge: for Alice's portrait he stripped to the waist, baring a belly seamed with gunshot scars, and shut his eyes, the great voyeur yielding his own vulnerable body to Alice's view.

Perhaps because she had herself lived unconventionally, sexual liberation became a Neel specialty. She painted gay and gender-nonconforming couples; she encouraged respected art-world figures to take their clothes off for her. When a young curator named John Perreault approached her for a show of male nudes, she talked him into posing. Her image of him lounging on a bed, tanned and furry, is as sexy as Manet's *Olympia*, yet Perreault, critic as well as subject, looks ready to turn his appraising eye on the result. Sitting for Alice felt like a collaboration, he recalled: "We were both being wicked."

Alice was quick to embrace women's liberation, while second-wave feminists were delighted to discover her work. She served on the board of New York's Feminist Art Institute and found friendship—and often practical assistance—from younger admirers. Some fellow artists thought her feminism was self-serving, but others celebrated her as a woman who was "out of bounds" in a way often associated with men. At a time when restroom access in public spaces was a feminist issue, Alice once, at a conference, turned her inability to wait into an impromptu protest by lifting her skirt and peeing on the floor. "If she couldn't help it," Ginny said, "she wasn't going to be embarrassed or apologize."

Insisting that her art wasn't only for or about women, Alice complained that feminist critics "respect you if you paint your own pussy" but weren't interested in other kinds of social justice. Still, it was partly pressure from feminist groups that got Alice her first major exhibition, a 1974 retrospective at New York's Whitney Museum of American Art. Only after that show, she said, when she was seventy-four, did she truly feel justified in being an artist.

In 1962, she moved to a large, light apartment on West 107th Street, near Columbia University, where Hartley was an undergraduate and

Richard was in law school. Alice's bond with them remained close. Ginny, who met Alice as a student in the 1960s, said, "I always thought of them as a troika, all for each other, out in the world handling it together. Her sons felt that she would support them no matter what they did."

With John Rothschild's help Alice found a patron, the psychoanalyst and philanthropist Muriel Gardiner, whose annual stipend of $6,000 lifted her out of poverty. For affection she had John, who moved in with her in 1970. No longer isolated with small children, she was now the matriarch of a supportive family, and she began to explore motherhood not just as a condition but as a subject of her art.

When her sons brought their friends over to meet their cool mom, Alice painted them, in playful, admiring portraits that suggest her pleasure in their company. Her portraits of her sons as young men are among her most moving canvases. They glow with pride and concern while they hint at a mother's sensual pleasure in her boys' good looks.

Richard became a lawyer, Hartley went to medical school. Independent, they were still her allies, as were her daughters-in-law. When Ginny and Hartley moved to a Vermont farmhouse, they built Alice a studio, her first space of her own. When she visited, Ginny posed for her and acted as her assistant, stretching canvases and making runs for art supplies. Later Ginny would become a tireless advocate for her artistic legacy.

Nancy Greene, who married Richard, was Alice's assistant in New York City and modeled for some of Alice's most remarkable pictures of pregnancy and motherhood. In *Mother and Child* (1967) Alice painted Nancy holding her first baby, gazing at the viewer—and Alice—with a frank plea for help as her daughter wriggles in her arms. She painted Nancy hugely pregnant with twins; Nancy with the twins; Nancy alone; each image thick with self and meaning.

Her portraits of pregnant women shocked some viewers: one squeamish critic called her portrayal of a nude, pregnant Nancy a "grisly prenatal odalisque." But long before Beyoncé Knowles posed for a series of photographic portraits, pregnant and beautiful, Alice argued that child-

bearing was an aspect of a woman's sexuality that deserved artistic representation. "I feel as a subject it's perfectly legitimate, and people out of
false modesty, or being sissies, never showed it, but it's a basic fact of life."

According to critic Mary Garrard, Alice "observed that the whole picture of women without pregnancy is trivial, saying that that was treating
them as sex objects." In her portraits of pregnancy and maternity Alice
attended to her own lived experience, while she satisfied the desire she felt
as a child under the blossoming pear trees: for someone to see, to make
sense of what was there, to tell the story.

Her awareness of parental entanglements often gets into her portraits.
In *Linda Nochlin and Daisy* (1973), Nochlin, the feminist art critic, tries
to hold a pose while her small daughter leans forward, too curious about
Alice to sit still. Alice, having once sketched herself in the same situation,
recognizes a mother trying to have an adult interaction while keeping
track of a child with other ideas.

That didn't mean parents always had her sympathy. When she painted
the art-world power couple John Gruen and Jane Wilson and their daughter, Julia, Alice portrayed them as two self-possessed adults and a girl like
Alice once was, squeezed into the margin. Julia Gruen recalled, "Alice
looked very benign, like a nice old lady, but underneath she seemed to
be made of steel. In the end, I found the portrait to be a little too scary,
far too revealing. But that's the price you paid for sitting for Alice—to
be revealed."

There was still one blind spot in Alice's vision. As a grandmother she
was especially fond of her sons' eldest daughters—maybe, Ginny thought,
because they reminded her of Isabetta. But though Isabetta and her family
had emigrated to the US during the Cuban Revolution, she didn't try to
get in touch with her mother and Alice didn't ask where she was.

Beautiful and intelligent, Isabetta had been brought up to be a traditional woman, but she wasn't happy in married motherhood. She divorced
and settled with her children in Miami, where she worked as a real estate
broker. The loss of the Enríquez family home and her exile in America

were difficult for her, and when her children were grown she turned to partying and relationships with married men. "She was always traveling, always having affairs," one friend said of Isabetta in her forties. "She wanted to live a bourgeois life, but at the same time she had a wild streak that was something unbelievable."

She began drinking heavily; her health was poor. In 1978 she made one last attempt to contact her mother. Alice came to town to give a lecture, and Isabetta sat in the front row. Alice, who had cataracts and didn't know Isabetta was living in Miami, didn't recognize her. Later, at the reception, Isabetta walked right past Alice, who still didn't see the daughter who looked so much like her. Too upset to introduce herself, Isabetta left and went home.

Four years after Alice's lecture, Isabetta committed suicide. When Richard told Alice, she said she'd dreamed about her daughter the night before.

THE MOST IMPORTANT of questions about creativity and art is also the most unanswerable. Did Alice's mothering make her art better? Many creative mothers have argued that their relationship with their children has deepened their sensibility, broadened their range, brought them, as Ursula Le Guin put it, "closer to the bone."

How true this holds for Alice is impossible to know. Yet the eye of the outlaw mother surely helped Alice make pregnancy and families her brilliant late subjects. And when Alice did a nude portrait of herself, in 1980, four years before her death, it became a last, magnificent statement on herself as mother, lover, and painter. Eighty years old, she painted herself on a striped chair on which she had often posed her sitters. From one of her hands a white painter's rag hangs limply, mimicking the sag of her breasts and belly. In her other hand she holds her brush ready. Behind her glasses her cool eye evaluates the result of her work, while her expression carries the authority of intense concentration. Her self-portrait reveals both the mother's embodiment and the artist's mastery.

It was around this time that Alice wrote of herself and her art, "What will they think of me afterwards? You know, I had to do this. I couldn't have lived, otherwise."

All the Time

◆

There *is* a heroic aspect to the practice of art; it is lonely, risky, merciless work, and every artist needs some kind of moral support or sense of solidarity and validation. (URSULA K. LE GUIN)

Maintenance is a drag; it takes all the fucking time (lit.) (MIERLE LADERMAN UKELES)

IF THE IMAGE OF the writer is of solitude and perseverance, the image of the artist tends to be more physical: a picture of complete, bodily devotion to the work. The heroic stance of the male creator explicitly rejects the work of care, but the practice of art really does require more focus than writing, more hours of the day, more dedication. Mother-artists have needed even more permission than mother-writers, and more autonomy.

The authority of the artist has been identified with his uninterruptibility. In 1893, critic Walter Pater wrote:

Manliness in art, what can it be, as distinct from that which in opposition to it must be called the feminine quality there,—what but a full consciousness of what one does, . . . tenacity of intuition and of consequent purpose, the spirit of construction as opposed to what is literally incoherent or ready to fall to pieces, and, in opposition to what is hys-

teric or works at random, the maintenance of a standard. . . . There
will be . . . no "negligence," no feminine forgetfulness of one's self.

Experiencing their time and attention "in pieces," women artists have
worked accordingly. The brilliant English sculptor Barbara Hepworth,
who had four children (one plus triplets), said that throughout the 1930s
and '40s she "lived a life of work and the children were brought up in it, in
the middle of the dust and the dirt and the paint and everything":

> *A woman artist is not deprived by cooking and having children. . . . One*
> *is in fact nourished by this rich life, provided one always does some work*
> *each day; even a single half hour, so that the images grow in one's mind.*

She had practical ways of dealing with interruption: "If I was in the
middle of a work and the oven burned or the children called for me, I used
to make an arrangement with music, records, or poetry, so that when I
went back to the studio, I picked up where I left off." But she also sought
to set herself apart from other, less dedicated women:

> *My home came first but my work was there always. . . . I never had*
> *much patience with women who said, "Well, I can't work this week or*
> *next week or the week after, but maybe I'll work in six months' time or*
> *maybe in a year's time." I found one had to do some work every day, even*
> *at midnight, because either you're professional or you're not.*

One such postponer was the Australian-English painter Stella Bowen,
who lived from 1918 to 1927 with the writer Ford Madox Ford. During
that time she was unable to do her own work. She wrote in 1941:

> *My painting had been hopelessly interfered with by the whole shape of*
> *my life, for I was learning the technique of quite a different role: that of*
> *consort to another and more important artist, so that although Ford was*

always urging me to paint, I simply had not got any creative vitality to spare after I had played my part towards him and Julie [their daughter] and struggled through the day's chores. . . .

Ford never understood why I found it so difficult to paint when I was with him. He thought I lacked the will to do it. That was true but he did not realize that if I had the will to do it at all costs, my life would have been oriented quite differently. I should not have been available to nurse him through the strain of his daily work; to walk and talk with him whenever he wanted, and to stand between him and circumstances. Pursuing an art is not just a matter of finding the time—it is a matter of having a free spirit to bring it on. . . . I was in love, happy and absorbed, but there was no room for me to nurse an independent ego.

Grace Hartigan married at nineteen and had her son the same year, 1941. In 1975 she said:

My son bitterly opposed my painting. He would stay after school and would come in at five o'clock, look at me, and say, "I know, you have been painting again." When he got to be twelve and his father had remarried, I sent him to California. I have never seen him since. It is a very bitter relationship.

There are other bitter relationships among artists and their children. In her 1991 documentary *Finding Christa*, Camille Billops explored her decision, in 1961, to give her four-year-old daughter up for adoption so that she could begin a new life as an artist. When Christa contacted Camille as an adult they tried building a relationship, but Camille admitted in the film that she couldn't open her house or heart to her daughter: "She took up space in a way that was threatening to me."

Artists felt that their gender or race set limits on what they could say. In the early 1970s, caring for small children, filmmaker Kathleen Collins wrote:

Men become themselves out of a refusal of certain kinds of limitations, women out of an acceptance of them. Women are bound. They must come to terms with a whole centrifugal force of taboos that they cannot violate without doing severe violence to themselves. We are in bondage to life.

The great painter and fabric artist Faith Ringgold observed,

No other creative field is as closed to those who are not white and male as is the visual arts. . . . After I decided to be an artist, the first thing that I had to believe was that I, a black woman, could penetrate the art scene, and that, further, I could do so without sacrificing one iota of my blackness or my femaleness or my humanity.

Ringgold had grown up assisting her mother, a fashion designer, and she dealt with the practical problems of her work in the 1960s and '70s by enlisting her mother and two daughters as collaborators:

Painting is a thoroughly self-absorbed activity, but still you need some-one to look with you, to see what you see. I tried to draw my family—my mother and the girls—into my work to help make up for the fact that I had no one else.

Painter and stepmother Helen Frankenthaler quoted the poet Joseph Brodsky, who believed that a writer or artist "has two subjects to han-dle: one is life and the other is art, and you cannot be successful in both. Sooner or later you realize that you must fake one." She disagreed:

One cannot simultaneously, with equal love and gift, handle (the cli-ché) of a "full life" and make beautiful and original art, [but] one can handle the problem of both. . . . I think that if [you are] in the grips of the torment in the gap between art and life, that your very survival is

threatened because you can't handle it. And rather than pretend, you will settle on just the art, or you will try to settle on just the life, which is impossible if you are a real artist.

In 1965, sculptor Eva Hesse addressed the problem of interruption and said a woman could practice one kind of artistic heroism, endurance.

To achieve an ultimate expression . . . requires the complete dedication seemingly only man can attain. A singleness of purpose no obstructions allowed seems a man's prerogative. His domain. A woman is side-tracked by all her feminine roles from . . . cleaning house to remaining pretty and "young" and having babies. . . . She also lacks conviction that she has the "right" to achievement. She also lacks the belief that her achievements are worthy. Therefore she has not the steadfastness necessary to carry ideas to the full. . . . A fantastic strength is necessary and courage.

Artist Mierle Laderman Ukeles thought otherwise. In 1969, after the birth of her child, she decided to accept cleaning as the essence of her art. In a spirit of subversion she organized performances—such as washing the floor of a museum gallery—that linked maternal labor to other under-compensated forms of maintenance work. Among her achievements, she became artist-in-residence at New York City's Department of Sanitation. Describing her moment of insight, she said,

I had a huge crisis. I had a child, and I became a maintenance worker. I was feeling like two separate people. I loved that baby. . . . I felt like I was rediscovering the world with every discovery, millions of discoveries that she was making. The world became new to me through her eyes. But it was also extremely boring. Boring! I felt like my brain was going to say to me, "Goodbye. I'm out of here. I wasn't made for this. I'm made to be free." . . .

One night I just said to myself, "If I am the boss of my freedom, then I call maintenance, art." What am I doing? I'm taking a Western notion of art as freedom, and taking a non-Western notion of repetitive systems, and saying that's art. I'm crashing them together, actually. It's not such a happy union. But I said, if I have this freedom to name, like my [honorary] grandfather Marcel [Duchamp] gave me, I choose maintenance and I call it art. I call necessity art.

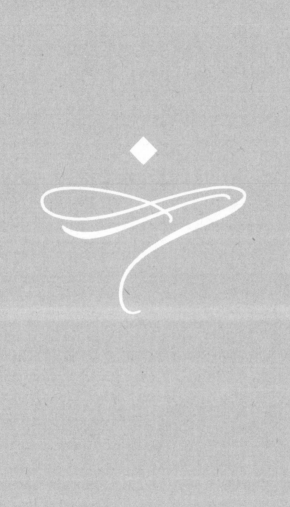

The Discomfort Zone

SEX AND LOVE

◆

I *BEGAN THIS BOOK* *determined not to criticize mothers' choices. I didn't want to judge Alice Neel for not providing a quiet home life or be shocked by Doris Lessing, while she was pregnant, sleeping with a man who wasn't the father of her child. As it turned out, though, thinking about mothers awakened my desire for safety and conventionality, and some things mothers did made me uncomfortable. I couldn't take a dispassionate view, and I didn't trust my uneasiness not to lead me to disapproval and control.*

I decided to make a space for what I wasn't sure about: the Discomfort Zone. To begin with: mothers, sex, and unconventional love.

THE BODILY PLEASURES of mothering can be intense. "Lovers make you a gift of your body; so do children," Kate Moses writes. "The erotic shimmer of motherhood, the light-on-water of physicality that underscores contact with our children. . . . Can the erotic and the sensual, the spiritual and the corporeal, ever be completely separated after you've become a mother?"

Louise Erdrich writes that caring for babies threw her into a "joy of the physical emotions, a religious and fixated delight that seizes me so thoroughly that the life of the imagination sometimes seems a spare place."

But that other great source of pleasure, sex, often gets censored out of mothers' lives. The institution of motherhood, Adrienne Rich wrote, demands of women that they be "beneficent, sacred, pure, asexual, nourishing." Or if not completely asexual—for contemporary mothers, there can be pressure to get your body back and look hot again—then restricted: available to one partner only.

Poet June Jordan recalled learning from Dr. Spock that a mother shouldn't even look attractive. In her words: "Do not wear miniskirts or other provocative clothing because that will upset your child, especially if your child happens to be a boy. If you give your offspring 'cause' to think of you as a sexual being, . . . you will derail the equilibrium of his notions about your possible identity and meaning in the world."

As the parent of a son she briefly tried to wear colorless, plain clothes, "hoping thereby to prove myself as a lusterless and dowdy and, therefore, excellent female parent." Then she gave it up, concluding that this attempt to control her bisexual, polyamorous, desiring, maternal body was an attack on her "self-determining power."

Of the mothers in this book, some, including Le Guin, Walker, and Carter, preferred monogamous relationships, limited or lifelong. Several others, for different reasons, opted out of monogamy in their search for authenticity and independence. Audre Lorde's open marriage to a gay man was a practical way to raise children as a lesbian. Doris Lessing's writer friend Naomi Mitchison was looking for more love and better sex when she chose polyamory, as well as a way to claim her freedom against the institution of marriage.

Born in 1897, Naomi Haldane wed army officer Dick Mitchison in the middle of the First World War, when she was eighteen and he just a few years older. Neither one knew anything about sex, and their first attempts disappointed them both. "I got little or no pleasure" from making love, Naomi wrote. "The final act left me on edge and uncomfortable. Why was it so unlike Swinburne? Where were the raptures and roses? Was it going to be like this all my life? I began to run a temperature." In 1918 she heard about *Married Love*, the new sex manual by birth-control activist Marie Stopes. The discovery that information could turn bad sex into good sex was an eye-opener. While she and her husband learned new techniques, Naomi began to see sex in general as a project worth pursuing.

Dick returned from the war and he and Naomi had the first of their seven children. When her son was a baby she began to write fiction and plays, sometimes balancing a notebook on the pram as she wheeled him through a London park. While she nursed she read novels for review: "If the books were not very good, I could manage two [infants] at a feed, one for each side." Sex and pregnancy nourished her creativity, she claimed, while the Mitchison family's wealth, and the servants and boarding schools that went with it, gave her time to write. She published novels and nonfiction, including a 1930 pamphlet on birth control that daringly mentioned as potential users "temporary or semi-permanent lovers."

By then Naomi and Dick had decided together to explore sex outside marriage. Influenced by socialist critiques of marriage as, in effect, sanctioning men's social and economic ownership of women, Naomi saw polyamory as a way of making love less proprietary and, potentially, more equal. First Dick took a lover, a married woman who was—and remained—the couple's close friend. Shortly afterward Naomi began a sexual relationship with Theodore Wade-Gery, an Oxford professor of classical history who gave her material for her celebrated historical novels set in ancient Greece and Rome.

Ironically, the Mitchisons' socialist ideas were supported partly by an upper-class British family structure that relied on the maternal labor of others. Not being her children's primary caregiver left Naomi free to travel with her husband and other partners: once she, Dick, and both their lovers went to Greece together while Naomi was pregnant with her fifth child by Dick. Lessing, meeting Naomi years later, idealized the Mitchisons' marriage as "the essence of good sense and civilized behavior" and appreciated Naomi's "exuberance" and honesty.

There was sorrow in an open marriage, too. When Wade-Gery broke off their relationship to marry another woman, the separation, she wrote, caused "deep heartache which for me went on long after." And though she and Dick remained close, they discovered that frankness didn't eliminate the pain of jealousy. "Perhaps we were too truthful," Mitchison mused, "since it is the minor details which hurt." Still, she felt that even these currents of emotion "turn[ed] the mills" of her work. She was careful to use contraception with her other partners, so that all her children would be conceived together with her husband, but hoped that her daughters "would be able to have children by several chosen fathers, uncensured."

During the most despairing period of her life, after she and Dick lost their eldest son, nine-year-old Geoff, to meningitis, Naomi felt guilty, and was blamed by others in her circle—she hadn't been home when Geoff developed the ear infection that turned deadly. Her brother and sister-in-law, who couldn't have children (though Charlotte Haldane wrote a scientific overview of mothering titled *Motherhood and Its Enemies*), were especially judgmental. But she never regretted her choices in her marriage. Love, she wrote in her memoirs, "sharpened and intensified all my abilities," while in her writing she encouraged others to live differently, with greater freedom than before.

IN GREENWICH VILLAGE in the 1950s, sexual experiment and multiple partners were not only necessary to becoming your own person, they were part of a larger project, too, the beginnings of the sexual revolution, the stirrings of gay liberation. In that generation, poets Audre Lorde and Diane di Prima approached sex and mothering as related acts of self-making and defiance. Lorde saw her adventures with women, and occasionally with men, as a safe way to bridge the distance between herself and others. Di Prima saw her adventures with men, and occasionally with women, as a way of being open to experience without having to give up too much of herself.

Di Prima was the red-haired, brilliant child of Italian immigrants, a high school friend of Lorde's who, in the 1950s, dropped out of college and found her way into the Beat poetry scene. High-spirited and intrepid like Mitchison, she took advantage of the sexual freedom of the time. Sharing apartments with her gay men friends, she slept mostly with partners who didn't make claims on her.

Then, at twenty-two, she began to want a baby. Her body "had its own agenda," she wrote, one that put it on a collision course with her poetry. "My physical being . . . wanted to flower, to put out fruit and seed. . . . I knew with certainty that if I foiled it I would not and could not live happily and long."

She didn't want a child with a partner. Her early experience with an abusive father made her determined to keep paternal control and violence out of her home. "No one, I vowed from the first, would ever tell me how to raise my children. . . . No one owns me in any way, my body, my love. No one by 'providing' . . . would buy the right to tell me what to do."

Instead she got pregnant without telling the father and had a daughter, Jeanne, as a single mother in 1957, when she was twenty-three. She improvised a family: her women friends supported her, her parents came around, the lesbian couple upstairs pitched in, and her gay friend Freddie pretended to be her husband at the hospital so she wouldn't be pressured to give up her "illegitimate" baby.

As a mother, like Neel, she felt protected by "the pragmatism and hard-headedness" of her new role, which kept her from taking risks that might have hurt her art. One night at a party at Allen Ginsberg's, Diane said she was leaving because her babysitter expected her. From the floor, a stoned, sprawled Jack Kerouac proclaimed: *Di Prima, unless you forget about your babysitter, you're never going to be a writer.* She believed she wouldn't have been a writer if she'd stayed. To write and to come home on time, she argued, required "the same discipline throughout": a practice of keeping her word.

Even the adventurous Beat poets had unwritten rules about sex. Diane broke one of them when she started sleeping with a man who was already taken, her fellow poet LeRoi Jones (later Amiri Baraka). His wife, Hettie, who was Diane's friend, hadn't agreed to an open marriage and was hurt despite her attempts to be "cool" about it. Their friends disapproved, and Diane's difficult situation was made worse by the pregnancy that followed. Roi pressured her to have an abortion that wasn't her choice; after she went through with it, she felt wracked by grief and anger. Pregnant again a year later, she defied his arguments and had his child.

As Mitchison had dreamed, Diane had five children by four different men; about the white gay man whom she took as her lover on the rebound from Roi, she said, "I knew that he was a man I'd never fall in love with, so he seemed like a good person to marry." Inevitably motherhood sometimes cost her the freedom of her working hours. In a letter to Lorde in the mid-Seventies she said that for time to write she was "waiting for the next rift in the curtain of days—days of driving kids to school, to dentist, doing laundry, groceries, garbage. . . . Can there be an unquenchable thirst and no time to drink? What is that about? When does time xplode?"

She thought of her work and her motherhood as arising from one source, openness to experience. She called it being "available, a woman's art I saw as a discipline, a spiritual path. To be available, but stay on course somehow. Self-defined in the midst of it all: my work, my life."

Audre Lorde believed that her sexuality and the pleasures of the body were central to herself and her art, at a time, the 1950s and '60s, when even to publish a lesbian love poem was a radical act. "Our erotic knowl-edge . . . becomes a lens through which we scrutinize all aspects of our existence," she wrote in her essay "Uses of the Erotic: The Erotic as Power." She urged women to explore the erotic—understood as "that power which rises from our deepest and nonrational knowledge"— as a source of personal joy and artistic agency as well as a gift of freedom to one's children.

Audre first started having multiple partners as a socialist in her twenties. Later she translated the socialist embrace of sexual freedom to a feminism that celebrates pleasure as a power source. "The aim of each thing which we do is to make our lives and the lives of our children richer and more possible. Within the celebration of the erotic in all our endeavors, my work becomes a conscious decision—a longed-for bed which I enter gratefully and from which I rise up empowered."

If Lorde is right, sex is not separate from but at the heart of maternal subjectivity, a necessary form of self-knowledge for the hero-mother, whether she is settled in a monogamous marriage or making other arrangements. If you're tempted to lose yourself in motherhood, erotic power can bring you back to yourself. "When we begin to live from within outward, in touch with the power of the erotic within ourselves," Lorde went on, "then we begin to be responsible to ourselves in the deepest sense. For as we begin to recognize our deepest feelings, we begin to give up, of necessity, being satisfied with suffering and self-negation."

Doris Lessing with Peter, 1946, in a photo sent to John Whitehorn.

Incompatible Pleasures

DORIS LESSING (1919–2013)

◆

If you look for the provenance of the feminist writer, mother is the key. The women who really nailed patriarchy weren't on the whole the ones with authoritarian fathers, but the ones with troubled, contradictory mothers: you aim your feminism less at men than at the picture of the woman you don't want to be, the enemy within. (LORNA SAGE)

A woman who has experienced her own mother as a destructive force—however justified or unjustified the charge—may dread the possibility that in becoming a mother she too will become somehow destructive. (ADRIENNE RICH)

ONE THING EVERYONE KNOWS about Doris Lessing is that she abandoned her children to pursue a writing career. At twenty-three, in 1943, she was the mother of a three-year-old son and a one-year-old daughter, married to a civil servant and living in colonial Salisbury, Southern Rhodesia (now Harare, Zimbabwe). She sat down on her suburban lawn with her two toddlers and explained that she was leaving them. She said she was going, not to be a writer—she didn't know that yet—but to fight economic injustice and racism, the "color bar" that was Rhodesia's version of apartheid. She thought they understood, or if they didn't yet, they would. Besides, because of her own childhood experience, she thought that only if they didn't have a mother could they really be themselves.

This scene seems to illustrate everything that is liberating about Lessing's work and life, and what's troubling, too. She later remarried, had a third child, got divorced, and moved to London as a single mother, leaving her two eldest children behind in Africa. She became a great novelist who drew on her own experience of love, motherhood, and politics to expose the gaps and seams in women's lives. In *The Golden Notebook*, in a series of autobiographical fictions she called *Children of Violence*, in short stories and plays, she explored relationships between men and women, mothers and children, wondering whether they were as fixed as they seemed, bringing what had seemed "natural" into the daylight realm of political action and change.

The idea of a woman who leaves her children is fascinating, almost exhilarating, like any forbidden thought. One mother will comment on it to another, envying the suggestion of freedom, before turning back to her own children with guilty devotion, thinking: well, at least I'm not as bad as *that*. It can also serve as inspiration for rethinking one's own motherhood. But in Doris's case, the story that she walked away from her two eldest children and never looked back turns out to be, more or less, a fiction.

The evidence against abandonment lies in a collection of over a hundred letters that Doris wrote between 1945 and 1949. The recipients were two Royal Air Force cadets, John Whitehorn and Coll MacDonald, who had come to Rhodesia for flight training at the end of the Second World War. The letters are remarkable for the assurance of their style: at twenty-five, Doris is funny, self-revealing, and already making the astute observations of people and situations that would later animate her writing.

The letters portray her as both capable and vulnerable, confident and guarded. They show her hoping and longing to see her children and thinking about them with pleasure and concern. They show her not abandoning her children but entering into painful arguments with her ex-husband to get more time with them.

Motherhood looms large in the letters, fascinating Doris, but putting her on the defensive, too. One side of her, she writes, would like to have a lot of children, cook, sew, and live a peaceful life. Another side tended to "get bored, restless and unhappy" in that life and would rather "run a newspaper, write novels, meet people, take part in the class struggle etc. These two things don't fit together, you must admit."

The letters show a woman who left an unsuitable marriage at a time when the law gave her no legal rights to her children, and who wrestled with that choice. In her memoirs, written years later, she plays down her complicated feelings, perhaps to protect her children's privacy. But in both letters and memoirs she reveals a pride and defiance that keep her from trying to exonerate herself from the charge, always serious and so easy to reach for, of being a bad mother.

"WE USE OUR PARENTS like recurring dreams, to be entered into when needed; they are always there for love or for hate," Lessing observed, and over and over, in fiction and memoir, she wrote and rewrote her relationship to her parents, trying to understand what had brought them to Southern Rhodesia, what her mother wanted from her, how she could keep from becoming like her. Doris's motherhood and her writing both began in her own childhood, and especially in the tug-of-war between mother and daughter over selfhood, self-determination, and the limits of maternal power.

To begin with, neither of Doris's parents seemed to be entirely in contact with reality. On the family's failing farm, her father wrote letters to the newspapers opining that proper composting would contribute to world peace and that "one should only drink water that has stood long enough in the direct sun to collect its invisible magic rays." Her mother unrealistically projected onto Doris all the English, middle-class ambitions that had slipped out of her own grasp when her husband took her to Africa. Doris's truth-telling in her fiction partly reflects her long struggle to claim her own identity from her parents' illusions.

Doris was the product of their first false hope, that in marriage and parenthood they could make up for the damage done to them by the First World War. She was born Doris Tayler in Kermanshah, now Bākhtarān, in Iran, on October 22, 1919, nine months after her parents' wedding. They had met in a London hospital, where Alfred Tayler was recovering from the loss of his right leg, from "shell shock," and from grief after the other men in his company all died at Passchendaele. Emily Maude McVeagh was a nurse in her thirties also suffering from what would now be called PTSD. She had spent the war tending to horribly wounded and dying soldiers; the doctor she had loved was among the dead.

Emily and Alfred sought consolation with each other, and when they married they decided to erase the past. They took new first names: he chose Michael, after the youngest brother in *Peter Pan*; she became Maude. Then they left England to start over in colonial Persia, where Michael had been offered a job clerking in an English bank.

They had a comfortable life in Kermanshah, and Maude enjoyed the luxuries of the expat life: friends and parties in the British community, servants, a house with a garden. But Michael, despite his wooden leg, had always wanted to be a farmer. On leave in England in 1924, he read about good money to be made growing corn in the new colony of Southern Rhodesia. When the Taylers paid for a thousand acres of bushland and made plans to move to Africa, they pictured themselves as rich planters, like the English settlers in Kenya, and Maude packed her silk evening dresses in anticipation.

When she found herself instead living in a mud-walled house in an isolated rural district of a backwater colony, with no hope of getting out of debt to the British South Africa Company, married to a husband who didn't want to leave, she took to her bed with a "bad heart" and refused to get up for a year. Out of a sense of duty she finally pulled herself together and went on, but only by giving up herself, her desires, her ability to assert her own reality.

Doris struggled to cope with the unadmitted needs of a parent who had lost her way. This was true for many twentieth-century mother-writers.

But in particular Maude Tayler and Olive Stalker, Angela Carter's mother, each projected onto their only daughter their own frustrated aspirations, encouraging her to succeed but cautioning her to be ladylike, judging her looks, policing her body, overidentifying with her success. Maude was proud of her clever child but possessive of her too, wanting her to repay the debt of her own self-sacrifice. It's the eternal story, in Rebecca Solnit's phrase, of "the mother who gave herself away to everyone or someone and tried to get herself back from a daughter."

Energetic and active, Doris might not have been an easy child to parent under any circumstances. As a baby she cried. At five, angry at being left alone aboard ship, she cut up her mother's dress. At eight she played with matches and burned down the storage shed. But she hated it when she overheard her mother blaming her for her unhappiness, telling the other farmers' wives what burdens she and her brother Harry were, "how all her own talents were withering unused, how the little girl in particular (she was so difficult, so naughty!) made her life a total misery."

In this drama of emotional deprivation, Maude and Doris took turns playing the rejecter and the rejected. In her memoirs Lessing wrote that when she was born, Maude had been so sure her child would be a boy that she had no name for a girl and had called her "Doris" at the doctor's suggestion. But this seems unlike Maude, with her romantic approach to naming, and to John Whitehorn Doris told another story in which she herself defeated her mother's plans. Maude had in fact thought long and hard to come up with a girl's name that sounded serious, one that couldn't be corrupted into some silly diminutive. But when Doris was nine, she announced that from then on she would answer only to "Tigger." The new children's book *Winnie-the-Pooh* had just arrived from England, and Doris, seeing herself in the bouncy, difficult, lovable tiger, followed in her parents' footsteps by choosing a name for herself. In her letters to John she confessed to having second thoughts, but she went on signing her letters "Tigger" right up until she moved to London at twenty-nine.

From her father she absorbed his distrust of the British ruling classes and his love for Rhodesia's wild beauty. Like many colonial Europeans, Doris enjoyed far more privilege than she would have had at home, including the freedom to roam the land; she was too young to understand that it was stolen and just the right age to fall in love with it. She spent hours alone or with her younger brother, at first populating the anthills with goblins and fairies from her mother's bedtime stories, later exploring the veld around their farm, hunting small game, listening to the birds, feeling the sun on her skin. While Maude played Chopin on the piano and wrote letters to her friends in England, Doris gave her heart to the open country, the distant hills, even their improvised house, where a tree sprouted through the earth under her bed every rainy season and the mud walls were always on the point of dissolving into the bush. It was her father's gift to her: a space big enough for her imagination to grow.

Culturally, though, Rhodesia's insular and conservative white community offered her no clues to what a brilliant girl might become. Sent to boarding school, Doris was lonely and homesick, and when she went home with a case of pink eye at fourteen and refused to go back, that was the end of her formal education. Maude hoped she might win a scholarship to study in England, but even if Doris had trusted her mother's plans for her, her parents' home country seemed to her then "as far away as the stars."

The scene that opens her first autobiographical novel, *Martha Quest*, is of a teenage Martha slouched on the porch, glowering at Mrs. Quest and pointedly reading the radical "sexologist" Havelock Ellis. While Alice Neel was learning love and defiance in the Village, Doris was hearing faraway echoes of the same message, and her pose as a sexual rebel, she later said, was "pure extract of *Zeitgeist*." It was also a weapon aimed at Maude, with her disappointing life and sexless marriage. Sex by itself wasn't enough to solve a woman's problems, but you wouldn't know that from reading D. H. Lawrence. She hung around the house, daydreaming about a bohemian life in Paris, repeating to herself, "I will not. I will not be like that. I am never going to be like them."

At the same time she started to perceive the foundational deception of white Rhodesian society, one her parents believed along with all the others: its claim of racial superiority. But she hardly knew anyone who saw what she saw. At seventeen she taught herself to type, wrote novels, tore them up. At eighteen she got a job as a telephone operator and moved into a rented room in Salisbury. She had no money, no education. All she knew was who she wasn't and how she didn't want to live. Into that vacuum, as so often happens, stepped a man.

The capital of Southern Rhodesia was a frontier town of fewer than twenty thousand Europeans, served by a parallel city of perhaps four times that many Africans. The settlers were a hard-drinking, philistine lot, with fewer young women than men, but Doris thought of herself as a "man's woman," and the men could appreciate an attractive, outgoing girl like "Tigger" Tayler. Caught up in a group for the first time in her life, she drank, danced, stayed out late. After years of loneliness she was thrilled with the attention. Doris may have longed for a brilliant career, but she wasn't ready yet to begin, and Tigger was losing her resolve. The admiration and fun was so seductive to this "raw young woman out of the bush" that within a year she was not only flirting with the boys, she'd married one.

WHY DID INTELLIGENT, ambitious Doris take a wrong turn, marrying a man she didn't love and having two children she wasn't ready to care for? In her autobiography she claimed it was because it was 1939 and war was in the air, making young people live only for the present. She blamed alcohol—all the young people drank heavily—and the sexy popular music of the time, music about "yearning and longing and wanting." (When she published her first memoir in 1994 she took the title from one of those songs, Cole Porter's sultry "Under My Skin.") She suggested that it wasn't she but Tigger who was getting married.

For saying these things Doris has been accused of not taking responsibility for her feelings, trying to "locate the cause for her actions outside the sphere of her free will," or claiming to be a "victim of History." Yet a bright young woman making an impulsive marriage is the oldest story in the world. For a lonely nineteen-year-old in flight from childhood, searching for affection, approval, and a sense of belonging, marriage and the motherhood plot are right there waiting, promising all: love and fulfillment, adult privilege and sexual satisfaction, maternal bliss and a happy ending.

Tigger and Frank Wisdom even seemed to have a lot in common. Ten years older than his wife, Frank was "one of the boys," but he also had progressive ideas and was willing to question Rhodesia's status quo. He too had begun to intuit that whites' oppression of the Black majority was wrong. He "claimed to despise anything that might be called 'bourgeois,' from mortgages to fidelity." He supported her writing, or said he did.

Her emotional needs and her ambitions were in conflict, but she didn't want to see it. Like Alice Neel, she went through with the marriage, feeling powerless to stop. "I seemed to have no will," she recalled. "My intelligence watched what I did but was helpless." A month or two later, having said she wasn't going to have children, she became pregnant.

She had always felt herself to be different from other women, and in *Under My Skin* she wrote that she hadn't imagined she could have a baby: "There is an absolute barrier between the idea of oneself standing there inside one's young strong body . . . , a body that is *yours*, so you think, and really, but *really* knowing how easily you can get pregnant." She and Frank both thought she should get an abortion but had no idea where or how. Frank suggested Johannesburg, so Doris took the train there, a two-day trip. But when she found the house of a doctor she'd heard performed the procedure, she arrived in the middle of a party. One of his friends took Doris aside and advised her not to do it: "He had been struck off the Medical Register for operating drunk. If I valued my womb I would thank him and say I had changed my mind."

She found another, more professional doctor who examined her and told her she was already eighteen weeks pregnant; he wouldn't perform an abortion so late. So she went home, a little relieved and hoping for the best. In September 1939 war broke out in Europe. In October she celebrated her twentieth birthday. That summer, in February 1940, she gave birth to her son John Wisdom, ten months after the wedding. Her first child was assisted into the world by those two fertility goddesses of the modern age: contraceptive failure and hope.

THE TROUBLE WITH MOTHERHOOD, Doris wrote John Whitehorn eight years later, is not the work itself but the conditions under which it is done. Her generation of women had been promised careers and freedom, only to find themselves back in "captivity" after their first baby. Her English grandparents had had nannies. Her grandchildren, she hoped, would have access to reliable day care. But among her contemporaries, she observed, "I haven't yet met a woman who isn't bitterly rebellious, wanting children, but resenting them because of the way we are cribbed cabined and confined." She loved her child but had a bad relationship to her motherhood: the lack of independence and the erasure of self were more than she could bear. In her first marriage, as she put it, "the best part of me was in cold storage."

She had been sure she wouldn't have a difficult labor—after all, she was stronger than other women—but it was difficult nonetheless, and John was not an easy baby. Although Frank was a proud father, he went off to his government office every morning, leaving his young wife behind with an active, unsleeping infant who never rested or wanted to be held. Doris admired her son's energy and saw in it "the exuberant health he inherited from me." But she was exhausted by it, too. In a state of dreamy boredom she pushed his pram through their suburban neighborhood over "Himalayas of tedium."

Work and fatherhood seemed to change Frank, tempering the sense of adventure that had made Doris hope he and she could be different from the rest. Now he encouraged Doris to spend time with other young mothers, the wives of his civil service colleagues, because the connections would be good for his career. Doris also ambivalently wanted a community of new mothers, to reflect back to her her commonplace, extraordinary experience of new motherhood. Together she and her neighbors shared the slow time of infant care, exploring this new state whose feelings were so overwhelming, primal, impossible to explain to anyone else. "I was bored, I was rebellious, I hated the morning tea parties," she recalled. "I craved them, and hated myself for craving them." When she instead stopped by the Sports Club, where she used to go to parties, her former friends looked right past her. "Eighteen months ago I—and all the other girls—had been competed for by every man in sight and now I had become invisible. I was treated as respectfully as if I had been fifty, in spite of my again slim body and my girl's face." Exclusion gave her perspective: on the veranda of the Sports Club, holding a cigarette in one hand and rocking the pram with the other, Doris listened as the young colonials talked, gathering material that she would eventually use in her first novels. In her daily life she had little time to write. She had servants, as all but the poorest white Rhodesians did; her middle-class comforts depended on Black labor. But to ask a Black person to care for her child was not done and would have caused a scandal.

Besides, when Doris wasn't catering to Frank, who liked to bring colleagues home for lunch, she was fending off her mother, who paid visits to criticize her daughter's parenting style. Defining and defending her boundaries without guilt and drastic measures would be a problem for Doris even at her most self-possessed; she had grown up knowing only self-sacrifice and passive-aggressive reaction. Her alter ego Anna in *The Golden Notebook* comments on her partner's sense of entitlement to her time and attention and her inability to assert her own needs. Since she can't picture a solution, she tries to live with her discontent, calling it "the disease of women in our time. I can see it in women's faces, their voices, every day. . . . The woman's emotion: resentment against injustice, an impersonal poison."

All Doris knew at twenty-one was that she was in danger of sharing her mother's fate. In her fantasies she saw herself as a calm, radiant nurturing figure, but in her fears she became controlling, embittered, a mental health hazard to her child. Neither of these visions left room for her real capacities and desires, or for her to grow into an authentic relationship with her son, though in her second autobiographical novel, *A Proper Marriage*, Martha Quest hopes that "she, Martha, the free spirit" will be strong enough to protect her child from "her, Martha, the maternal force." Meanwhile, the motherhood plot was still pulling her along. When John was nine months old the Wisdoms decided to have another child—or so Doris later wrote. At any rate, she became pregnant again, and their daughter, Jean Wisdom, was born in 1941.

To keep from going under, she clung to her intellectual life; like Martha Quest, she tried to "keep brightly burning that lamp above the dark blind sea which was motherhood. She would *not* allow herself to be submerged." Sitting on a blanket in the garden she recited poetry to her babies. In the park, in a trance of slow hours and "rich, pleasurable melancholy, which is like a drug," she wrote poems in her head. Some of them mildly criticized racial injustice, and these made Frank angry: he had always shared her dislike of the color bar, but now he had his career to think of, and a segregated society does not look kindly on dissent. She was growing away from him. He started lapsing into grim silences that lasted for weeks.

At some point she realized she'd been fooling herself, living as much in an illusion as her parents had. She also realized that, under Rhodesian law, if a wife left her husband for any reason, he was granted full custody of their children. When Jean was a baby, she wrote in *Under My Skin*, she unconsciously avoided getting too attached to her infant daughter, who was quieter and more cuddly than her son—and more obviously wanted her mother. "I was protecting myself, because I knew I was going to leave. Yet I did not know it, could not say, I am going to commit the unforgivable and leave two small children." She tried to convince herself she was liberating them, but if she believed it at the time, she soon thought it was madness.

She couldn't say to herself that she was leaving for the "selfish" act of writing. Her plan was to live in Salisbury, go on seeing John and Jean—she hoped Frank would allow it—and work for political change. At twenty-three she had chosen to acknowledge and be shocked by the restrictions on Black and Colored Rhodesians: the "locations" reserved for those whose land the Taylers and others now occupied, the passes, the curfews, the lack of access to education and training. She saw the beatings, murders, and humiliations. She saw with new eyes what the British Empire had done to her father, how he had been used and broken in the army, "then flung aside for the rest of his life." An acquaintance invited her to a political meeting, and Tigger Wisdom became an activist in Rhodesia's tiny Communist Party.

You can't be out of step with your culture on your own; that's a position only for the mad or desperate. These were the first people Doris had ever met who discussed ideas, questioned white supremacy, debated the proper roles of men and women, tried to imagine change. They read and learned, essential work for those, like Doris, who had had little formal education. They offered her a close-knit community, a new encounter with her own abilities, and a meaningful project.

Soon enough she would doubt the effectiveness of their isolated group, and in time she would realize how crazy their blind idealism and trust in Communist ideology had been. But at first their belief that they could see what others didn't—that they weren't deluded like her parents, her husband, all of white Rhodesia—was irresistible. Doris went on to become a brilliant writer on the lies people tell themselves, whether they're in an unhappy relationship, about to leave their children, or following a demagogue; and it was her motherhood that taught her how easy it was to be deceived.

DORIS'S STORY IS OFTEN told as if she left her children in Rhodesia and went straight to London. But a dramatic escape was never her plan. The first thing she had to do, like Alice in Greenwich Village, was reencounter herself, take stock, and look for a way forward. She moved into a rented room in Salisbury, got a job as a typist in a law office, and worked at making what she felt she needed: a home where her children could stay with her and "an identity . . . that would justify my having left them."

She also had to mourn her lost maternal self and the children she had left, and to get over the shock of her new independence. After office hours she rushed around town, attending meetings and canvassing for causes, all the while feeling "full of division." Like Alice, she worked frantically by day, then had terrifying dreams. In her sleep she stood looking down into a chasm or saw her childhood house on the farm crumbling into dust, demolished by insects, the earth around it blackened by fire. Her nightmares "insisted in a hundred ways that I was dangerously unhappy about the infants I had left, about my [parents], and because I wanted so very much to have time to write, but could not see when that would happen." She had been wrong about Frank: for the first year after she left, he wouldn't allow her to visit John and Jean.

She was looking for herself in political work, but it wasn't only politics that filled the new empty space in her life. When she finally collapsed from the strain, one of the comrades who came to see her was Gottfried Lessing, a refugee from Berlin who was one of the leaders of the little Communist group. He had seemed to her sophisticated, analytical, and aloof, but as she later assessed, "men who find it hard to break out of a shell of shyness enjoy being kind to sick girls in bed." He was probably the only one in the group who was her intellectual equal.

She didn't love him, she later said, and they could never get the sex to work. But within months of her leaving Frank they married, mainly to keep Gottfried out of a refugee camp. Theirs was a marriage of convenience, according to Doris, and the convenience was mostly his. On the other hand, Doris liked him and admired his intellect, and he approved of his wife's political work and didn't expect her to make him his tea. His willingness to grant her her independence came partly from his Marxist disapproval of the bourgeois family and his commitment, at least in theory, to gender equality. The insight central to *The Golden Notebook*, that domestic life has social relevance—that the personal is political—had its origins in Doris's Communist reading. On Communist principle he also agreed, reluctantly, to her request for an open relationship. She didn't want to do without satisfying sex or give up the power—and boundaries—that came with sexual freedom.

If Doris's first marriage stood in the shadow of domestic bliss, her second went on under the sign of political devotion. In those years challenging the color bar was an unheralded uphill battle. To John Whitehorn she admitted there were times when she feared that her meetings and canvassing and monthly column for the *Labour Forum* were a waste of time and energy and would never make "the dimwits of Salisbury any less complacent." To Coll MacDonald she said she struggled not to be absorbed into her country's "prevailing fog of dumbness." But then she saw the real suffering around her and came back determined to work harder.

Her years as an activist in Rhodesia left Doris with an oppositional stance that gave her energy, a sense of self, a counterstory to the motherhood plot. She would probably never get over "spending all my life consciously rebelling," she wrote Coll in 1945, and she wasn't wrong, but her rebelliousness helped her make her bold way in the masculine postwar literary world while telling truths about women's lives.

In Salisbury, gradually, she started owning her vocation as a writer. She wrote articles for little leftist papers, had a few satirical sketches published in a local magazine, and began thinking about writing a novel. That plan became more real about a year after her marriage to Gottfried, when she found friends she could talk to about writing as well as politics. One of them was John Whitehorn.

Starting in 1940, the Royal Air Force had sent thousands of servicemen to Southern Rhodesia for flight training at hastily constructed air bases. Some of them had socialist leanings, and late in 1944 a group of friends formed that included Doris, Gottfried, and three RAF cadets: Whitehorn, MacDonald, and Leonard Smith. All just twenty to Doris's twenty-five, they had been students at Cambridge before they joined the service and were the first people Doris had met who shared her passion for literature. In her first letters to John, written while he was still based near Salisbury, she resumes a conversation about Proust as a social critic; wishes she could ride off on a white horse like the cross-dressing adventuress Mademoiselle de Maupin, from the novel by Gautier; and reports, "I have been writing some rather bad fin-de-sieclish poetry. Great fun."

Finding an intellectual community was as big a change for Doris as finding a political one. In their little group she became closest to John, though she slept or attempted to sleep with all three of them (including Leonard, although he had told her he was homosexual). And it was in her friendship with them that she began remaking herself as a "free woman," an autonomous intellectual and artist. The group began taking weekend trips to a hotel in Macheke, about sixty miles from Salisbury, where they drank, danced, slept off hangovers, went on walks in the bush, and talked. For Doris, their discussions, silent longings, individual and collective sense of connection added up to a formative meeting of minds and bodies. The excitement of it spilled over around Christmas 1944, when during a long night of drinking and dancing Doris and John slipped away from the hotel, ran into the veld, and made love in the tall, rain-soaked grass. When they couldn't find their way back afterward they climbed a kopje, a rock outcropping, and sat pressed together in the dark, waiting for the sun to rise.

Doris had never done anything so romantic, and she cherished that night and her feelings about it ever afterward; a fictional version features prominently in *The Golden Notebook*. But when she returned to the hotel, dazzled and enamored, she found a wounded Gottfried waiting for her. Despite his agreement to an open marriage, he hadn't really wanted it and was hurt that she had so openly put it into practice. Several weeks of domestic turmoil followed, as reported by Doris, now writing in secret, to

John. She hated to make Gottfried unhappy, she wrote. She loved him, he was "the perfect husband," and she respected his rationality and his kind heart. But she couldn't pretend she was attracted to him and didn't want to give up on an open marriage.

The situation resolved itself when John was posted away from Salisbury, though Doris continued to write to him. She couldn't help it, she said: "In this most bloody place one is bound to fall in love with anyone one can talk to." In her letters she asserts her intellectual as well as emotional independence, noting what she saw around her and trying out her literary voice. Despite her praise of Gottfried, there was more than one reason she was looking elsewhere: she was starting to take herself seriously as a writer, and she couldn't talk to him about her art.

Within a few months she gave notice at her job and began drafting a novel, a decision that took her even further from her husband. Though Gottfried respected her political skills, Doris wrote John, he didn't think any writing was worth doing that didn't serve the Revolution. How was lying in the bathtub reading poetry supposed to advance the class struggle? he asked. What good to anyone were her second-rate sonnets? She replied that she didn't know but didn't plan to let that stop her. To Coll she reported the following exchange: "Do you think, I say meekly, that Lenin would have liked Virginia Woolf? No, says G firmly."

Though she could joke about it, Doris realized she was stuck in yet another marriage where she couldn't think her own thoughts. She told John that Gottfried claimed, " 'When people have a relationship such as we have, love outside marriage is a betrayal.' Well, I agree with him, except I am horrified and frightened by his saying that, when half the things I think I can't tell him, because he disapproves."

Some of her confessions were serious, but she also loved gossip: the letters show her as a sympathetic but keen observer, gathering material for her fiction in her own and other people's lives. She had a sense of humor that she reserved for private writing, mixing politics and art with the low comedy of everyday life: "I have the curse, a headache, depression and cold feet. (When we are married, can I have a hot water bottle? G says they are sissy.)" Beginning with the body, she was practicing her later openness about women's concerns.

The other drama that plays out in the letters is of Doris arguing with Frank to get more time with John and Jean. Two years after they had separated, Frank had begun letting Doris take the children on occasional weekends, usually after long lectures on her political views, her "bohemian" lifestyle, and especially her remarriage. That Frank too was remarried, to a woman who was now raising Doris's children, was beside the point. In March 1945 Doris described to John what ensued after she phoned to ask if she could have the children for Easter. First Frank said he wanted to see her in person. Then, as they stood outside on the street, he lectured her for "neglecting" John and Jean after the divorce.

Me. Since I was forbidden to see them at all it is difficult to see what else I could do but neglect them.

He. Still, it showed lack of feeling.

Me. Apart from marrying you, or staying married to you I couldn't do anything else.

He. Precisely.

Later on she went to talk to Frank at his office, and after an hour of arguments and reproaches, when she had almost given up, he suddenly relented and said she could have the children for the weekend. "Complete collapse of me, but that's all right," she wrote John, adding that she hardly knew how to care for them, what they liked to eat, what they would wear. She asked her son if he would like to come with her to Macheke. "He gives me a considering look for some time and then says 'I don't see why I should, do you?'"

If her son's coolness hurt she didn't say so; in letters to John Whitehorn she wrote admiringly of his independence. (Later on, after eighteen-year-old John Wisdom came to see his mother in England, they developed a good relationship.) In the spring of 1947, after she had had the children again for Easter, she wrote glowingly about her children's brains, her daughter's beauty. John still kept his distance, she wrote, and she respected it. She adored five-year-old Jean, "an affectionate and sensitive infant. I wish I could have her, but I can't, so that's that."

Frank Wisdom continued to appear in the letters as both a bore and a tormentor: the pain of being kept from her children ran deep. In early 1946 she wrote Coll that she couldn't reconcile his ordinary appearance with the figure who kept appearing in her dreams: by day he seemed too small and banal to be so menacing at night.

In July 1945 she told Coll that she had finished a draft of a satirical novel about Southern Africa and joked, "One of these days you will be able to say 'the novelist Tigger. Of *course*, I know her *very* well!'" Rhodesian civilians could travel overseas again, with the war in Europe over, and she was talking with Gottfried about moving to England. Her vision of herself as "the novelist" was becoming clearer, though her sense of her vocation still conflicted with her emotional needs and her thwarted motherhood. Writing Coll that a mutual friend was pregnant, she said she was jealous. "I can't think which is more satisfactory, having a baby, or writing a novel. Unfortunately they are quite incompatible."

As it turned out, she was going to have to negotiate a compromise. When she did go to England, in 1949, she took with her both her first novel and her third child, her son Peter.

MATERNAL IDENTITY IS ALWAYS a work in progress. Parent-child relationships change dramatically over time, and so do mothers' relationships to their maternal selves. Doris had contact with and visited all her children as adults, but because Peter lived with her, it was their relationship that was most often redefined. It was happy when he was a baby, grew in tandem with her literary career, then became both close and fraught in adulthood, when Peter suffered from mental illness. Where Doris separated herself from her first two children, partly out of fear of damaging them, perhaps it was partly out of guilt that she kept Peter close to her.

The enigmas of Doris's relationship with Peter begin with his conception. In *Under My Skin* she describes her third pregnancy as a deliberate decision that she and Gottfried had made with "practicality and common sense." They both wanted a child, she says, and it would be some time before they could get British passports. Until then, they had to stay in Salisbury and stay married. Why not have a child? If the marriage didn't hold together beyond that point, they could stay friends and share the parenting.

At the time, she told her RAF friends that the pregnancy was an accident—the result, she told Coll, of an ill-judged experiment "with a newfangled form of contraception." Coll passed his letters on to John, so this may have been a lie for John's benefit. Still fantasizing about their future together, Doris told John she wished it was his baby and that she regretted not leaving Gottfried earlier: "Now I can never live singly, but will have to be divided." Yet she wasn't completely unhappy about it: she still missed John and Jean terribly, she wrote, and hoped the new baby would make her feel less lost without them.

At the start of her pregnancy she made a break for freedom. She had already made plans to spend a few months in Cape Town, and in early 1946 she went ahead with the trip, working as a secretary at *The Guardian*, the South African Communist paper, and canvassing for the Party. Looking ahead to a future of evenings at home with Gottfried and the baby, she started sleeping with a bohemian painter named Gregoire Boonzaier. He had a wife from whom he was separated, a mistress who was expecting his child, and at least one other lover; in other words, he could be loved and discarded, and Doris enjoyed their friendly affair. (She apparently didn't know about the pregnant mistress at the time; back home in Salisbury, she urged him by letter to take better care of her.) Unlike Gottfried, Gregoire took "sensual delight" in Doris's pregnant body, in her breasts already making milk—or so she reported to the other party in all this, John.

On her return she told Gottfried and their marriage continued on a strained basis until their son Peter was born, just before Doris's twenty-seventh birthday. Shared parenthood did bring the couple together. Gottfried enjoyed caring for his infant son, and with his support Doris could love the new baby without losing herself. But it brought tensions too. In the heat of a fight shortly after Peter's birth, Gottfried told Doris she would never be a good mother and that he wanted custody. He later apologized, and she was willing to overlook the insult, but his attempt to claim Peter was unforgivable. Whatever happened, she was not going to let this child be taken from her.

Meanwhile Maude was horrified by this new proof of her daughter's irresponsibility, and even Michael asked, "Why leave two babies and then have another?" By then Doris's father was terminally ill and disappointed with his life and his two children, who had lost the infinite potential of their childhood and now seemed to him "second-raters." Once as he watched John and Jean playing he turned to Doris and remarked, "Yes, that's what you were like too, such lovely little things you were and look what you turn into. It's not worth it."

Frank naturally disapproved, and told John and Jean what he thought. When Peter was about a year old, six-year-old Jean asked her mother over the breakfast table if she was going to give the new baby away, too. When Doris denied that she'd "given them away," John replied, "That's what Frank says." The conversation left her "feeling as if beaten all over, like steak."

Yet this time around, with Peter in day care every afternoon from about age one, and with a committed partner and a plan for the future, Doris was able to find a balance between life and care. Peter was a good-natured baby and with him she enjoyed one of parenting's great rewards, the tranquil closeness between parent and infant, the intimacy that she once wrote was possible "only between an adult and a child, confiding and trustful, and as easy as breathing."

Slowly she reworked her satirical novel into something darker and more serious. Her RAF friend Leonard Smith read drafts and sent encouragement from England. She "was developing the habit of privacy, writing when she could, increasingly thinking her own thoughts, increasingly self-critical." After an affair with a married man gave her a sudden longing for another pregnancy, she protected herself from her impulses by having her tubes tied. By the time she left for England in early 1949, she had a publisher for her novel, now called *The Grass Is Singing*.

Her first published book was a tense, intimate drama about a society poisoned by race prejudice, and it would be acclaimed for exposing the treatment of Black Africans in the British colonies. But in the character of the doomed farm wife Mary Turner, Doris had also gathered together a number of female types she disliked or wanted to leave behind her: efficient office worker, "woman's woman," impulsive bride, asexual prude, victim of illusions about how women should act. Then she murdered her.

The woman who sailed from Cape Town to London in April 1949 had had some practice, both politically and personally, in refusing to be a victim of illusion. Having acquired material she would draw on for a decade's worth of fiction and essays, she was going north to claim the creative, political, and sexual life of a woman writer.

A FAMOUS CLIP OF Doris Lessing as a literary celebrity: in 2007, she steps cautiously out of a cab, a white-haired woman of eighty-seven, followed by a middle-aged man holding a string of onions and an artichoke. When she asks why there's a camera crew in front of her house, a reporter tells her she's won the Nobel Prize. "Oh, Christ!" she exclaims, then sets down her shopping bag and starts thinking of something suitable to say. "I've won all the prizes in Europe, every bloody one," she offers, looking increasingly cheerful. "I'm delighted to win the whole lot."

To thrive in public life, to write good books, to be a parent, to find love are all different projects, and from the moment she arrived in gray, postwar London with her manuscript, Doris not only had to negotiate new private identities, she had to deal with becoming a public person. She began turning her old life into material, using it in the Martha Quest series as well as her brilliantly observed short stories with African settings. It was partly an effort at self-definition, she later wrote. "While I was seeing my early life more clearly with every new person I met, for a casual remark could question things I had taken for granted for years, I was nevertheless confused. While I certainly 'knew who I was' . . . , I did not know how to define myself as a social being [or] see myself in a social context."

At first, as she threw herself into writing, she found both social and literary success. The writer Jenny Diski lived with her as a teenager in the 1960s, when Doris was in the full flush of her career. Peter was then in boarding school, leaving Doris with whole days free, and Diski recalled that the "shotgun sound of typing went on continuously for hours" as Doris wrote her first drafts at top speed. She worked until a book was finished, and only then did she emerge to see friends for gossip and political talk—both of which still nourished her as much as they had when she was writing to John Whitehorn.

The day job she took when she first arrived lasted only a few weeks: she quit when she found that being a secretary and caring for Peter left no time over. By publishing almost a book a year—novels, short stories, nonfiction, poetry, plays—she was able to support herself and her son. She taught herself to work in short, concentrated bursts, suppressing the urge to take care of daily business—shop, make phone calls—in favor of "the flat, dull state one needs to write in." This way she made use of days that turned with the clock of school, meals, bed. Anna in *The Golden Notebook* says that "the control and discipline of being a mother" has come hard to her, as it must have to Doris, but when Peter came home from school she put her work aside. When he was older she sometimes sent him to stay with friends while she was writing, or to acquaintances in the country who took in children for pay. For several years she shared a house with another single mother, her friend Joan Rodker, who often cared for Peter when Doris was out in the evenings. Their maternal reciprocity, she later said, was "the most important thing about my life then."

Her combativeness and political instincts had helped get her out of the provinces, and in the Fifties they were essential to her success. She wasn't afraid of difficult subjects: race, her conflict with her mother (a daring topic in the years before feminism), her own conflicted motherhood. And as the Nobel Prize clip illustrates, she wasn't shy about claiming her successes. In the 1950s, the style among men in the arts was alpha-male arrogance. In response, Doris adopted a brusque, contentious public pose that let her stand on an equal footing with that generation's "angry young men" while helping her maintain her boundaries. Several women in this book had a reputation for argumentativeness (Le Guin, Lorde), rude remarks (Neel, Carter), even verbal abuse (Sontag). Jenny Diski said that those who were close to her knew well the experience of "being told off by Doris."

Like Carter a generation later, Doris emphasized her outsider status and the license it gave her to be "open, straightforward, honest to the point of tactlessness." At one point in their correspondence, John Whitehorn teased her that she should have been an eighteenth-century French lady of letters, a *salonnière*, with him as her lover dressed in silk. She replied that she liked the second idea: "Silk breeches would be such fun to take off. But not a salon darling. I have no manners."

Gottfried Lessing arrived in London shortly after Doris did, and for a little while, though they were now divorced and lived separately, they shared custody of Peter. She assumed this sensible arrangement would continue, but when Gottfried couldn't find work—refugee German Reds being not in high demand in postwar Britain—he left, over Doris's protests, for East Germany. He took a position in the idealistic new Communist government; the next year, Peter spent the summer with him in Berlin. Shortly afterward, though, the government began discouraging personal ties with the West and Gottfried was instructed to end all contact with his son. Doris never saw him again.

Now Peter, like John and Jean, had lost a parent. He cried because he missed his father, while Doris was frustrated by the "day-in, day-out slog of it all, trying to be what is impossible, a father as well as a mother." She felt guilty, too. Not having a father was supposed to be bad for a son, and like all other failures in children's upbringing, it was held to be the mother's fault.

Doris had assumed that she would marry again in England, and that her real emotional life would finally begin. But she was also reluctant to be claimed, a dilemma she resolved, as one does, by getting involved with unavailable men. (She and John Whitehorn resumed their friendship but not their affair.) Not long after she came to London she met the love of her life, a Czech refugee psychoanalyst who was married, with children, but insisted that his marriage had been a youthful mistake and that he was morally free. When he broke up with her, she was devastated. Afterward she got involved with a man who was available, but whose solicitude made her feel "an irritable need to escape."

Small children give stability and solidity, but that steady work of the heart and the clock falls away as they get older. When Peter, at age twelve, went to boarding school at his own request—he had been unhappy in school and resentful at home—Doris stumbled and felt lost. "Peter had been the one constant in my life, my ballast, what I held on to through thick and thin—which is of course why he had had to go away from me, because it was not good for him—but now he wasn't there."

She had recently sustained other losses. In 1956, at the end of a trip home, she was banned by the Rhodesian government, so that she could no longer even think of visiting her country or her children. The next year Maude Tayler died suddenly, leaving Doris full of guilt for her mother and grief for her unmothered self: a "chilly grey semi-frozen condition," she wrote, "as if I were miles under thick cold water." In between, she left the Communist Party after realizing they had been lying to their members. She had been faithful to an idealized version of the Soviet state, and when she allowed herself to see that the Party had covered up Stalin's crimes, her loss of faith made her question her activism and herself.

She started a love affair with a footloose young American, Clancy Sigal, that gave her new creative energy but also made her miserable, especially when he exploited her affection. ("I'm not your mother, your psycho-analyst, your confessor," she wrote him, but she spent time being all three.) Her status as a "free woman," the term she coined in *The Golden Notebook*, wasn't keeping the discord among her daily activities—work, politics, love, mothering—from feeling like fissures in her soul. Without a story to understand what was happening to her, she thought she was going mad.

So she wrote that story, drawing on her confusion and her inability to make one narrative out of her selves that were mother, lover, author. She couldn't see clearly which elements were relevant, so—raw courage being one of her artistic powers—she threw it all in. The result was the long, messy, radical novel that was her masterwork: *The Golden Notebook*.

The novel's central character, Anna Wulf, is a writer and single mother whose life has become structured around other people's expectations, and who sets down her experiences in different notebooks because she can't seem to bring them together. When the book was published in 1962, many of its readers, women and men, realized that they had been living like Anna, doing what others expected of them, without access to their emotional or intellectual power. Lessing had voiced thoughts about the fragmentation of women's lives that seemed awkward, unconventional, better left unsaid—and found that she'd spoken for her generation.

The Golden Notebook was acclaimed as a feminist novel, though Doris frustrated many younger women by never taking up the feminist cause. She sometimes claimed that she actually resented women's praise for *The Golden Notebook*, because it had made it harder for men to read it. Like Alice, she wanted credit for her socialist insights more than her feminist ones. She was wary of the doctrinaire side of feminism as well as of its emotional truth-telling—even though this last was her specialty as well. Yet her 1973 novel *The Summer before the Dark* is unmistakably a feminist work, in which a middle-class wife and mother goes in search of a new self after her children leave home. Doris recognized that maternal identity persists and changes over a lifetime and that mothering can take many different forms.

One recurring plot in Lessing's fiction, especially in the dreamlike *Memoirs of a Survivor* (1974), is of a woman who is handed a child, not her own, for whom she must care. In 1963, after Doris had bought a house with her earnings from *The Golden Notebook*, Peter wrote home about one of his boarding-school classmates, a fifteen-year-old aspiring writer named Jennifer. She had been expelled from school, had attempted suicide, and was being housed in a mental institution because neither of her divorced parents was stable enough to give her a home. Doris, flush with spare rooms and unexpected income, impulsively offered her a place to stay and financial support. Jennifer—later Jenny Diski—lived with Doris until she was eighteen, while Doris paid her school fees and taught her by example that being a writer meant hard work and "getting on with it."

Jenny was the same age Doris had been when she had been at war with her mother, and it may be that Doris saw taking her in as a way of rescuing herself. But that didn't mean she was prepared to be emotionally responsible for a teenager, any more than she'd been able to cope full-time with the demands of lovers or, arguably, her first two children. Her second memoir, *Walking in the Shade*, in some ways reads as a ledger of her expenditures of emotional labor, whether in support of African emigrés, Communist comrades, or lovers, and she remained wary of others' needs and her own susceptibility. Instead of telling Jenny what she expected of her, she got angry afterward when she couldn't guess the rules. In her ambiguously titled memoir of their relationship, *In Gratitude*, Jenny writes that she felt uncertain of her welcome: What if Doris didn't like her and sent her away again? But when she said this to her new—what? foster parent? she and Doris never worked out what they should call each other—Doris responded with a furious letter accusing her of emotional blackmail.

Reading that letter, Diski said, was a "shattering" experience, and though she and Doris went on seeing, and caring for, each other for the rest of their lives, she never got over this early abandonment. Doris "did do something generous and positive but as soon as anything emotional came into it, she just froze, couldn't cope with it. And that was always the case. . . . What's wrong with most people is that they were too emotional, she would say. And so living with her, you learnt that you weren't to be emotional. Which is sort of difficult at fifteen."

Struggling with depression, Jenny went to a therapist who eventually called Doris in and told her, "The problem with Jenny is that because you've taken her on, she doesn't feel that she can be critical or say anything is wrong, as a normal child would in a normal family." Afterward Doris turned to Jenny and asked, "You don't feel like that, do you?" It was, Diski noted, "a masterpiece of manipulation." Yet she remained tied to Doris by mutual loyalty, and the two were more alike than not. They both wrote with fierce honesty and were, in the affectionate words of Diski's daughter, Chloe, "independent, determined and ruthless when they needed to be."

Over time Doris became closer to her two eldest children. In about 1958 John came to London for a few days on his way to study forestry in Canada. He and Doris had had almost no contact for nearly ten years. "He had never heard anything good about me, and he had been forbidden to write to me," she recalled. "It could not have been easy for him to decide to see this problematical mother." But she wrote in her memoirs that they got on well together. (According to her, the worst he ever said to her about her desertion was "I understand why you had to leave my father, but that doesn't mean I don't resent it.") When her books started bringing in money she bought him a coffee farm in Rhodesia, where he lived until his death from a heart attack in 1992, and where she visited him after 1980, when Rhodesia became Zimbabwe and she was again allowed in.

Jean also came to visit her in London, though Jenny recalls that Doris didn't take time off from her writing but instead enlisted her to show Jean around. That may have been a way for Doris to cope with an encounter that for her was fraught with almost unbearable tension. (Nonetheless, Diski adds, "It was never clear whether she knew how painful or disastrous her actions or pronouncements could be.") Still later, Doris went to South Africa to visit Jean and her two daughters. At her mother's memorial service, Jean remembered her with affection.

In her last four decades, the man Doris made her life with was her son Peter. In adolescence he evidently began to suffer from mental illness. Doris apparently didn't help him seek treatment—possibly because illnesses such as schizophrenia were still blamed on bad mothers—but kept him close to her, in an apartment next door to hers. One interviewer who came to her house saw him returning from the public library with an armload of science fiction books for Doris. Another noted that Peter "shuffled in to say hello, wearing a tea cosy on his head," though he suspected the tea cozy was a joke for his benefit. Mother and son "shared a dry, ironic sense of humour. They were a bit like the Odd Couple . . . a double act."

The novelist Margaret Drabble took a more somber view of Peter, writing that her friend Doris "was locked for more than sixty years into a mother-son embrace of peculiar intensity, married to a son whose strangeness, whose incapacities, whose gifts . . . remained undiagnosed, indefinable." In the Nobel Prize clip, it is Peter who stands behind her, one arm in a sling, holding the artichoke they presumably will share. Peter had developed diabetes by then, and they were in the cab on the way home from the hospital. Peter died in late 2013, at age sixty-seven. Doris's health was also declining and she died just a few weeks after her son.

Even though, or because, her mothering was frustrated, interrupted, discarded, reinvented, Lessing was able to make motherhood one of the great subjects of her work. She layered contradictory emotions into her literary portraits, portraying the satisfactions, temptations, frustrations, the guilt and anger of mothering at a time when few women felt able to say in public that the institutions of marriage and motherhood had failed them. Ambivalent love is one of her great subjects, from the autobiographical revelations of her early work right up to the eroticized mother-son bonds of *The Grandmothers* (2003) and the disastrous maternity of *The Fifth Child* (1988), in which a son's extreme needs tear a happy family apart. Realizing early on that if you said what seemed unthinkable it might turn out to be what everyone else was thinking, she made a career of bringing up uncomfortable subjects. Maybe it's inevitable that even now she is viewed askance, forever placed by public opinion outside the comfortable circle of the good mothers.

Among her contemporaries, there were some who went further than she did down the road of sexual defiance in their search for freedom. In the early 1960s, Doris got a visit from the older writer Elizabeth Smart. She had a books column in *Queen*, the hot magazine of swinging London, and was a glamorous figure on the Soho literary scene. Meeting her made Doris grateful that motherhood had kept her home in the evenings, away from the harsh, late-night edges of Bohemia. Elizabeth came for lunch, Doris recalled, then "drank and wept and wept and drank from midday to seven at night and was savagely witty about her life and the lives of women. I would not describe her as an advertisement for the joie de vivre of Soho."

Smart had confused freedom and authority with romantic rebellion and self-destructive passion. The result was one brilliant book, four children, and an example to other women of how not to live.

Elizabeth Smart with Sebastian, Christopher, Georgina, and Rose Barker
at Tilty Mill House, their home in Essex, 1948.

The Discomfort Zone

THE UNAVAILABLE MUSE

◆

ELIZABETH SMART's literary and maternal career commenced in a London bookstore in 1937. Or it started when a man got off a bus in California in 1940. Or it arrived in 1936, when Smart, as a twenty-two-year-old debutante in Ottawa, wrote in her journal, "I must marry a poet. It's the only thing. Why don't I know any?" but also "How can I possibly marry and sign away my life?"

Or it began in 1913, when Elizabeth was born into a stifling, upper-class Canadian milieu. Her lawyer father and her socially ambitious, emotionally abusive mother humored her writing but ultimately disapproved of too much intellect or fantasy, believing it would harm her chances of a good marriage. She was educated at snobbish schools where she recalled "keeping covered all I knew, & my mad delight in learning." When she explored the forest around the family's summer house, tracing the meanings of the natural world, her mother warned her not to go "mooning about by yourself in the woods—people will think you are queer."

She drafted the book that made her name when she was pregnant with her first child. Unmarried, hiding her condition from her family, she went to stay in a fishing village in British Columbia. The English poet George Barker, her lover, installed her there and went off with a boyfriend, but since he was her irresistibly sexy muse and writing partner, she forgave him everything. Connected to him through his child growing inside her and experiencing the "beginning of that silence necessary for hearing my own voices," she wrote her epic novel of erotic obsession, *By Grand Central Station I Sat Down and Wept*. In touch with the primal and liminal states of female sexuality, she felt powerful as she never had before—and seldom would again.

The pursuit of love was Smart's great subject, the romantic wish to find and lose oneself in passion, generosity, and heartbreak. In her work and life she made vital connections between sex and creativity, that link so casually assumed by male poets but not often claimed by women of her generation. Yet the independence she gained with illicit love was partly undone by her selflessness in motherhood. Her career started with, and suffered from, her dedication to her unavailable muse.

Elizabeth as a young woman was impatient and romantic, full of raw talent, without much discipline or confidence. Her childhood had been a gilded cage, her beauty at odds with her brains. She thought she would have to choose between writing and the body:

> I am going to be a poet I said
> But even as I said it I felt
> The round softness of my breasts
> and my mind wandered and wavered
> Back to the earthly things
> and the swooning warmth of being loved.

To the end of her life she feared that if she wrote her own truth she would be cast out, would "have to repudiate every kind of human love."

On a trip to Mexico, she had a lesbian affair with the French poet Alice Paalen, a sexual connection that fueled her artistic agency and inspired her early writing. But she had already, fatefully, discovered George's poetry in a London bookstore and had fallen in love with the idea of becoming his wife.

Knowing what the world knows now, that George was a drinker, charmer, and liar who would go on to father at least fifteen children by several partners, the reader of Smart's biography wants to shout, "Look out! Stop fooling yourself!" But when she finally met him and his wife Jessica in Monterey, California, Elizabeth claimed him as her destiny: ditching Jessica, the two of them hit the road. They wrote together in bed, wrote in each other's diaries, finished each other's sentences, praised each other's work. Their travels together through America, their separations (she once spent three days in an Arizona jail because her passport wasn't in order, while George made himself scarce), his hookups with men, and Elizabeth's obsession with him all went into *By Grand Central Station I Sat Down and Wept.*

In this female road novel, published a decade before *On the Road*, two lovers go on the run from his wife, her parents, the law, and even, at times, each other. In loosely connected scenes the unnamed narrator describes her joy in intense feeling. "I am suddenly so rich, and I have done nothing to deserve it, to be so overloaded. All after such a desert. All after I had learnt to say, I am nothing, and I deserve nothing." She insists to her lover that she is his destiny: "What you think is the sirens singing to lure you to your doom is only the voice of the inevitable, welcoming you after so long a wait. I was made only for you."

Love reveals the narrator to herself, and so does her pregnancy, the child that lies within her "like the fated and only island in all seas . . . the one focal pinning me to my own center." Looking forward to childbirth she demands nothing short of self-transformation: "Pain, pain that will bring me my son, step through the curtains of the officious housewife nature, and give me the truth first, or give me nothing."

George made her brave enough, she once wrote, "to face the murderous act of stepping resolutely into my own life." But like a lover, a self once found can be lost again. By the time George and Elizabeth's daughter Georgina Barker was born in 1941, George had gone back to Jessica, his wife, leaving Elizabeth to support herself and the baby. After a year and a half of transcontinental pursuit and evasive maneuvers, Elizabeth moved to England in 1943, pregnant again and hoping George would follow. At that point George was living in New York, where Jessica was pregnant with twins. Then he moved back to England, too, though for several years, until Jessica ended their relationship, George went back and forth between the two women, making promises to both.

If George didn't provide money or stability, he offered a different kind of nourishment, the emotional intensity on which Elizabeth thrived. But for Elizabeth, unlike Alice, what gave her creative energy—love, children, friendship, freedom from a bourgeois life—also kept her from the hard work of creation. She lived for a while in the Cotswolds on her allowance from her parents, her bohemian poverty making her feel alive, but with small children she had neither time nor privacy to write. "Nothing will ever be right until he wants more children," she wrote in her journal, but when George was with her she put his writing time ahead of hers. She told a friend that she didn't like to let her infant son cry "in case he gets on George's nerves," and that she felt "homicidal but helpless." This kind of self-abdication not only made her vulnerable to the daily interruptions of mothering, it led to long periods when she was barely writing at all.

She had good reasons for having children. She loved the immediate awareness of her body that pregnancy gave her, and the astonishing experience of bringing new life into the world made her feel close to the divine. She saw pregnancy and birth as a central part of her sexuality. Her affectionate care for and closeness to her children may have helped heal the wounds of her own mother's disapproval. Yet mothering can also be a way not to face the fear of writing. Looking at the unsettling aspects of creative solitude, Adrienne Rich writes, "The void is the creatrix, the matrix. . . .

But in women it has been identified with lovelessness, barrenness, sterility. We have been urged to fill our 'emptiness' with children. We are not supposed to go down into the darkness of the core."

By Grand Central Station was published in 1945, just after the birth of her third child. The book into which she had poured her heart was judged "full of promise" by the reviewers and sold modestly. Her scandalized mother bought up all the copies on sale in Ottawa and burned them. A few years later, when Elizabeth briefly turned her attention to another man, George sat down and wrote a cruel reply to her book in which he portrayed her as an egotistical home-wrecker and invalidated her delight in motherhood. Observing his lover's pregnancy, the narrator of George's novel *The Dead Seagull* sneers, "Her fulfillment in the child seems likely to be so perfect that everything else will be forgotten. . . . I cannot help suspecting that the woman exists in a lower category of spiritual consciousness."

In 1946 she broke up with him, writing,

> I see no beauty in lopsided true love. It really is in sorrow & not in anger that I say: I do not want you any more because *I simply cannot bear it.* It isn't only the unfaithfulness. It's the loneliness, the weeks & months of being alone, . . . receiving perhaps a postcard saying I fuck you as you pause for breath in fucking somebody else. . . .
>
> I've had my fuck, but I've lost my love. My womb won't tear me to pieces now, maybe, but my heart certainly will. Goodbye. Elizabeth.

Yet in 1947, having moved to a village in the west of Ireland to live more cheaply, Elizabeth had a fourth child with George. The birth of her daughter Rose made her feel "arch-angelic," she wrote a friend. "It's wonderful the way youth & vitality & sanity & possibility & initiative RETURN after a baby—it's so strange to feel things again." But the sublime is twinned with the banal in mothering, and her allowance was no longer enough even for her to feed her children. After George came to visit, ate up all her food, drank up all her money, and absconded, she ended the affair, moved back to England, and got a job.

Her vision of herself was of a woman who had accepted her fate, had her pleasure, and now was paying for it in hard work and loneliness. The price was high, and that made her bitter, but she never came to the realization that it wasn't a fair bargain. Her biographer Kim Echlin, who focuses on her motherhood, believes she was burning with rage in her years of supporting children; but it was her unmet need that came to define her. Critic Anne Quéma likens her sexual rebellion to anorexia, a mutinous self-denial that "freezes the rebel in poses of futile and painful extremism."

Ironically, when she looked for work, Elizabeth discovered that her bourgeois upbringing had given her monetizable writing skills. She began turning out feature stories for *House & Garden* magazine, then went into advertising, one of the few lucrative fields open to women. She became legendary for her fashion ads, maybe because she had such an intimate knowledge of fashion's essence: carefree passion masking a longing to be loved. Within a few years she was said to be the highest-paid woman copywriter in England.

She settled the children in a house in the country, where a gay couple, both painters named Robert, looked after them. The Roberts were kind and caring during the week. On weekends, though, Elizabeth came home from her apartment in London, friends arrived, everyone drank, and chaos ensued. The next morning, the children would wake to find that their caretakers had smashed the furniture or thrown the bedclothes through a window. Eventually Elizabeth sent her children to boarding schools, Rose from the age of six.

At work Elizabeth coped by chain-smoking, sniffing layout glue, and using what she called "brilliancy pills." Evenings, instead of writing, she drank with the mostly male crowd in Soho, listening to the poets and painters opine that women couldn't make real art. Despite her own unhappiness, she tried to "give, sympathize, entertain. . . . I think: their needs may be greater than mine. I suffer. But I haven't the courage to direct things my way."

Soho was where George held court, and she still wanted his friendship, though the door he had once opened for her no longer led into a place where her genius was recognized or served. She saw other men, but only temporarily, avoiding George's jealousy. She had sexual relationships with women that she conducted in deepest secret. She spent these years, she later wrote, in "Love. Children. Earning a living. Friends. Drinking. Pushed too far to do too much. Silent years. Desperate from hating."

Fay Weldon, who worked with Elizabeth in the late 1950s, recalled that in those days "it simply did not occur to us that if men misbehaved, the answer was to have nothing more to do with them. That 'love' was a trap not worth falling into. The female response at the time was still to feel more love, have more babies, write more poetry, sink yet further into masochism."

The times changed. Elizabeth began writing for *Queen*, where in her books column she praised women writers, saying how thrilled she was to see "women talking; women daring to tell the truth about themselves . . . speaking unmasked straight out of deepest experiences." In 1966, when she was fifty-three, *By Grand Central Station* was reissued to critical and popular acclaim. Her children were independent. She got a grant so she could write fiction again.

Then Rose got into trouble. Intelligent and sensitive, a vulnerable beauty out of a Rosetti painting, she was in and out of schools until she left home at sixteen. A year later she had her first baby, and not long afterward, in the midst of the swinging Sixties, she began using heroin. She struggled with addiction, while Elizabeth cared for her two children, until she died of liver failure at age thirty-five.

Time is often on the side of mother-creators. A writer or artist may regain her footing, get her second wind, or even begin her career after her children leave home. But Elizabeth had waited too long, drunk too much, depended too much on pills and the excitement of the moment, kept too few hours for herself. She published another novel, *The Assumption of the Rogues & Rascals*, in 1978, thirty years after her first, in which she looked back at her life among the poets, shaking her head at "the untenable position of love." She wrote fragments of her truth about motherhood, especially her relationship to her own mother, but was afraid to venture far into that unwritten territory. She died, in 1986, without recovering the momentum of her early years.

In the 1970s Angela Carter, who was nearly thirty years younger, met Elizabeth at a party and found her, as Lessing had, drinking and bemoaning women's lot. Unnerved by what she saw as her "self-inflicted wounds," Carter was inspired to reject the plots of women's suffering she'd been writing and think about alternatives. Describing the party to her friend Lorna Sage, she added that she hoped "no daughter of mine should ever be in a position to be able to write *By Grand Central Station I Sat Down and Wept*, exquisite prose though it might contain. (*By Grand Central Station I Tore Off His Balls* would be more like it, I should hope.)" By then Weldon had also realized that men taking advantage of women's hearts was, in fact, injustice, and began spinning plots about women's awakening and their revenge.

Not all mother-writers needed to break with convention in order to win their creative freedom. Ursula Le Guin wasn't raised to sacrifice herself, and though she had a taste of heartbreak she was never really tempted to suffer for love. Instead she married a man who genuinely supported her writing and shared the childcare so she could do her work—a life that, if she'd written about it at midcentury, would have sounded like science fiction.

"Poems Are Housework"

BOOKS VERSUS BABIES

◆

To think ["mother" and "intellectual"] together . . . requires that one buck a long tradition by challenging both the exhaustiveness of these two identities and the contradictory associations that present them as incompatible. (GAIL WEISS, "MOTHERS/INTELLECTUALS: ALTERITIES OF A DUAL IDENTITY")

You were supposed to choose between boys and books, because for girls sex was entirely preoccupying, your sex was *more of you* than a boy's appendage, you *were* your sex, so you had to do without if you were to have enough energy, self-possession, and brains left over to do anything else. (LORNA SAGE)

I N THE MID-TWENTIETH CENTURY, educated women were told that they could write if they wanted to, but there was a catch. To have a life of the mind, they would have to give up all claims to love and family life. This was not presented as a practical problem of access to resources. Motherhood was morally at odds with an intellectual's power, an artist's autonomy.

That women have no right to their own time and mental faculties is an opinion as old as art itself. Poet Robert Southey famously told Charlotte Brontë:

Literature cannot be the business of a woman's life: & it ought not to be. The more she is engaged in her proper duties, the less leisure she will have for it, even as an accomplishment & a recreation.

Another literary concern troll, reviewing the work of poet and mother Elizabeth Barrett Browning in 1862, amplified the theme:

> *It is very doubtful if the highest and richest nature of woman can ever be unfolded in its home life and wedded relationships, and yet at the same time blossom or bear fruit in art or literature with a similar fulness. . . . A mother's heart, at its richest, is not likely to get adequate expression in notes and bars, if it were only for the fact that she must be absorbed by other music.*

Psychology assigned to this judgment on women's nature the status of a twentieth-century science:

> *Freud appeals both to the bio-psychological description of women as intellectually less able and the psycho-moral prescription, that they had best leave the things of the mind alone, since these interfere with the exercise of their sexual function. . . . In . . . charging that sexual and intellectual are incompatible in women, Freud exhibits again his belief that the two qualities are basically opposed.*

In the 1950s, when Susan Sontag wrote the above words to be published under her husband's name, she already had a child and an advanced degree. In her teenage years her stepfather had paraphrased Freud's view—You'll never find a husband if you don't stop reading all those books—and she had married partly to prove him wrong. But even after the divorce she still thought her intellect and body were in conflict:

> *Where do I want my vitality to go? To books or to sex, to ambition or to love, to anxiety or to sensuality? Can't have both.*

It was in her generation, born in the 1930s, that writers struggled most with the moral and social implications of the mind-baby problem and the fear that they were mutually exclusive. This was especially true for women in college: the "ivory tower" depended on the romance of the lonely, heroic thinker.

The mind-body problem of an intellectual woman in the 1950s was . . . one of rigorous conflict. In those days the body required sex and childbearing, and quite likely the death of the mind alongside. My thesis supervisor, Helen Gardner, truly believed that women scholars should be nuns, renouncing the body for higher things. (A. S. Byatt)

Both in their personal life and their writing, [American women writers] in the Fifties depicted intelligence, studiousness, erudition, and literary vocation as defeminizing to the point of deformity. Their heroines are mercilessly punished for their intellectual hubris. (Elaine Showalter)

When I was in my twenties [in the 1950s] I was going through a very sort of female thing—of trying to distinguish between the ego that is capable of writing poems, and then there is this other kind of being that you're asked to be if you're a woman, who is, in a sense, denying that ego. I had great feelings of split about that for many years actually, and there are a lot of poems I couldn't write even, because I didn't want to confess to having that much aggression, that much ego, that much sense of myself. (Adrienne Rich)

If you're a woman writer, sometime, somewhere, you will be asked, Do you think of yourself as a writer first, or as a woman first? *Look out. Whoever asks this hates and fears both writing and women. (Margaret Atwood)*

African American women also saw the division between books and babies: like Sontag, the autobiographical heroine of Gwendolyn Brooks's *Maud Martha* is warned by her family that reading will doom her marriage chances. But at the same time, at all education levels, they saw it as the norm to mother while working outside the home.

> *Black women seem able to combine the nest and the adventure. They don't see conflicts in certain areas as do white women. They are both safe harbor and ship; they are both inn and trail. (Toni Morrison)*

In the 1970s and '80s, Black women argued that their creativity was not separate from the rest of their lives.

> *[In] the Black aesthetic, the feminist aesthetic, . . . art and poetry become part and parcel of one's daily living, one's daily expression, the need to communicate, the need to share one's feelings, to develop in oneself the best that is possible. (Audre Lorde)*

> *What has been called "women's work" traditionally includes the nurturing of young people, maintaining a house, providing the wherewithal so that people can keep going. . . . My work is closely related in purpose to the traditional work. It just takes a different form. (June Jordan)*

Or, as interviewer Alexis De Veaux summarized Jordan's words, "Poems are housework."

If Black women escaped some of the social pressures that kept white women at home, they often had fewer material resources and less artistic support. Under those conditions, they struggled to find joy or pleasure in mothering. Writer and filmmaker Kathleen Collins told her daughter:

> *I couldn't possibly allow myself to love you children except by being a good caretaker and a good provider. I, literally, put my love into that and kept my heart closed. It was all the love I could handle, all I could provide. I was going through my own life keeping up, coping, holding on, trying not to fall apart.*

But Morrison said her work was necessary for herself:

All of my life is doing something for somebody else.... Whether I'm being a good daughter, a good mother, a good wife, a good lover, a good teacher.... The only thing I do for me is writing. That's really the real free place where I don't have to answer.

The most self-destructive frustration was reserved for women who were brilliant, had been encouraged, but were unable, in the context of the times, to make sense of either their artistic vision or their personal pain. This is what happened to Sylvia Plath, her friend Fay Weldon thought. Weldon's sister, Jane, a poet, had had "the same hot line to the appalling infinite":

What my sister had was a notion that there was something out there, just beyond vision, which had to be reached no matter what. Trying to grasp it rendered a woman desperate and emotionally fragile. Before people talked so much about "creativity" as something to be desired, ... we were left with the vague and painful mystery of ourselves. We had no language for what was wrong. What drives the artist is an urge as powerful as sex and if denied, if the times are against her, if she doesn't find the words, doesn't find her audience, looks inside and finds only muddle and misery, why, it's enough to send a woman mad.

In the generations of African Americans whose genius was denied expression, Alice Walker wrote of women "driven to a numb and bleeding madness by the springs of creativity in them for which there was no release."

Even now, writers hear the message of choice, along with the guilt that can come from a refusal to choose.

Writing depends on authority, the belief that what we say matters. But I'd weigh every paragraph of that necessarily crappy early draft against my children's needs, and the paragraphs mattered little. Fear made me doubt the desire I'd relied upon. I couldn't write as Mama. (Heather Abel)

But what if creativity and child-rearing can benefit each other?

Everyone was telling me that becoming a mother would take away that existential drive to make work—but it was the opposite. I have never felt more full of life and death, and it made me become reborn as a writer. . . . And also this constant cautionary tale that I would not be able to write. . . . I felt I had something to react against, to try to transcend. (Kate Zambreno)

One day as I am holding baby and feeding her, I realize that this is exactly the state of mind and heart that so many male writers from Thomas Mann to James Joyce describe with yearning—the mystery of an epiphany, the sense of oceanic oneness, the great yes, the wholeness. There is also the sense of a self merged and at least temporarily erased— it is deathlike. . . . Perhaps we owe some of our most moving literature to men who didn't understand that they wanted to be women nursing babies. (Louise Erdrich)

Imagining motherhood opens the door to imagining every power relationship, every profound connection. . . . Far from depriving me of thought, motherhood gave me new and startling things to think about and the motivation to do the hard work of thinking. (Jane Smiley)

Art is supposed to be about this kind of intensified experience of life. . . . And that is totally what raising kids does to you, too. . . . Everything becomes heightened, and the range of experience becomes so much greater. Your heart is so much more open. All of those things that we think of when we think about what the artist's experience is are embodied in this idea of having children. (Justine Kurland)

"Mothering" is a queer thing. Not just when people who do not identify as heterosexual give birth to or adopt children and parent them, but all day long and everywhere when we acknowledge the creative power of transforming ourselves and the ways we relate to each other. Because we were never meant to survive and here we are creating a world full of love. (Alexis Pauline Gumbs)

I remember when I was pregnant with my first child: I was at a book festival and a writer of my own age, who will remain nameless, sat opposite me and said, "God you're having a kid huh?" It was a man. He said, "I guess you're going to lose a lot of time and you must be worried about falling behind." I was about seven months pregnant. . . . I said, "Yeah I guess so" and then, "You must be worried about just a complete lack of human experience that you're now going to be 40 and then 50." His face went so pale. (Zadie Smith)

Some simply took their chances. Margaret Atwood, who came of age in the 1950s and had her daughter in her mid-thirties, in 1976, said,

I'm of that generation that was told by all of the social historians and literary writers, that of course women writers had to dedicate them-selves to their art and they couldn't have both. So I thought to hell with that. I didn't see why it had to be either/or. . . . If you have a job in the daytime, you write at night. It's all a question of how much you want to do it.

When Diane di Prima decided to have a child as a single mother in the 1950s, she had a heated argument with the spirit of her favorite poet, Keats:

He told me, as he often had before, that . . . women didn't do it right,
the art thing, we wanted too much of the human world besides. That
no one had done the thing I wanted to do. At least in hundreds, if not
thousands, of years. That I probably wouldn't succeed.

I told him I knew the risks, but I had to try. Not at all sure it would
work, sure only that I was putting the one thing I loved most in jeop-
ardy. Because of some urgency I couldn't explain. We said goodbye, me
knowing I couldn't be sure when I'd "see" him again. If I'd see him
again. I simply couldn't be sure I would still be a poet.

But I was damned if I refused to try.

Ursula Le Guin, who like Atwood shared the childcare with her husband,
recalls lamenting the dilemma, not to a dead poet, but to her childhood
best friend and getting a more encouraging answer:

[Having children] was something I had thought about ever since I was
seventeen or eighteen. And at one point, the way young people will do,
I said, "Well, I can't get married, because you can't write and be fair to
your family."

And Jean said, "Well, why the hell not?" She was John Steinbeck's
niece, and had seen that he couldn't do it, but that didn't convince her.
She just didn't believe that shit.

Ursula K. Le Guin with Caroline on the Oregon coast, 1960.

All Happy Families

URSULA K. LE GUIN (1929–2018)

◆

Art is two things: a search for a road and a search for freedom.
(ALICE NEEL)

IN 1964, a thirty-four-year-old woman and her family move for the
year, for her husband's academic fellowship, to a house in suburban
California. Her two daughters are in school but her son is a baby, so her
days are not her own. Their subdivision has no sidewalks to push a baby
carriage. There are no city buses. She doesn't drive. Even at home in Portland, Oregon, her mobility is limited to fifteen blocks downhill to Safe-
way and back up again, about all she can manage with a stroller and a few
bags of groceries. It's hard to go anywhere with a baby, in the days before
disposable diapers. On a cross-country trip one summer she and her husband ran out of clean laundry, so they drove across Texas with a wet cloth
diaper flapping out the window to dry in the wind, like a white flag of
surrender.

She is starting to come back to herself after her most recent pregnancy,
which she spent in depression and despair. She isn't unhappy as a mother:
she feels more herself in the midst of a family, not less, and hasn't stopped

writing. But she hadn't wanted a third child and had been afraid a new baby would end her writing career, just when she had finally found an audience. The birth made the depression lift a little, and she loves the new baby, but she still has the same problem all new parents have: there aren't enough hours in the day, and it feels like there never will be again.

Every evening, after her husband has put the children to bed in their rented house, she does some work on a new novel, different from the ones she's written before. By day she suffers from anxiety and "cabin fever," but at night she follows the quest of a young man exploring an unfamiliar world. Dreaming up his adventures gives her a lightheartedness that has to do with letting go of high literary ambitions and enjoying herself. A journey across a planet with four moons, on the back of a giant flying cat? That's one way to get out of the house. The imaginative distance from her daily life frees her up and gives her the "inventive spark" she needs.

Her husband believes in her talent, respects her time, doesn't demand her attention, knows that writing and mothering both give her emotional balance. By the end of their suburban year, in the summer of 1965, her first science fiction novel, *Rocannon's World*, has been accepted for publication.

Ursula Le Guin dealt with mothering and writing by keeping the two in separate spheres of thought. When she was "tied down" in her daily life, she sought her freedom in her imagination. Neel and Lessing used their motherhood as material, but Le Guin approached mothering and writing as two distinct projects that happened to occupy the same place and time. Nourished by the security of a family, she claimed authority by leaving home in her work, writing about male protagonists in invented worlds. Ambitious and proud, she wrote about the deeds of heroes, while she limited motherhood's claim on her selfhood by becoming, in her fiction, a man.

Where Lessing and Neel ditched the motherhood plot to raise children outside traditional marriages, Le Guin claimed a space of her own within it. For Le Guin, as for Lessing, it was the loss of her maternal self when her children left home that made her want to put the narratives of mother and writer together. But for a long time she didn't know how to write about her own experience in a genre in which mothers are seldom subjects. She didn't see how a mother could be a hero.

IN THE LATE 1930S, in a tall house in Berkeley, California, a girl climbs out the attic window onto the roof in search of solitude. If she scrambles far enough up the redwood shingles she can reach her own Mount Olympus, the roof's peak. From here she can gaze out over the rough blue of the bay to the city of San Francisco, rows of white houses climbing the hills above the water. The city is strange to her—she rarely ventures so far from home—but the view is hers, and splendid. Beyond it she knows there are islands, with a magical name, the Farallones. She imagines them as "the loneliest place, the farthest west you could go."

Inside the house, the children's father is at work, thinking about myths, magic, songs, cultural patterns—the proper territory of a professor of anthropology. "Don't bother him right now, honey, he's in his study," her mother says, but she knows that in an hour or so he'll come out and be available to her. From him she will take a model for writing in the midst of a rich family life, as well as the belief that the real room of one's own—or the baby on the fire escape—is in the mind. "What you need is the conviction that what you are doing is of real importance, and really worth doing, and you have to do it; and that conviction creates the sacred space around you."

Ursula Kroeber was born October 21, 1929, the youngest of four children and the only girl. Unusually for her generation, her creative ambitions didn't put her at odds with her parents or even make her different from them. The Kroebers were a family of scholars and writers whose occupation and pleasure was the reading, recording, telling, and making up of stories. She grew up listening to her great-aunt Betsy's tales of pioneer childhood and Native Californian stories retold by her father, the anthropologist Alfred L. Kroeber. Ursula absorbed them together with the books she read: not only children's classics but Norse myths, Irish folk-tales, and early fantasy. In her father's library she found Romantic poetry and Eastern philosophy, especially the Tao Te Ching. Together with her brother Karl she read science fiction. She formed herself as a writer not in opposition to her family but within it.

Ursula's mother, Theodora Kracaw Kroeber, known as Krakie (with a long "a"), didn't start writing until her children were out of the house, but she had a lively intellectual life and close friendships with artists and academics, while Elizabeth Buck, Krakie's Aunt Betsy, who lived with the family, did much of the day-to-day child-minding. Krakie was psycho-logically astute and sympathetic to her children's emotional lives, while Alfred liked to pose philosophical questions or puzzles over the dinner table or ask what they were reading. "We were a talkative and discursive and argumentative lot, with the kids encouraged to take a responsible part in the conversation," Ursula recalled, though as the smallest she rarely got a word in edgewise. "There were too many people and I was outshouted by everybody else." Eventually she learned to hold her own and argue back.

She began writing in early childhood. ("It wasn't that I wanted to write; I did write," she liked to say. "You don't say you 'want to play the piano.'") Her parents took her vocation as seriously as she did and gave her encouragement and assistance. When she was a teenager, her father sug-gested that she train for an academic career, like her three older brothers, so she could support herself and live independently. When she was in her twenties, he acted as her agent for poetry, sending her work out to maga-zines, and he and Krakie were the first readers for her work. Not only were they supportive, their help—unlike the efforts of, say, Adrienne Rich's tyrannical father or Sylvia Plath's well-meaning mother—made her feel seen and recognized.

Still, she also learned from them that harmony in an intense family isn't easy to maintain. "All happy families are alike," begins *Anna Karen-ina*, but looking back on her childhood and her motherhood, Ursula dis-agreed. "The only interesting families are unhappy ones? The hell with that. Tolstoy was wrong. They're the ones that are all the same. But a happy family—which doesn't mean that everybody's 'happy' all the time—the so-called happy family is a fascinating thing. The interplay of power and control and love and dislike and frustration: it's endless."

IF IT WAS sometimes difficult to be the youngest of the Kroeber children, the family was also an island of safety and recognition in a larger world that didn't value bookishness or difference. It was outside the house that Ursula felt like "an exile in the Siberia of adolescent social mores." At Berkeley High, all that seemed to matter was sports and popularity. The fashions for girls were strict—wide skirts, short "bobby sox"—and the expectations low. Later, when Ursula described her teenage years, she spoke of loneliness, confusion, and the pain of being among people who have no use for one's gifts. "You're just dropped into this dreadful place and there are no explanations why and no directions what to do."

She found refuge in the public library, encountering Austen and the Brontës, Turgenev, Dickens, and Shelley. Because the foreign-language section was often empty she started reading in French, weeping silent, adolescent tears over *Cyrano de Bergerac* and Baudelaire. California in the 1940s felt provincial, and for Ursula and Susan Sontag, another precocious teenager then devouring the same classics in Los Angeles, Europe seemed like an intellectual's promised land. Ursula fell in love with Prince Andrei in *War and Peace* and once, at thirteen, defaced a library book by cutting out a still of Laurence Olivier's Mr. Darcy and taking it home to look at in private, guilty rapture. In real life she suffered from unrequited loves and must have felt thwarted and lonely. Years later, when she wrote about a teenage girl's emotional awakening in *The Tombs of Atuan*, she made her heroine the priestess of an underground labyrinth in the middle of a desert.

She thought of her teenage unhappiness as being "out of balance," as if she were "walking a high wire: *If my foot slips, I'm gone. I'm dead.*" Balance would become a central metaphor in Le Guin's great works about adolescence, her Earthsea novels. In the first volume, *A Wizard of Earthsea*, a lonely teenager with a gift for sorcery learns that a true magician must choose equilibrium over power. There's little resemblance between the wizards' school in Earthsea and Harry Potter's Hogwarts. But there is some resemblance between Ged, the provincial boy with a chip on his shoulder, and Ursula Kroeber, the Californian in jeans arriving at Radcliffe College in 1947, all books and opinions, never before out of her home state, eager to prove herself as a poet. Her Radcliffe friend Jean Taylor, who became her sister-in-law, recalls that before she and Ursula bonded over jokes and wordplay she found her "a little frightening. It's not that she meant to be, but that's the way it came across. You knew she was highly intelligent, and that there was a good chance that she was ahead of you, in wherever the conversation was going. And so one rather brief acute remark could set you back on your heels."

She realized she didn't fit in with the literary culture when she and a friend signed up to read submissions for a new Radcliffe literary journal, *Signature*. Its undergraduate contributors included Edward Gorey, Harold Brodkey, and Adrienne Rich, but the editors accepted nothing of Ursula's, and she found them "cliquish and unfriendly": "Their comments on what we submitted ourselves, even the comments on our comments, were often remarkably savage and dismissive. We got out again and gratefully went back to our invisibility."

Radcliffe was Harvard's college for women, with its own campus and a separate but second-class status. It offered an excellent education, but its students were on notice: their studies were only an interlude in the motherhood plot. When Ursula began freshman year, she and her classmates were told by the president of the college that "we were there to learn gracious living." She brushed it off and headed straight for the library, with intense pleasure, but Adrienne Rich, her classmate, recalled that she "never saw a single woman on a lecture platform, or in front of a class," while she was there: scholarly women weren't taken seriously. The English department was especially known for its sexism. Four years after Ursula left Radcliffe, a Harvard English professor told grad student Susan Sontag that he didn't believe in graduate education for women. Sontag transferred to the philosophy department. Ursula majored in French.

To reinforce the message about books first, babies later, colleges policed their female students' sexuality. Radcliffe women had to be in their dormitories by 11 p.m., while Harvard men were free to come and go. Couples often parted at the front door with lingering embraces, a practice known as "vestibuling." For Ursula the mind-body problem was reduced, for most of her college career, to sitting "forlorn and loveless listening to everybody else kissing in the front porch between 10:30 and 11:00."

Meanwhile she drafted fiction about the same character in different guises, an artistically gifted, misunderstood young man. Then in her senior year she met his real-life equivalent, a graduate student in mathematics and talented musician. Ursula fell hard for Norman, though her friends warned her about him. He's a New Yorker, Jean said; what you think is reserve is really arrogance. Ursula wouldn't listen. That fall the two of them went to his family's summer house and slept together for the first time.

But even the open-minded Kroebers had never told their daughter about contraception, and Norman knew for a fact that if you made love twice in one night you didn't need to use a condom the second time. At Christmas, while Ursula was staying with her parents in Manhattan—Alfred was teaching at Columbia University that year—she realized she was pregnant. She went to see Norman, expecting to marry him. It would mean leaving Radcliffe, which didn't allow married students, but she would be expelled anyway if the pregnancy were discovered.

Norman broke up with her on the spot. He wasn't ready to settle down, he said, and didn't want to marry outside his Jewish faith. At her parents' house Ursula cried for days, refusing to tell Alfred and Krakie what was wrong, until they finally guessed. They told her that if she wanted to have the child they would support her, though it would be the end of her education, but if she didn't they would help her get an abortion. When Ursula worried that it would be unethical to end the pregnancy, Alfred replied that even if that were so, it was a lesser sin than "sacrificing your training, your talent, and the children you will want to have" to bring an unwanted child into the world.

The normally law-abiding Kroebers inquired discreetly in their circle and got the phone number of an abortionist on the Lower East Side. His fee was $1,000—a year's tuition, room, and board at Radcliffe—payable in cash. The Kroebers were willing to pay it, and Krakie went with Ursula in a taxi. The office was clean, the procedure professional, the word "abortion" never spoken. She returned to Radcliffe, finished her senior thesis on French Renaissance poetry, and applied to graduate school, all in a state of shock and misery. She wouldn't fall for arrogance—or for a Harvard man—again.

As a graduation present and to cheer her up, her parents gave Ursula and her brother Karl a trip to Europe in the summer of 1951. As the Kroeber children visited cities, churches, and castles, Ursula started writing a historical novel set in an imaginary Eastern European country she called Orsinia.

Women writers born around 1930—Rich, Lorde, Toni Morrison, Sylvia Plath—felt their way tentatively forward in the Fifties, unsure of their direction, lacking models. American literature was still under the spell of Hemingway, Faulkner, Richard Wright; both masculinity and realism held sway, and there was little interest in play or fantasy. "I was going in another direction than the critically approved culture was," Ursula said, looking back at her first years of writing. "I was never going to be Norman Mailer or Saul Bellow; I didn't know who my fellow writers were. There didn't seem to be anybody doing what I wanted to do."

Yet she knew there was something in her that needed to be said, and she felt she had to follow it if she could. One day in the spring of 1952, when she was living in New York and studying medieval French poetry at Columbia, she had a vision of an open door, and of stepping through it into the unknown. It marked a change for her, an acceptance of her vocation as a writer and a decision to trust her intuition. In a notebook a few years later, thinking of this "opening of the door," she wrote, "I don't ask where the great wind bears me, so long as it blows, so long as I am able, if nothing more, to accept, to feel/make my freedom, or my necessity, mine."

"Freedom" was a powerful word for her. Before the second wave of feminism, political engagement seems to have empowered creative women. Those who had an activist background, like Lessing and Lorde, understood their situation better than writers and artists, like Smart and Sontag, who were trying to make purely emotional or intellectual sense of their lives. Ursula wasn't yet politically active, but she was concerned about intellectual repression, both in Eastern Europe, where the Iron Curtain was falling, and at home. After she married a historian, she became fascinated by Europe's nineteenth-century campaigns for political liberty. She wrote: "I was looking for something I needed in my own life. It had to do with just thinking and being, in a society that really did seem to be shutting the doors and windows and becoming more closed and more stifling. I felt: Let me out! Let me breathe."

For two years after her marriage, from 1954 to 1956, she lived in Georgia, her husband Charles's home state. She had known about segregation, but witnessing it daily made it harder for her to accept. Not knowing how to write about American politics, she instead worked on a novel set in Orsinia, about a young man in the 1820s fighting for his ideals of equality and free thought. Reading and writing about the unsuccessful European revolutions of 1830 gave her, she wrote, "the distance that I needed, and probably have always needed, between me and the raw, implacable fact that's going on right now. I've never really been able to handle that. If it's right in my face I can't see it."

After she exchanged the "small and stony" ground of realism for a nonexistent country, her imagination began to flourish. She was still writing about men, but being a man in her fiction had advantages. It allowed her to keep her writing and her private self separate in her mind. With her children, she was a mother, with a mother's shared identity and interests.

In her fiction, she could write about people who were solitary, searching, alienated, learning to be themselves.

When she became a man in her fiction, though, it was also because she couldn't imagine what a woman's liberty might consist of. She didn't know how to give any women, especially mothers, the powerful destinies she dreamed of for herself.

In September 1953, a graduate student in French literature stands on the deck of the ocean liner *Queen Mary*. In her cabin are notes for a PhD thesis she will never finish because by the time she docks in Le Havre her long exile of the heart will be over. She is there because she has a Fulbright grant to spend a year in France researching Jean Lemaire de Belges, an obscure fifteenth-century poet, and because she is bored with academic life and wants to get away. Her brother Karl, who has come to see her off, thinks she seems fragile and sad, standing there alone. She has been, but that very night she falls in love.

Charles Le Guin was another Fulbright scholar, a handsome historian with a soft, melodious Georgia voice who was writing a thesis on the French Revolution. Ursula was drawn to his "foreign" accent. He judged her "awfully snooty and shy." Once they got over their first misapprehensions, they became inseparable. In Paris they moved into a hotel in the Quartier Latin with two new Fulbright friends: Ursula and her roommate on one floor, Charles and his on another, with shared toilets down the hall. They went together to plays, concerts, museums, enjoying the romance of Paris. In their rooms the four friends played games, dressing up and staging scenes from operas, discovering a shared sense of fantasy. A few weeks after Ursula and Charles arrived, as they were walking back from a concert through the Tuileries, they paused under the arch and Charles proposed.

Deeply in love, Ursula began picturing the family that she and Charles would make together. In a letter from Aix-en-Provence, she wrote him that she had been to visit friends in the country, and watching their small daughter playing with a cat in the garden had "set me to thinking of an autumn afternoon in our garden with a little one and a minou [kitty-cat] and all, and I must say this is a persistent picture in my mind. You have no idea, Charles, how vastly and intensely bourgeoise I am."

But she also wrote that she'd dreamed she and Charles were flying, supported by books. He was confident; she worried about downdrafts. He was good at steering, while she kept "laughing and losing altitude." It wasn't hard to do: "You simply attach a book to the front end of a sort of surf-board, and spread-eagle yourself on it with your feet over the edge, and trot a little, and woop! there you are gliding. The book is for balance."

If you grow up with a family that has been an island, having children of your own can give the same sense of refuge. When Ursula and Charles married in Paris in December 1953, having known each other for three months, they both felt they wanted kids. Charles was still a penniless grad student, though, and Ursula began her marriage determined not to have another accidental pregnancy. At first they had the gross of condoms they'd been given for a wedding present, and then Krakie, about the same build as her daughter, mailed her a diaphragm in her own size. Ursula also began her marriage with an omission. Not wanting to hurt Charles's feelings, she didn't tell him about her earlier pregnancy—a silence she would keep for thirty years.

One trap for women of Ursula's generation, if they were not ready to believe in their own ambition, was to pursue vicarious success by marrying high-flying, high-maintenance men. But in Charles Ursula chose a man whose gifts and interests complemented hers, and who would let her do her bookish gliding. From a family of farmers, he had been raised by strong women and didn't feel a need to look manly. He had a domestic streak and liked raising children and baking cakes. Where Ursula was a worrier and an arguer, he was easygoing and even-tempered.

They shared a love of history and literature and a quiet indifference to convention.

Ursula envied her Radcliffe classmate Adrienne Rich her early success, the two acclaimed books of poetry that she published while barely out of college. But Rich had married a Harvard economist and though he helped with their three children, she felt in the 1950s that his professional life was "the real work in the family," while her writing was "a kind of luxury, a peculiarity of mine." In her marriage to a different kind of man, Ursula was able to maintain her boundaries and claim an equal role. Thinking back to her ambitious Harvard boyfriend, she would come to realize how lucky her escape had been.

As soon as she was married, Ursula abandoned her own academic prospects. "I went to the Bibliothèque Nationale with Charles sometimes and fiddled around with Jean Lemaire. I loved handling the old books, and the language and all. But I wasn't serious. Charles was doing real research and building up his thesis. I had got free." She cast Lemaire back into obscurity, to await the compassion of future graduate students; began reading and learning from Charles about revolutions; and devoted herself to writing poetry and fiction.

In the next few years a novel she submitted got encouraging rejection letters, while Charles and her parents read her work and affirmed her talent. Three years later, in Moscow, Idaho, where it was so cold in winter that the books in Charles's study froze to the wall, she had her first child, her daughter Elisabeth, and kept on writing.

WHAT DO NEW PARENTS DO, in the first days and weeks after they cross the divide? Ursula and Charles change diapers and wash them. They learn to clean, feed, dress, and carry a cross-eyed, wriggling creature no bigger than a cat, and to gaze upon it with improbable adoration. They enter a state of slow time and heightened emotions, their heartstrings pulled taut and singing with love and distress, fury and delight. They are vulnerable, but they also become part of a delicious new physical intimacy and involvement; Ursula called caring for a baby "thinking with one's whole body." Without support, parenting an infant can be hell. Shared, it has moments of heaven.

Motherhood didn't push Ursula out of her life but centered her in it, partly because she and Charles enjoyed doing it together. Their three children "never would have had a diaper on right without him," she later wrote a friend. "I vividly remember facing an extremely small shitty seven-day-old Elisabeth and attempting to pin this vast mass of cloth onto something about the size of an overgrown hamster, and Charles came and said I think it goes like this. And it did." Charles had been delighted with his newborn daughter, she added, the two gazing at each other "with exactly the same total mutual admiration and self-sufficiency" as any Renaissance Madonna and child.

The matter-of-fact way in which Charles undertook to share fatherhood made it possible for Ursula to go on working—which in turn spared her Lessing's "Himalayas of tedium" and Rich's frustration. Charles, Ursula later recalled,

> was out of the house all day working, but I could rely on him: when he was here, he was *here*. So I didn't have that despair that women get when they're doing it all alone. Even women who have husbands. Even now.
>
> One person cannot do two full-time jobs: writing is a full-time job, and so is children. But two people can do three full-time jobs. So even though I did a lot of the work, there was that ease of knowing that he was there. It didn't always work, and of course we got mad at each other. But overall it did.
>
> And as the kids began to go to bed at a decent hour and sleep the night, because I had the energy of my age, I would go upstairs and work from eight to about midnight. It wouldn't be the time that I'd choose, but I had it, and I got a lot done.

She observed that there was chance involved, too, in having children who didn't need extra care, and good fortune in having the gift of concentration. She didn't shut the study door like Alfred did, "because I was the mother, not the father," but when she was working she wasn't thinking of anything else.

And because she saw her vocation and her family as being on different planes, she said, "I didn't have guilt feelings about writing, or about having children, which obviously so many women do. And that was, I think, an unmixed blessing."

As Elisabeth grew out of her earliest babyhood, Ursula began writing again. Full of energy at twenty-seven, she wrote poems and sent them to her father, who managed to place several of them in little magazines. In 1958 she finished a contemporary novel about a San Francisco family caught up in the Communist witch hunts. J. R. R. Tolkien's editor at Houghton Mifflin turned it down but urged her to send more, praising qualities that would stand out in all her later work: "a good prose style and a profound awareness of the moral relationship of people." She appreciated the encouragement but was more and more frustrated to be writing for her desk drawer. "Writing was always my inmost way of being in the world and the only thing I was ever sure justified my existence as an individual (rather than as a wife, mother, social being). That I could not get anything but a few poems published was therefore increasingly painful, to the point that I suffered a good deal from the contradiction between knowing writing was the job I was born for, and finding nowhere to have that knowledge confirmed."

That year, 1958, Ursula's next pregnancy miscarried at about twelve weeks, a "terrifying and very depressing" experience. First came a little blood and cramping, she recalled, and then "it just happens: the child is not going to make it, you just lose it. It's so easy; it's too easy." Afterward she and Charles rearranged all the furniture in the house, to do a "restart," and when Elisabeth turned two, in the summer of 1959, Ursula was pregnant again.

That year was the start of a series of changes that shaped Ursula's identity as a writer. Charles had taken the job in Idaho partly to get out of the South: although they both loved Charles's parents and Georgia's natural beauty, they chose not to live with segregation or among the narrow minds of those who maintained it. But the University of Idaho was parochial in its own way, and Ursula missed the West Coast. Charles went job hunting and was hired at a new urban university, Portland State. In October 1959 she and Charles celebrated her thirtieth birthday in a little rented house near the campus. Two weeks later their daughter Caroline was born.

A few months later the Le Guins moved into a big Victorian house on a hill above the industrial district, with a view of mountains from the upper windows and enough room in the attic for two desks. When one of Charles's colleagues told them their new neighborhood "wasn't socially acceptable," they thought of that as a plus; it would be their home for the next sixty years.

In October 1960, when Ursula was thirty-one, her father died suddenly of heart failure at the age of eighty-four. "His death was a loss—a pure, simple, large loss," she later wrote. "Life is diminished by such a loss." Where motherhood had been a gain, no longer being her father's daughter felt like a new, painful coming of age.

Theodora Kroeber, Ursula's mother, began to see her own art flourish. Drawing on her husband's notes, she had just published a book with her retellings of California Indian legends, *The Inland Whale*. Then she wrote a book on one of her husband's informants, the last survivor of the Yahi people. *Ishi in Two Worlds*, published in 1961, became an immediate and enduring success, a revelatory work on one Indigenous culture and its near destruction.

As Krakie went on writing and publishing, mother and daughter became literary allies. Ursula sent her mother manuscripts to read, wrote her with news about her growing daughters, and shared with her "the pleasures and anguishes of writing, the intellectual excitement, the shop-talk." Not long after *Ishi* came out, Krakie burst into tears over Ursula's latest rejection slip and cried that she didn't care about her own career, only her daughter's. She couldn't possibly mean that, Ursula thought, and why should she? But she was moved nonetheless by her mother's solidarity.

Around this time a friend loaned Ursula some science fiction magazines—she hadn't read the stuff in years—and in 1961 two of Ursula's stories were accepted for publication in the same week. One, set in Orsinia and dealing with the sacred duty of the artist to his art, was published by a small literary journal that didn't pay. The other was bought for ten dollars for the magazine *Fantastic*, by an editor who wanted to see more. That story, "April in Paris," was about a second-rate academic who abandons his study of Renaissance poetry and steps instead into the world opened to him, one rainy night in his garret, by an act of magic.

Magic was the element that had been missing in Le Guin's work. Fantasy gave her imagination plenty of room, while science fiction gave her a context and authority for talking about politics and as much distance as any writer could want. Although SF was in those days written mostly by men, it was a small, open, and accepting field with a lively community of fellow writers and readers.

It was also a genre that invited readers into sympathy with beings and concepts that had previously been alien to them. In 1962–63, the year of the Cuban missile crisis, Charles taught at Emory University in Atlanta and the Le Guins again lived in Georgia. Emory was for whites only; across town at historically Black Spelman College, Alice Walker was demonstrating for civil rights. Having to send her daughters to segregated schools made Ursula feel more personally exposed to racism than she had before. She barely kept a journal that year, but in the spring of 1963 she wrote:

> Why does it hurt so much, increasingly, this difference between what
> I want and what my people, my countrymen want? . . . Because the
> rift has become an abyss, maybe? And yet at the same time, through
> my children and my present domicile, all the anti- and pseudo-art
> and thought and feeling, all the Distractions, have a bridge to me

across the abyss, and besiege me, and the children. And because of the fostering of hatred and war-spirit. Because I fear the government more than I trust it—as if it were a foreign government. And because there is absolutely no place to go. Nowhere but in.

If "in" means a descent into her own imagination, that is where she sought refuge, but it was also where she could think about race and difference. Departing from her early Eurocentrism, she gave many of her characters dark skin, inviting the reader to identify with protagonists of color. At a time when almost all science fiction characters were white, even the hint of representation had an important effect, especially on a generation of young Black and brown SF readers and writers.

Having stumbled into science fiction, Ursula wrote more of it. By the end of 1963 she had sold several stories to *Fantastic*. But then, just as her career was getting going, she discovered that her diaphragm had failed and she was pregnant again. Her two daughters were six and four. Only another year or two and they'd both be in school. Longing to get her days back, Ursula didn't want to start over with another baby. She didn't seek an abortion: it was still illegal, and her unhappiness didn't seem to her to justify ending a married pregnancy. But for months she was despondent. What had been a space of reassurance had become one where she didn't have control.

She was still bitter about the birth of her daughter Caroline, in which she'd had no say at all in her care. She'd requested natural childbirth, but when she arrived at the hospital, none of the doctors on duty was willing to assist at a natural delivery. Charles couldn't advocate for her, because he wasn't allowed on the ward, and she was left to labor mostly alone, frightened because she was bleeding and no one would tell her why. "I suppose I could have yelled and howled, but no, I wasn't brought up to yell and howl and say, 'Somebody look after me, I'm scared!' I wasn't able to tell anybody that. . . . Oh, it was unspeakable."

When her son Theo was born in June 1964, on Charles's birthday, the worst of her depression lifted. "There he was, a little bitty squally guy, he was the biggest of my babies but he was still only seven pounds. And I said, all right, I'll keep him." Though she fell in love with her third child as she had the other two, for the next several years she went through periods of depression, "dark passages that I had to work through. And then getting through it may not be a big triumph and bursting out into the light. After a period like that there are gains and losses."

As she recollected herself, her writing gained in power, in light and shadow. Motherhood didn't make her writing milder; if anything it had the opposite effect. (Speaking of a particularly violent story that she wrote while planning Elisabeth's fifth-birthday party, she commented, "It's funny how you can live on several planes, isn't it?") Ironically, though, even her maternal experience was inscribed in her stories through a male perspective. She wrote her depression into her Earthsea novel *The Farthest Shore*, sending the wizard Ged on a journey into a silent, lightless underworld from which he returns in a hard journey across his own barren Himalayas, the Mountains of Pain. Later, when Ursula wanted to write about a female character in that world, she couldn't: she didn't know what an adult woman in Earthsea would do. But for now her strategy was working. From Theo's babyhood, Ursula emerged into the most productive writing period of her life.

As Ursula published, in quick succession, the works that made her famous—*A Wizard of Earthsea* in 1968, *The Left Hand of Darkness* a year later, *The Lathe of Heaven* in 1971, two Earthsea sequels, short stories, novellas, and in 1974 *The Dispossessed*—she balanced her growing literary reputation with a comic, down-to-earth private self. In her letters to friends she described cats, children (in 1977: "Caroline (17) just emerged from the basement singing a Christmas carol and her brother (12) kicked her and it went like this: 'Quem pastores laudavere screw you!'") and herself in their midst, busy with a story, "blinking remotely at my poor family as they pass by and mumbling jussamint lemme finshssentence, and four hours later emerging dimly to make dinner." The "bourgeoise" in Ursula enjoyed her domestic life immensely, but was defensive when she felt taken less seriously as a mother, a West Coast author, or a writer of science fiction. It was with a chip on her shoulder that she referred to herself as a "Portland housewife."

Though the Sixties weren't as life-changing for her as they were for younger writers like Carter and Lorde, they created a context in which her work made sense. In the 1960s, science fiction was maturing as literature, and Ursula's ideas—including her politics of liberation—found an audience open to change. From not knowing where she was going, she emerged at the forefront of her genre, expanding its political, philosophical, and literary horizons. *The Dispossessed* is an influential thought experiment about an anarchist society in which work—including the raising of children—is done voluntarily and communally. The short story "The Ones Who Walk Away from Omelas" asks its readers whether they can accept a society built on the exclusion of others. *The Left Hand of Darkness* takes place on a world whose human inhabitants have no fixed gender. They make love only during a brief monthly sexual mode, at which point they may become either female or male, can get pregnant with a child or father one. This arrangement, among other things, seems to create space for Ursula's own strategy of being maternal in her private life, a man in her writing.

During the Sixties the Le Guins did let their hair down—literally, when Charles grew his past his collar. In 1970 he stood with his students when they barricaded Portland's downtown Park Blocks, creating an autonomous zone to protest the war. Ursula demonstrated against nuclear testing, volunteered for antiwar candidates, and danced in a conga line with Allen Ginsberg when he came to speak at PSU. When she sold a short story to *Playboy* for $2,000, almost as much as her advance for *The Left Hand of Darkness* (though the magazine insisted on the byline "U. K. Le Guin" to conceal its female authorship), Charles traded in the family station wagon for a new VW bus. She stayed away from drugs— "my consciousness does *not* need expanding, rather the reverse," she commented— but took in the decade's "youthful ferment" with pleasure.

After Theo went to kindergarten she was "walking on air for a while, because I'm a morning worker, and I had the morning back. That was the end of the period when every aspect of my writing depended on what the kids needed." She settled into a rhythm of working from nine to three, and with energy, focus, and a sense of urgency she got a lot done. Afterward she shopped, did housework, and cooked, but since she didn't drive she wasn't stuck taking the children to music lessons; that was Charles's work. If other mothers wished she would be more involved in school activities, she didn't notice; her mind wasn't on the maternal tribe.

She also resisted, at first, invitations to give talks or take on a public role, partly out of introversion, partly out of a fear of upsetting the balance she'd achieved. Writing her agent, Virginia Kidd, to turn down a speaking engagement, she added, "I walk a rather narrow path, between the needs of my family and my own psychological badlands and abysses. If I don't try either them or myself too far all is well and books get written and mutual security and cooperation prevails."

She still couldn't write full-time, especially not during summer vacation, when her children were home. She was sometimes impatient with the "loose ends quality" of summer, loving September when she could go back to her desk and write for hours. She often started with an idea in the fall and had the first draft of a novel ready by spring. When she wasn't writing, she was liable to be moody. In March 1971 she complained to her writer friend Eleanor Cameron that she had hit a dead end on a book she had started and for the moment had no project to work on. "Oh woe, oh damn! Confound it! And my poor family. I am remote when in spate, but when not in spate, I am just plain MEAN and grumpy."

On one hand, she felt impinged on by others. "I feel very sisterly with Austen, Gaskell, Oliphant, Stowe, writers not able to take much control of their life, working away in the parlor or kitchen with the house life going on around them. I always managed some kind of corner, as I guess Austen did. But . . . with kids under seven or so, *time* is what you have almost no control of. Maybe the absence of control is important in itself? You live with that? This really has not been much written about."

On the other hand, she rejected the idea that writing should go on in isolation. "The degree to which some male writers protect themselves from other people always amazes me. It seems all wrong to me. Yes, you want time to get your work done, and that time is precious and somehow it's very hard to come by, but to achieve it by isolating yourself from commitment to other people—it just does not make sense."

Mothering allowed her to take imaginative risks, she once observed, by giving her a place to come back to. "An artist can go off into the private world they create, and maybe not be so good at finding the way out again. This could be one reason I've always been grateful for having a family and doing housework, and the stupid ordinary stuff that has to be done that you cannot let go."

In 1968–69, and again in 1975–76, Charles went on sabbatical and the Le Guins spent the academic year in London. Both times Ursula lost her writing momentum. On the first trip, the trunk with her notes for a new novel disappeared en route; her children remember how unhappy she was until it turned up. Although she had enough focus to write a novella that year, "The Word for World Is Forest," a lot of care work also fell to her. Putting the children in new schools, doing the grocery shopping in a foreign country, sightseeing on weekends, and not having a desk of her own distracted her from her writing self, so that "the novels didn't happen, evidently because I didn't have some kind of rooted connection I need."

When she was available, she enjoyed being with her children: musically talented Elisabeth; Caroline, a reader and lover of horses; precocious Theo, who at age six liked to wear white dress shirts and a clip-on bow tie, and who at nine went out the door saying, "Goodbye for now, my dear overprotective Ma!" Theo was protective of her: she was still anxiety-prone, and as a small child he would offer comfort and tell her not to worry. Mother and son remained close.

If there was a problem, it may have been that it was difficult to be ordinary in the Le Guin household. If Ursula wanted to re-create the Kroeber family as a safe space for her work, the Le Guins didn't have quite the right temperament, starting with Charles, who disliked argument and raised voices. Elisabeth in particular felt burdened by her mother's passionate belief in devoting oneself to one's art. Elisabeth practiced the cello for hours at a time and was planning a career in music, but at heart she suspected it wasn't her true calling. She later got a doctorate in musicology, and she and Caroline both went into the family profession, academia.

Later Ursula clashed with her daughters about their partner choice. "Around the time Caroline married, she had to cast me off for a while," she recalled. "We always got on so well, so when she had to sort of break that bond, that was tough. And I had to sit there and think, OK, she *has* to do this. And you just have to wait it out and hope that she can come slowly around back to affectionate, easy relationship. It took a long time."

Ursula felt painfully the loss of her role and her children's company as they got older. With Elisabeth, as the eldest, she recalled feeling "a literally physical bond. It was umbilical, in a sense, when she was twelve or thirteen and began to leave home overnight. Oh, that was very tough." When Elisabeth went to college at seventeen, forty-five-year-old Ursula mourned. The first copies of *The Dispossessed*, about a physicist, Shevek, working on a revolutionary theory of simultaneity, arrived in May 1974. Ursula normally resisted comparing her novels to her babies, but now she complained to Virginia Kidd, "All my children are growing up and leaving home, Shevek today, Elisabeth in a month, O menopause, bewilderment, tremblement, confusion—"

For ten years she had been caught up in the urgent, simultaneous time of writing and mothering. "Sometimes in my forties," she said, "I felt like

I was in the middle of a big current that was carrying me—the current of life—and all I could do was try to keep my head above water." In 1971, at the height of her run, she wrote a friend that she thought she worked almost too fast: "Now that I have this incredible expanse of working time from 9 to 3, I rush to my desk and set to work in the same passionate haste as when I had an hour during naps. . . . It's a good habit in some ways, but bad in others. A compulsion to finish can be as bad as a psychological bloc against finishing."

But after *The Dispossessed*, she complained that her inspiration was drying up. At first it just seemed to be a post-project depression, when she was "written out" and an idea for a new novel wouldn't come. She quoted the German artist Käthe Kollwitz, who said that when her children were away she could "work the way a cow grazes": steady, devoted, but no longer "sensual" and "passionately interested in everything."

She missed her own mother, who was no longer such a loyal writing ally. In 1969, at seventy-two, Krakie remarried. Her new husband, John Quinn, was twenty-nine. He was handsome, bisexual, and probably after her money, the Kroeber children thought, but Krakie seemed to think he was worth it. Ursula's writer friend Harlan Ellison remembered arriving for dinner in Berkeley in the early Seventies to see Ursula's beautiful mother and her blond husband coming down the stairs, having clearly just gotten out of bed. John looked exhausted, he thought, "like she had ridden him hard and hung him up wet. . . . And she looked *radiant*, absolutely glowing." He asked Ursula if it was what he thought it was; her look spoke volumes. Still, Krakie had always held up the ideal of a close family, and her children felt betrayed.

Maybe the greatest problem Ursula faced in her writing was the growing pressure she felt, from critics, from readers, and from herself, to incorporate feminism into her work, and especially to write from a woman's point of view. To write from her own experience was what the feminists were demanding, to produce the raw, personal truth-telling of novels like

The Golden Notebook. But for Ursula that would mean breaking down the separation she had maintained between writing and mothering, with its indirect truth-telling and its productive work-life balance.

Ironically, it was partly the support she had always felt from her father, her brothers, and Charles that made it so hard for her to accept feminism. Feminist anger made her uncomfortable, and so did the movement's critiques of mothering. Some feminists, influenced by Simone de Beauvoir among others, identified motherhood as the source of women's oppression. Shulamith Firestone, in *The Dialectic of Sex*, agreed with the socialists that the traditional family was an oppressive institution, but took it further to snarl that "pregnancy is barbaric," and that ideally babies should be gestated in bottles and brought up communally. Rachel Blau DuPlessis asserted, "Motherhood under patriarchy means the death of the self." Mothers were guilty of allowing themselves to be exploited; any woman who enjoyed traditional mothering was lying to herself.

This kind of thing upset Ursula and made her doubt herself. If women's writing, as one feminist scholar claimed, was made possible by "a child-free space," then she must be "wrong to keep on writing in what was then a fully child-filled space." It seemed to her that feminists were holding motherhood up as "the paradigm of brainless enslavement, which wasn't calculated to rouse feelings of solidarity and self-confidence in a woman who had three kids and found the work of being their mother terrifying, empowering, and fiercely demanding on her intelligence."

During feminism's second wave, emotional strategies that women had built their lives on—Elizabeth Smart's self-negation, Lessing's strategic affairs—fell apart, and so did the traditional plots of genre fiction. Ursula felt the loss, and the trepidation of having to reinvent. In 1977 she told Virginia Kidd she couldn't go back to writing from a male viewpoint but didn't know how to go forward. "There is no doubt that I have to find out how to write all over again because I am in a different country where the language is different; I don't speak this language yet. It really is maddening, Virginia, because I *know* how to write the old language now, I really have learned my trade, and to have to abandon all that and start all over— ! But there is no option."

To narrate an unfamiliar truth, she wrote elsewhere, is to "feel like a foreigner in your own country, amazed and troubled by things you see, not sure of the way, not able to speak with authority." And yet years later Ursula said she couldn't have gone on writing from a male point of view. "I think if I hadn't gone through with it and learned how to write from my own being as a woman, I probably would have stopped writing."

At Christmas 1978, Krakie phoned to say she had terminal leukemia. She died six months later, at eighty-two, leaving Ursula grieving and illogically angry at her mother's final abandonment. Ursula came to think of this period of doubt and loss as "the dark hard place."

She made her way out partly by questioning her own narratives of solitary male heroes. To replace them with women in the same roles didn't satisfy her. Instead she tried letting communities and family relationships serve as models for new fictions in which, she wrote, "the Hero and the Warrior are a stage adolescents go through on their way to becoming responsible human beings, where the parent-child relationship is not forever viewed through the child's eyes but includes the reality of the mother's experience." She wrote a series of short stories set on the Oregon coast and dealing realistically with women's lives. She played with collective heroism in her funny and brilliant short story "Sur," about an all-female Antarctic expedition. She went back to Earthsea, rewriting it to look at how its women lived.

To recuperate the mother's experience, Le Guin chose to examine the high fantasy tradition "from outside and underneath," from the perspective of those who had not previously been given a voice. "The ones who can't do magic. The ones who don't have shining staffs or swords. Women, kids, the poor, the old, the powerless. Unheroes, ordinary people—my people." In discarding the "Hero," though, she also set aside the hero in the broader sense of a central character who over the course of the story acquires agency or self-knowledge. Despite what she knew about mothering—that it was "empowering and fiercely demanding"—she didn't portray women in Earthsea as empowered by their maternal work. She chose not to unite motherhood and magic.

She did choose, in her own life, to step into the public eye. She broadened her range as a writer, publishing poetry, realistic fiction, new Orsinian stories, essays, work that brought her new audiences. Early in her career she felt uncomfortable doing events, but now she overcame her introversion and started giving readings and talks. She discovered that teaching workshops gave her inspiration. She reviewed books, putting the argumentativeness she'd learned as a child to good use. She was particularly critical of the realist genre she called the "suburban dysfunctional family novel," saying, "If the family is only something dysfunctional that you want to rail at and run away from, you're losing a large piece of the reason for having novels."

In 2014 the National Book Foundation awarded her its annual Medal for Distinguished Contribution to American Letters, and in a speech to an audience of publishers she chided them for treating books as commodities. "We live in capitalism, its power seems inescapable—but then, so did the divine right of kings," she told them. "Any human power can be resisted and changed by human beings. Resistance and change often begin in art. Very often in our art, the art of words."

Even then, it may still have been easier for her to think about her mothering from a male point of view. In 1993 she wrote "Another Story, or, A Fisherman of the Inland Sea," set on the planet O, where a marriage consists of four people, two men and two women. In that story a young man decides to forgo marriage to become a temporal physicist, exploring the theory of simultaneity and its potential for instantaneous transport. He lives a solitary life, devoted to his work. Then he offers himself as a test subject and one day, instead of translating himself through space, finds himself pulled back in time. Unable to return, he decides to marry and devote himself to family, living the other life he hadn't had. If time is what you can't control as a parent, then time travel is an answer: the hero solves the riddle of work and parenting by living two sequential stories, each one "completely different and completely true."

IN 1987 a woman in her fifties is standing onstage at a university, commanding the attention of her audience. She still lives in the same house on a hill in Oregon and writes constantly, but now she also travels around the country to teach and speak. All her children have left home and her eldest has made her a grandmother. Her "Portland housewife" disguise has worn a bit thin after so many books, awards, and honorary degrees, and she is much in demand as a lecturer. At nearly sixty she has become comfortable in the public sphere.

These days she often speaks about feminism. Several years ago, when she was asked to give a talk to an abortion-rights group, she spoke in public about her abortion, breaking her thirty-year silence. Before she did it she broke a private silence by telling her husband her story.

Today she is giving a talk called "The Fisherwoman's Daughter," on writers who are mothers, who have refused to choose (she says) between creation and procreation. She warns, "The difficulty of trying to be responsible, hour after hour day after day for maybe twenty *years*, for the well-being of children and the excellence of books, is immense." But it is not, she says, impossible.

What must remain within the writer's control, she concludes, is not the time or place, but her writing self, for the duration of the time available. A writer doesn't have to have a room of her own or the goodwill of a partner, though they both help. What she needs is a pencil, paper, and the knowledge "that she and she alone is in charge of that pencil, and responsible . . . for what it writes on the paper. In other words, that she's free. Not wholly free. Never wholly free. Maybe very partially. Maybe only in this one act, this sitting for a snatched moment being a woman writing, fishing the mind's lake. But in this, responsible; in this autonomous; in this, free."

The Discomfort Zone

GHOSTS

In the face of [mother love] one's fat ambitions, desperations, private icons, and urges fall away into a dreamlike *before* that haunts and forces itself into the present with tough persistence. (LOUISE ERDRICH)

IN THE LATE 1940S the French American sculptor Louise Bourgeois, then in her thirties, with a successful career and three young sons, made a series of works she called *Femme maison*: "housewife" or, literally, "woman house." Each one depicted a building merged, like a mythical beast, with a nude female torso and legs, as if the house had taken over the woman's mind and left her body exposed. At the time, curators were losing interest in her and her career was collapsing. She was trying to combine her domestic life with the emotional intensity of her art, and she was failing. "There I was, a wife and mother, and I was afraid of my family. I was afraid not to measure up."

After her beloved and hated father died in 1951, she "lost her equilibrium," literally: she had dizzy spells and couldn't stand. Depression turned to anger: she lashed out at her family, then felt even guiltier for failing as a mother. When a fellow artist referred to her as a "housewife" she raged in her diary: "I could twist the neck of the world." At one point her son had to bar the door of her studio to keep her from destroying its contents. Though her husband tried taking charge of the children so she could work, anxiety attacks caused her to stop showing her art for nearly a decade. "I had the feeling that the art scene belonged to the men, and that I was in some way invading their domain. Therefore my work was done but hidden away."

Sometimes creative mothers fall into a silence that has to do with the daily demands of parenting: Diane di Prima's "waiting for the next rift in the curtain of days." Sometimes an artist holds still, listening for inspiration. But if mothering is a hero's journey, then there will also be times when a mother goes into a forest and loses her way, gets into a "dark hard place" and can't get back to daylight, enters a castle where she is besieged by shadows. Midcentury mothers used both houses and their ghostly occupants as metaphors for melancholy, self-loss, and the death of the spirit that is creative muteness.

Mother-writers suffered most in the conformist years just after World War II. They felt increased pressure to "measure up" to the housewife's role by giving up their own interests, while their careers were impeded by othering and rejection. The shift was hardest on women born in the 1910s, who were just entering their creative maturity when the silence descended. Those who stayed home sometimes got lost there, like the alienated heroine of Doris Lessing's story "To Room Nineteen," who has a seemingly perfect marriage but wanders through her house unable to fill her own emptiness.

Bourgeois, Shirley Jackson, and Gwendolyn Brooks all depicted lives limited by domesticity, interrupted by maternal judgment, "ghosted" by a set of expectations that denied their authentic self. Their maternal ghosts are passive and doomed or vengeful and dangerous, but all are figments of lost autonomy, imagination, and desire.

Shirley Jackson was a successful author who seemed to thrive on writing and parenting her four children. Ideas came to her in the midst of family life: she thought out her famous story "The Lottery" while she was putting away groceries, then wrote it in a few hours, with her daughter in her playpen and her son at kindergarten. But being a mother-writer also made her "different" and vulnerable to attack. "The Lottery" is a story about the kind of small-town hatred to which Shirley, living in an isolated community, herself felt exposed. She felt it most of all from the other mothers at her children's school, a small-minded maternal clique who looked the other way when Shirley's children were bullied but were judgmental about their uncombed hair.

Born in 1916, she had grown up with a toxically critical mother who expected her to look attractive, find a husband, and raise well-groomed children, while at the same time discouraging her gifts. This left Shirley, like Elizabeth Smart, confused, rebellious, needy, and insidiously tempted by the loss of identity that comes with conforming to the feminine ideal. We are all haunted, she once wrote (in the safe first person plural), by the fear "of being someone else and doing the things someone else wants us to do . . . , some other-guilt-ridden conscience that lives on and on in our minds."

Jackson's husband, Stanley Hyman, was on her side in the beginning. A critic and academic with a wide circle of friends, he helped make their household a place of lively intellectual exchange (along with the heavy drinking that was common in those years). But he became jealous when his successes didn't equal hers, and at home he was both tyrannical and useless: she cared for the children and did the cooking, at times with paid help, while he never ventured far enough into the kitchen even to make coffee. He was also a sexual harasser—one family friend said he came on to her like a "steamroller" —who had affairs and made a point of letting her know. Shirley didn't want an open marriage and had no desire to suffer for love, but she didn't feel strong enough to stand her ground against him. Instead she wrote him distressed letters she didn't send and had breakdowns in which she gave in to despair and self-loathing. She felt so unsupported that at times she feared insanity.

One way Shirley coped with these psychic assaults was by turning them into comedy. In her bestselling chronicle of raising children, *Life among the Savages*, she describes going into labor, a physical event that demands concentration and concern for the self, while her husband and children expect her to go on caring for them. In her account of trying to cook breakfast, then going alone to the hospital by taxi (Stanley couldn't drive), she plays her abandonment for painful laughs.

The erasure continues when she checks herself in at the hospital, where the desk clerk asks her name and occupation.

"Writer," I said.
"Housewife," she said.
"Writer," I said.
"I'll just put down housewife," she said.

Specters of lost female selves inhabit Jackson's work, including her 1959 novel *The Haunting of Hill House*, which reads like an extended metaphor for her own situation. The main character is a woman who has no children, having sacrificed love and marriage to care for her ailing mother. After her mother's death she decides she must live for herself and seeks refuge in the mansion of the title. But the house unleashes a flood of emotional abuse, seeking to seduce and entrap her, turning her into a *femme maison* while it vents its fury at her for not "measuring up."

The grim one-room kitchenette apartment inhabited by Maud Martha Brown, in the poet Gwendolyn Brooks's novel *Maud Martha*, is both a metaphor and a realistic depiction of a Chicago tenement, as seen by a young Black woman whose sense of self is dissolving into marriage and domestic obligations. Maud Martha's household is beset not by psychological forces but by the real economic and social pressures of white supremacy in this autobiographical book about race, class, housework, and the yearning for transcendence.

Born in 1917, Brooks was a girl like Shirley Jackson—too smart, too shy, not pretty enough—and *Maud Martha*, her only novel, records the pain of childhood exclusion. Early in her career, her chance of ever getting a book published seemed so remote that she considered burying her manuscripts, in the hope that they would be read and valued in a more understanding future.

Yet part of Black resistance was the encouragement of intellectually gifted girls by their family and community, and where Jackson's mother undermined her, Brooks had her parents on her side and early recognition for her talents. She also made fruitful connections with other poets in the racially mixed writing community of the Chicago Renaissance. She and her husband, Henry Blakely Jr., married in 1938, when they were both twenty-one, and had a son in 1940. Henry wrote poetry too but felt Gwen had the greater talent, so he took jobs as a mechanic, factory worker, and truck driver to give her time to write.

In a city where redlining and de facto segregation excluded Blacks from all but the poorest housing, the Blakely family moved from one cramped, leaky apartment to another. These dreary surroundings strained their marriage and made Gwen feel "grayed in, and gray." Then at thirty-three, one day while she was getting ready to take her nine-year-old to the movies because the lights in their apartment had been turned off for nonpayment, she got a phone call saying her latest poetry collection had won the Pulitzer Prize.

The $500 award may have made them hopeful: their daughter Nora was born a year later, in 1951, eleven years after the birth of their son. Still, buying a house—"a small wood frame house, small kitchen, small living room packed with books" —would have to wait until 1953.

Maud Martha, Brooks's unassuming heroine, is a secret lover of beauty who suffers from her ugly surroundings, in a building haunted by traces of others: the drifting fumes of the neighbors' frying onions, their ripe garbage in the hall, their long loitering in the shared bathroom, the roaches intruding on the kitchen. Her cultural interests are thwarted by her husband's insensitivity and lack of imagination. In one comic scene he reads a love manual in bed while she reads *Of Human Bondage*. As she watches, he falls asleep with his mouth open, still holding the book. "*Sex in the Married Life* was about to slip to the floor. She did not stretch out a hand to save it."

It's as a mother that she awakens and begins to regain herself. She laughs in joy at her baby's first cries and delights in "hearing that part of Maud Martha Brown Phillips expressing itself with a voice of its own." And it's for her child that she finally gets angry. When she takes her daughter to a department store at Christmas and the white Santa treats her coldly, Maud Martha imagines a murderous assault on Saint Nick, yearning "to jerk trimming scissors from purse and jab jab jab that evading eye." There's no playing this scene for comedy: the incident leads her to confront a resentment "she could neither resolve nor dismiss. There were these scraps of baffled hate in her, hate with no eyes, no smile and—this she especially regretted, called her hungriest lack—not much voice."

When the book was published in 1953, Mary Helen Washington writes, critics read it as a portrait of "a spunky Negro girl" instead of "a novel about bitterness, rage, self-hatred, and the silence that results from suppressed anger. . . . What the reviewers saw as exquisite lyricism was actually the truncated stutterings of a woman whose rage makes her literally unable to speak."

At least Maud Martha is aware of her authentic feelings, as Jackson's heroine is not, but her loneliness and frustration at her lack of opportunity and agency were phantoms that readers couldn't see. Still, Brooks was determined not to let her heroine be erased. In a period when independent, questioning female characters were such a problem that women writers regularly killed them off, Maud Martha stubbornly continues to seek a meaningful life.

Brooks proposed a sequel to her novel in which Maud Martha's husband dies in a fire, leaving her looking forward to a new freedom. Her white editor at Harper's, Elizabeth Lawrence, was uncomfortable with this scenario. (She also discouraged Gwen from publishing poems that were too critical of whites or didn't fit her narrow conception of African

American reality.) She turned the proposal down, saying she couldn't see how it followed from the previous book. Yet Brooks was relatively quick to regain her voice, partly through a well-known American maternal horror story: the 1955 lynching of Chicago child Emmett Till inspired some of her most coolly devastated poetry. In the work of African American mother-writers, most famously Toni Morrison's *Beloved*, murdered children have long maintained ghostly presences.

In the early Sixties Brooks published some of her best-known poems, including "We Real Cool," her comment on the early deaths of young Black men. The radical Black Arts Movement reenergized her work, and she began focusing on Black readers rather than trying to appeal to white ones. She left Harper's for a Black-owned publishing house, and in 1968, with her son grown and her daughter a teenager, she left her husband.

"Marriage is a hard, demanding state. Especially if you're a woman, you have to set aside yourself constantly. Although I did it during my marriage, I couldn't again," she said. Gwen and Henry got back together after five years of separation, partly after Henry accepted her new political views. In her later poetry she used her mastery of the sounds and rhythms of language to convey anger and urgency. "Words do wonderful things," she wrote. "They pound, purr. They can urge, they can wheedle, whip, whine. They can sing, sass, singe."

In the early 1960s, as Gwen's career was coming back to life, Shirley was becoming housebound. Afraid to leave Stanley, distressed by the loss of her mother role as her children needed her less, she became agoraphobic and unable to write. She had always thought of her writing as an escape from housework and from her anxieties: "So long as you write it away regularly nothing can really hurt you." Now she was physically and imaginatively stuck at home.

She had been drinking heavily and using prescription drugs, including tranquilizers and amphetamines, which she originally took for dieting. (She had an unhappy relationship to her body, which had often been the target of her mother's criticism.) Speed was helpful for writing, until it wasn't: it almost certainly contributed to her dysphoria and anxiety attacks. When she discovered one of Stanley's affairs she made scenes that frightened her children. Barry, the youngest, remembered sobbing out, "I don't want my mother to be crazy! I want my mother to be like everybody else!"

As hard work and therapy helped her recover her agency, she began a novel about a woman who leaves home for a new adventure. It was not yet finished one day in 1965 when her daughter went to wake her from a nap and found her dead of heart failure at age forty-eight. She'd left her new beginning until too late.

At the same age, with her sons nearly grown, Louise Bourgeois reached her nadir. In 1959 she wrote:

> I have failed as a wife
> as a woman
> as a mother
> as a ~~home~~ hostess
> as an artist
> as a business woman
> and I am 47 —
> as a friend —
> as a daughter
> as a sister —
> I have not <u>failed</u> as a
> truth seeker
> lowest ebb —

Around the same time, her reference unclear, she wrote in a notebook: "If I am abandoned again, I am going to set the house on fire."

But a woman wins her place as an artist, she once said, by "prov[ing] over and over that she won't be eliminated." She had never entirely stopped working, and as she entered her fifties, her endurance began to pay off. She played with sculpting body parts, often sexual; one was a larger-than-life penis she named *Fillette*, "little girl." In a photograph by Robert Mapplethorpe she smiles mischievously, holding the sculpture under her arm. She said she knew that the photographer of gay male sexuality liked to take pictures of people with big penises, so when she came to the photo shoot she brought hers with her.

After the death of her husband in 1973, when she was sixty-one, her career took off, as if the local representative of the patriarchy, however well-meaning, had to get out of the way before she could think her own thoughts. The next year she took imaginary revenge on both the parent who had belittled her and the family ideal that had eaten her brain, in an installation she called *The Destruction of the Father*. She claimed its abstract lumps of latex and plaster represented a patricidal family drama: "At the dinner table, my father would go on and on, showing off, aggrandizing himself. And the more he showed off, the smaller we felt. Suddenly, there was a terrific tension, and we grabbed him—my brother, my sister, my mother—the three of us grabbed him and pulled him onto the table and pulled his legs and arms apart. . . . We ate him up."

She made an apron covered in breasts and wore it in a performance. Because her mother had been a weaver, she started making giant sculptures of spiders that she called *Maman*, "Mother," claiming these scary figures as guardians, as if to incorporate her anger into a mothering that was still able to nurture and protect. She moved into a bigger studio, where she could assemble huge pieces from found materials, and hired an assistant, Jerry Gorovoy, who for thirty years smoothed the path of her career. Pouring her fears into her work helped her ease them in her life. She never stopped having bouts of anxiety, guilt, and anger, but she made them both the driving force and the subject of her art. Time was on her side: she hit her stride at the age of seventy and went on making brilliant work until her death at ninety-eight.

Sometimes when children leave and a partner leaves or dies, like water welling up from a deep spring, all the energy, ingenuity, insight, patience, and time that went into family-making returns to the self, giving new life to a ghosted creativity. This seems to have happened to Le Guin's mother, Theodora Kroeber, whose writing career began at sixty-two. It also happened to the novelist Penelope Fitzgerald, who began publishing fiction at sixty and became one of the great British novelists of her age. She too was a *femme maison*, and when she recovered her sense of vocation, it was partly because, with a symbolism straight out of Bourgeois's art, her actual home fell to pieces.

The Discomfort Zone

◆

I N 1960, broke and arguing bitterly about money, sometime writer Penelope Fitzgerald and her unsuccessful lawyer husband, Desmond, moved with their three children into the cheapest housing they could find: a semiderelict coal barge moored on the Thames. When the tide was out, *Grace* rested on the mud, listing slightly. When the tide was in and she was afloat, she took on water and had to be bailed. From the galley Penelope fed her family fried potatoes, fried eggs, fried bread, and canned stew. Desmond, who had a drinking problem, once lost his footing on the gangplank after an evening out, hit his head, and would have drowned if Penelope hadn't heard him fall. One morning their two daughters saw that their bedroom floorboards were wet. When they came home from school they found *Grace* awash and their possessions floating away.

Penelope Knox was born in 1916 into a family that valued cleverness and success, a clan of intellectuals and (mostly male) high achievers, including her formidable father, who edited the influential humor magazine *Punch*. She too was full of literary ambition, following in their foot-steps at Oxford, where she was a social and academic star. But though she got from her family a firm sense of entitlement and their blessing to pursue a creative life, her privileged childhood didn't give her the practical and emotional skills that she would need to make her way in a less sheltered postwar world.

In early adulthood she took some painful blows to her self-assurance. Her mother died just as she began Oxford; and when she patriotically went to work for the BBC during the war, she had a relationship with her boss that her biographer, Hermione Lee, describes as unrequited love and that Penelope, in her fiction, depicts as debilitating emotional exploita-tion. On the rebound she married Desmond Fitzgerald, a fellow Oxford graduate and newly commissioned officer in the Irish Guards.

It's hard to know what her plans were for writing, since her personal papers were lost along with *Grace*. But it seems clear that marriage inter-fered with her literary aspirations, practically and emotionally, in ways that probably neither partner could have predicted. When Desmond came back from Tripoli, Anzio, and Monte Cassino with a medal for bravery and a severe case of PTSD, Penelope found herself caring for a man who woke screaming from nightmares—and, increasingly, medicated his days with alcohol. Pregnancy brought more trauma for them both: though she eventually had three healthy and much-wanted children, she miscarried repeatedly and their first child died of a heart defect at birth.

The sudden postwar irrelevance of women, as they were pushed out of jobs to accommodate returning men, hit her hard. Desmond, who had trained as a lawyer, became the editor of a small literary magazine, where Penelope assisted and encouraged him though she most likely could have done it better. They lived in Hampstead, above their means, until the journal folded. Then the parties with fellow writers ended; the house went; the furniture was auctioned. Eventually Desmond's drinking cost him his law license.

It's not clear whether Penelope was too impractical to deal with disaster, or didn't want to upstage Desmond, or simply refused to cope as a kind of backhanded protest against her own feelings of devotion and self-sacrifice. She was an affectionate, though harried, mother and made sure her children got a good education. When they were little she freelanced for the BBC, scripting book reviews, educational programs for children, and features for *Woman's Hour* on subjects such as "What It's Like to Be a Librarian." Her own woman's hours conflicted with journalistic deadlines, though, and the BBC work dried up. In the mid-Fifties she wrote a serial about a farmgirl for a children's magazine, and once she took her eldest child with her to Mexico in pursuit of an inheritance that didn't materialize, but otherwise she seems to have undergone the long slide into financial ruin with a passivity that suggests depression, denial, and loss of self. Caught between the motherhood plot and her vocation, it could be hard for a woman to know her own mind—a state of indecision that she thought of, like living on the barge, as being "offshore."

Her second novel, *The Bookshop*, published in 1977, contains a fragmentary ghost story about maternal, or daughterly, grief and anger. During the novel's most tender scene, a moment of closeness between a middle-aged, childless widow and a ten-year-old girl, a poltergeist violently assaults the house, as if demanding a price for their half hour of happiness. "Don't mind it," the woman says bravely, determined not to be driven out of her home. The frightened child answers, "That doesn't want us to go. That wants us to stay and be tormented."

The sinking of the houseboat almost seems to represent the required patriarchal disappearance, taking with it the class conventions in which Fitzgerald had been raised and the selfless ideal of marriage on which she had pinned her hopes. (In *The Bookshop* she has the narrator say, "It sometimes strikes me that men and women aren't quite the right people for each other.") After this she pulled herself together and committed herself to a less normative life.

The Fitzgeralds moved into public housing: an anonymous but comfortable council flat in South London. The children went to private schools, then to Oxford like their parents. No longer burdened by expectations, Desmond stopped drinking, found work as a travel agent, and began sharing the housework, making trips to the launderette and doing the ironing. Though Penelope now slept on the living room couch, she still said she loved him, partly because she could relate to his inability to cope, partly for the same reason Alice loved Sam Brody: "Desmond always thought everything I did was right."

By then Penelope had begun teaching to support the family, coaching secondary-school pupils who needed help passing their A levels. At fifty she appeared to her students an improbable figure, disheveled and oddly dressed, wearing an old tweed jacket of her father's over homemade smocks. "I have tried dyeing my hair with a tea-bag, but it did not make much difference," she wrote her daughter gloomily, and she felt invisible and ineffective. (Her son-in-law said of her that she was "confident only in her fearsome sense of artistic rightness.") She disliked pretending to care whether or not her students did their essays; she encouraged the fainthearted but did not suffer fools. She and her much younger fellow teacher A. S. Byatt were prickly with each other, resenting small slights, probably in unacknowledged competition. Byatt recalled her as a good teacher, but said of her what could be said of any of the women in this book: she was a genius, and "geniuses are not nice people."

As her children left home, her old ambitions began to reawaken. In her fifties, with Desmond as her research assistant, Penelope wrote two nonfiction books, a biography of the artist Edward Burne-Jones and a book about her father and his brothers, whose brilliant lives had shaped her own. But as she once wrote, "Helping other people is a drug so dangerous that there is no cure short of total abstention." Desmond developed cancer in his late fifties. During his treatment she started work on a comic thriller, supposedly "to amuse [him] when he was ill." He died in 1976, and the book—her first novel—was published the next year. After that, her husband gone, her children settled, she gained her footing. A year later she published her brilliantly original second novel, *The Bookshop*. Then she wrote a book set at a moorage on the Thames, with a doomed but heroic cast of misfits. *Offshore* (1979) won the Booker Prize.

Failure became Fitzgerald's great subject. Her protagonists suffer defeat and their plans come to naught, but they keep their integrity (and ineptitude) and go out unbowed. Late in life she still hid behind her dishevelment: one friend, observing her careless clothes and her pointed remarks, wrote: "As sharp as a knife is old Penelope, and goes to great lengths to pretend not to be." She may have cured herself of helping other people, but not of hiding, not only her brilliance, but the originality that she had never quite permitted herself as a wife and mother.

Audre Lorde with her partner, Frances Clayton, and her children,
Jonathan and Elizabeth Lorde-Rollins, July 1978.

Mother, Poet, Warrior

AUDRE LORDE (1934–1992)

◆

Mother is the single most interesting and confusing word that I know. Next to Black. (ALEXIS PAULINE GUMBS)

The white fathers told us: I think, therefore I am. The Black mother within each of us—the poet—whispers in our dreams: I feel, therefore I can be free. (AUDRE LORDE)

WHEN SHE WAS PREGNANT with her first child, in 1962, Audre Lorde was delighted at the magic of making new life. She went to her job as a librarian in suburban Mount Vernon, New York, came home to her lawyer husband, Ed Rollins, worked on her poems, and felt the baby in her "blooming" with summer and "growing heavy against" the winter wind. She thought of how her daughter—she was sure it would be a daughter—was developing inside her: her hands forming, her teeth getting ready to appear, her hair starting to curl.

Audre and Ed were advanced parents for their time. They took childbirth classes together and made sure Ed got to be present for the birth. Afterward Audre insisted that the baby stay with her, not in a nursery. Making choices with an involved partner and getting the care she wanted, not setting aside her own needs, put Audre in a place where she could enjoy pregnancy and her new child.

Her pregnancy wasn't an accident: she had married because she wanted children. But she and Ed had made a marriage of their own design: a poly-amorous union between a Black lesbian and a white gay man who both sought the warmth and closeness of a family. At a time when male-female coupledom was the only safe option, they did what others they knew were also doing: they shared a home and had children while both still living "in the life."

Audre was a hard-headed New Yorker with a romantic heart; a vision-ary poet, memoirist, and essayist of racial and gender justice; an intellec-tual, dreamer, lover, activist who was already, as she walked the floor with her colicky baby, working out how to add "mother" to the list. An affec-tionate person who drew strength from nurturing those she loved, she felt empowered by parenting Beth and her son Jonathan, born the next year.

While she thought of herself as "wrapped in the cocoon of a nursing mother," she also thought of her writing with a growing sense of urgency. Twenty-nine when Beth was born, she was starting to find publishers for her poetry; and unlike Fitzgerald, she wasn't playing any waiting games. "Something in my body / teaches patience / is no virtue," she wrote. She had spent a lot of time in uncertainty and self-discovery, and once she finally claimed her vocation, her daughter Beth recalled, she "conducted her life like a house on fire."

Looking back, Audre called raising her two children not a position of self-loss but

a long and sometimes arduous journey toward self-possession . . . sweetened by an increasing ability to stretch far beyond what I had previously thought possible—in understanding, in seeing common events in a new perspective, in trusting my own perceptions. It was an exciting journey, sweetened also by the sounds of their laughter in the street and the endearing beauty of the bodies of children sleeping.

She was also aware that as a lesbian mother she risked ostracism, while as an African American mother she was parenting against a dominant culture that didn't support Black maternal bliss. If motherhood is a missing or unseen subject position to begin with, then Black, queer motherhood happens at an intersection of invisibilities. To be a mother in that situation, scholar Alexis Pauline Gumbs writes, is not normative at all. Instead it's a queer act, "where queer means a violent disjuncture between how our bodies are interpreted by the outside world and how we feel inside them, where queer means 'I am not supposed to exist,' but I do."

Audre observed, "As a Black lesbian mother in an interracial marriage, there was usually some part of me guaranteed to offend everybody's comfortable prejudices of who I should be." Her countermoves were to redefine motherhood as a place of both safety and defiance while giving her children the gift of themselves.

Her poem on her pregnancy, "Now That I Am Forever with Child," ends with the birth of her daughter, Elizabeth Lorde-Rollins, in March 1963:

I bore you one morning just before spring
My head rang like a fiery piston
my legs were towers between which
A new world was passing.

Since then
I can only distinguish
One thread within running hours
You, flowing through selves
Toward You.

BEFORE AUDRE BECAME A MOTHER, she had been a student, an activist, and a cute young thing on New York's lesbian bar scene, with a talent for seduction and a radiant smile that made the other "gay-girls" call her "dazzling." Friends saw her as intensely present, sexy, and full of life in whatever she was doing, whether it was writing, gossip, or love. When she slow-danced in the gay bars she knew herself to be "without peer or category."

Finding her way toward her motherhood and her career, she had first had to find herself. Alice Neel had made a home among artists, Doris Lessing in politics. But being a Black lesbian poet in the 1950s was another order of difficulty. Audre had done her exploring in Greenwich Village, where she'd lived with a woman lover, bravely putting both their names on the mailbox. She had done it at the Harlem Writers Guild, which nurtured young Black talent and gave her room to define her racial identity. She'd found an important clue to herself in her early twenties when she'd gone alone to Mexico and found romance with an older woman.

She'd tried on different selves the summer she was fourteen, when she and her best friend Genny had dressed up and roamed around the Village pretending to be bohemians, or had put on tight skirts and heels and followed respectable-looking men down Fifth Avenue, making what they thought were lewd remarks. Sometimes they had stayed closer to home and just walked around Harlem holding hands, not knowing whether what they had was companionship or love.

Poetry had been part of her since she was a little girl, with braids and thick glasses, whose parents liked to bring her out in front of company to show her off. Her performance then was reciting from memory: Walter de la Mare's "The Listeners"; Edna St. Vincent Millay with her romance and sly wit. Because she felt inarticulate—she hardly spoke at all until she was five—she communicated using others' words. When someone asked her about herself, she recalled, "I would recite a poem, and somewhere in that poem would be the feeling, the vital piece of information." She eventually started writing "to say things I couldn't say otherwise when I couldn't find other poems to serve."

IN A WAY both Audre's writing—her search for words for her experience—and her family-making seem like continuations of her parents' journey of self-reinvention. When Byron and Linda Lorde arrived in New York from Grenada in 1924, Audre's father left behind his first fatherhood: twin daughters, born to another woman, whose existence he never mentioned to Audre or her sisters. He also left behind his name. Balancing his pride in his origins with ambition and self-creation, he was Flavius Balgoven Lorde on his immigration forms but chose in America to be Frederick Byron.

Linda Belmar Lorde never stopped dreaming of her family's home, the tiny Grenadine island of Carriacou; with her husband she spoke a patois that Audre thought of as their "secret poetry." According to the family story, Linda's father had been a white Portuguese fisherman who was lost at sea. When she first came to New York she passed for white to take a restaurant job, then was fired when the deception was discovered.

The Lordes built a business together, managing apartment buildings and selling real estate in Harlem, working long hours while they pushed against New York's barriers to Black success. Together they made their family into an island in an unfamiliar world, teaching their daughters to trust neither white people nor African Americans, with home as the only safe space. Audre absorbed her parents' sense of exceptionality, though what she heard was a mixed message: "You're a Lorde, so that makes you special and particular above anybody else in the world. But you're not our kind of Lorde, so when are you going to straighten out and act right?"

Audre grew up feeling out of place, like the tail on the "y" that she dropped from her name: an awkward afterthought. Born on February 18, 1934, as Audrey Geraldine Lorde, she first renamed herself when she was just learning to write and loved "the evenness of AUDRELORDE." Her two older, better-behaved sisters, who were often left alone to care for her while their parents were at work, saw a "wild little girl" who was "always getting into things," while Audre just felt nearsighted and clumsy, the ugliest, the least loved.

The people you love most shelter you from the world's fury and rejection, yet the family can also be the place where anger burns brightest, where slights and fears collect like oily rags waiting to burst into flame. A day spent achieving in the eyes of others may end in a vicious snarl at a partner. Powerlessness to protect or help children can be acted out against them, and the Lorde sisters not only suffered but were punished for the consequences of poverty and discrimination. Audre longed for parental affection and recognition for her gifts. Instead her mother beat her for minor errors, from coming home late to losing a penny at the store. Even her attempts at comfort were rough, Audre wrote in her fictionalized autobiography, *Zami*, "as if her harshness could confer invulnerability upon me. As if in the flames of truth as she saw it, I could eventually be forged into some pain-resistant replica of herself."

It wasn't just the Lordes: in her Italian immigrant family in Brooklyn, Diane di Prima also felt on her body the violence of her parents' fears. When these two friends became mothers, Audre was strict, Diane more relaxed, but both were vigilant about protecting their children from others' anger and their own.

Linda Lorde also tried to overcome prejudice and poverty with lies and concealment. When she couldn't afford gloves, she told her daughters she didn't like to wear them. When white people spat on them, she pretended the wind had just been blowing the wrong way. "She had had to use these defenses, and had survived by them, and had also died by them a little," Audre wrote later, trying not to die of them herself. When Audre complained that she had no friends at her all-white Catholic school, her mother snapped, "You don't need friends."

It took Audre a long time to unlearn these messages. In the face of her parents' disapproval, she later wrote a therapist, "I was ALWAYS AFRAID. Because if power doesn't like what you are they hurt you. Or beat you. Or don't love you. So either become who they want you to be, or pretend and hide. I chose the latter."

She may have been tempted to hide, but all her life she fought bravely against it, too. Knowing fear, she learned to speak out. Having been lied to, she tried to tell true stories about herself. Having felt alone, she built a supportive community around her, maintained close friendships, and made sure she had pleasure in her life. As she wrote in one of her most quoted observations, "If I didn't define myself for myself, I would be crunched into other people's fantasies for me and eaten alive."

Audre began learning to define her difference after she passed the rigorous exam and became one of a handful of Black students at New York City's elite, all-girls' Hunter High School. Another, her partner in her ninth-grade dress-up games, was Genevieve Johnson, a talented dancer whose single mother encouraged her artistic ambitions. Other than Genny, her closest friends and allies were a group of Hunter girls, all white except for her, who turned insubordination and social rejection into badges of honor. They called themselves "the Branded," proclaimed themselves writers, penned verses in colored ink with quills, and held séances, summoning the spirits of the Romantic poets to be their muses. Like Le Guin, Audre was snubbed by the school's literary magazine (though she felt vindicated when a love sonnet that its editors had rejected was published in *Seventeen*). The Branded taught her to be an outsider, as together they "wrote obscure poetry and cherished our strangeness as the spoils of default, and in the process . . . learned that pain and rejection hurt, but that they weren't fatal, and that . . . not feeling at all was worse than hurting."

Friends saw her as imposing, quick-witted, and reserved behind her glasses, needing to feel in control of the situation before she spoke. Diane di Prima, another of the Branded's would-be poets, recalled her as "fierce, and in those days often unreadable. She kept us guessing with her eyes and her silence. A kind of knowing and a kind of contempt." She didn't know how much it hurt Audre not to be welcome in her white friends' parents' houses, or how insecure she was about her sense that she thought differently than other people, not logically, "step by step," but "in bubbles up from chaos that you had to anchor with words," so that "everything was like a poem, with different curves, different levels."

Inside the defenses that kept her "unreadable," she was a romantic who filled her notebooks, between her Latin homework and her confessions of love for her English teacher, Miriam Burstein, with poems about love and death, green trees and twilit vales with dryads dancing. A reader of science fiction, she drafted a story about a sentient light year who wants more from existence than just to carry light. In the end, when it hits the earth's atmosphere, it goes out in a meteor's blaze of glory.

To want more is to be vulnerable. Her friend Genny, now fifteen, had an argument with her mother and moved in with her charismatic, unreliable father. Not long afterward, for reasons Audre never discovered but could imagine, Genny committed suicide. Audre sat by her bedside in the hospital, but she'd swallowed rat poison and the doctors couldn't save her. In anguish Audre wrote in her journal, "I loved her so and I couldn't stop her."

Marking Genevieve's death in her calendar each year thereafter, Audre mourned her friend deeply and long. She began her first book with a poem, "Memorial II," imagining Genevieve looking out of the speaker's eyes. Black and gay lives were at risk, and Audre felt strongest when she could protect others. When she couldn't, she helped them grieve. Years later, when Diane's gay best friend, Freddie Herko, committed suicide, it was Audre that she phoned, and despite her small children and busy job, it was Audre who, knowing her pain, came to get her, drove her in her big car to Central Park, and let her cry against her shoulder.

Vulnerability taught Audre to look for allies, especially since, at this point, she didn't have a family to fall back on. She wanted to go away to college, like her friends from Hunter, and had been accepted with a full scholarship at elite, artistic Sarah Lawrence. Her parents had encouraged her to get a white, middle-class education, but faced with the next logical step, the one that would really take her away from them, they wouldn't allow her to go. They were frightened by Byron's failing health—within two years he would be dead of a stroke—but Audre felt abandoned and storyless in her parents' house.

When the tension became unbearable, she turned to the Branded, who helped her find a room to rent in Brooklyn. A month after she gradu-

ated from Hunter, at seventeen, she got a job as a nurse's aide and, terrified
in the present but hopeful for the future, set out on her own. Her proud,
stubborn parents didn't look for her for a long time, which hurt, but she
knew she didn't belong anymore at home.

IN 1951 it took an enormous act of imagination for any woman to claim
her own story, let alone a poor, Black, teenage lesbian dealing with childhood trauma. Just living on her own was unusual: for most women of
Audre's generation, college and marriage were the only options for independence. She experienced the next decade as "a period of war . . . when
things were bleak, and there was very little trust around and there were
so few of us. We were women-identified women, and it was us against the
world." She added, "I count myself as lucky. Every one of us who survived
that period did it through luck and love, and there were a lot of people
who didn't get enough of either."

At first, when she knew she loved women but not what to do about it,
she dated a Jewish boy about her age whom she'd met through the Labor
Youth League. She was deeply in love with Gerry, or the idea of him, and
slept with him because he wanted it, afterward in her journal lamenting
their "misunderstandings" in bed: "I love him so, and yet I can't—just
can't accept to conform to the sexual side of our relationship." That fall,
instead of stepping into the empty space in her life, he broke up with her,
leaving her miserable and—though she didn't know it yet—pregnant, presumably by him.

She left the doctor's office terrified and determined, "knowing I could
not have a baby and knowing it with a certainty that galvanized me far
beyond anything I knew to do." A friend of a friend had died from an
abortion, and she had nightmares "of myself upon the table, & the doctor's hand being bitten off by a razor-sharp pair of infant wolf-like teeth
that reached out from my womb." She couldn't possibly afford the safe,
expensive New York City doctor that Ursula Le Guin had been to the

year before, but eventually she found a nurse willing to induce a miscarriage for forty dollars, nearly two weeks' pay. Getting through the painful, bloody, and terrifying procedure made her feel brave and self-reliant. "Even more than my leaving home . . . this action was a kind of shift from safety towards self-preservation."

In the next year and a half she started putting together a diverse group of friends; went into therapy; moved to Connecticut, where she got a job in a factory; and met her first woman lover. Therapy would be an important part of her self-discovery, despite a bad start: she left her first analyst after she urged her not to "get mixed up with homosexuality." On the contrary: making love to Ginger, "gorgeously fat" and sweetly flirtatious, "was like coming home to a joy I was meant for, and I only wondered, silently, how I had not always known that it would be so."

In 1954, in Cuernavaca, Mexico, among a group of American expats who had fled persecution at home, she met another, older woman who helped her acknowledge and claim her sexual identity. Journalist Eudora Garrett taught Audre how to be made love to as well as to love, to call herself a lesbian and be proud of it, "how to love and live to tell the story, and with flair."

She came back to New York from Mexico knowing more about community and how to find it, and with more of the life and work skills she needed to support herself on her own. Now twenty, back in touch with her mother and sisters, she decided to resume the education she'd abandoned. Diane had dropped out of college and was freelancing as a typist and artist's model, but Audre didn't want a chaotic life, and being able to trust to chance was a privilege she didn't have. She began taking classes at Hunter College, the collegiate counterpart of Hunter High School.

It was there that she met, romanced, and found a lifelong ally in the student body president, Blanche Wiesen Cook. Blanche, a cofounder of Students for a Democratic Society and later a historian and biographer of Eleanor Roosevelt, was drawn to Audre's combination of intellect, bravery, and play. She once said of their friendship, "We have some very stormy times together, but we always have very full stormy times, and when we have fun we have full fun."

In the two years in the 1950s that Audre shared an apartment with her girlfriend Marion, they made "vows of love and forever," but their needs were greater than what they could give each other. In *Zami* she wrote, "Each one of us had been starved for love for so long that we wanted to believe that love, once found, was all-powerful. We wanted to believe that it could give word to my inchoate pain and rages; . . . that it could free our writings, cure racism, end homophobia and adolescent acne."

The loss was greater, then, when she and Marion broke up. In her journal, in 1958, she wrote out her raw, unpolished feelings of abandonment:

> I feel like winding myself into a puddle and weeping until I drown. . . . All the long years before, there was in me a dark and empty cavern where sometime shrieking howling winds ravened back and forth, and a sometime vacuum strangled all into silence, but this cavern lacked definition to make it final. Now, it is known and finalized, and its name is loneliness, that is an endless death.

She pulled herself together, but loneliness remained a threat. In her journal, Audre described lovemaking as part of her defenses, her way of playing "the safety game . . . giving freely in areas not commonly given yet holding tight the door to a more essential self." She was many women's first lover; Audre's biographer, Alexis De Veaux, writes that she "often loved people who hadn't had a sense of being truly loved before they met her."

In these years of travel, experiment, heartbreak, and introspection, Audre earned the self-knowledge that would make her later essays burn with insight. She saw that she could lessen her fears only by being more true to herself. She eventually learned to counter her impulse to hide by telling herself: "The only way to be strong is to do what requires strength.

The only way to be me is to do what requires being me. To feel myself. Not the picture of me, but me."

Knowing she could earn a living gave her a sense of strength. By 1961, she had a BA in English, a master's in library science from Columbia, and her library job in Mount Vernon. She moved into a comfortable apartment there, with a big bathtub ("when in doubt, bathe," she once advised), and enjoyed her new independence. A little later, she met Ed Rollins.

An attorney and community organizer from an old New England family, thirty to her twenty-seven, Edwin Ashley Rollins was serious about politics and fun to be around. He could look professional in a suit or as a volunteer for the Kennedy campaign, flamboyant and "très gay," Blanche recalled, when he wore a cape. Audre saw him as gentle, caring, and an outsider like herself. They got to know each other through mutual friends who were politically active and trying to move past traditional sexual roles. The married woman friend who introduced them to each other was sleeping with both of them, and at that point Audre had several intimate friendships with women and at least one other man. But she was tired of living alone, and Ed also wanted a family life.

At their wedding, Audre dressed in a tight-fitting Chinese cheongsam in white and yellow, showing off a slender waist that owed something to the amphetamines that she and all her circle used to combine their day jobs, lovers, and art or activism. (She didn't use them long, and eventually stopped trying to oppress her full figure.) Not everything came off quite the way she'd hoped. Though Linda Lorde, herself biracial, didn't mind Audre marrying a white man, Ed's whole family stayed home in protest. But aside from her ex Marion, who jealously called him "foppish" and "insincere," her friends were happy for her, Blanche recalled, and it was a glorious party. "We were celebrating."

It was a wedding for the woman who often found herself in "the farthest-out position" and wondered "why extremes, although difficult and sometimes painful to maintain, are always more comfortable than one plan running straight down a line in the unruffled middle."

WHEN BETH WAS FIVE months old, in August 1963, Audre weaned her so that she and Ed could leave her with her sister Phyllis and go to the March on Washington. Driving down with two other friends in their Rambler and picking up Blanche in Baltimore, where she was in graduate school, they made up a full activist carload on the way to the capital.

Audre's mind wasn't only on Martin Luther King Jr.'s "I Have a Dream" speech, or any of the other speakers that day. "With the heat and the crowds, I was very glad we had not brought the baby along, although I couldn't stop worrying about her. It was the first time we'd left her with someone else, and my breasts hurt," she wrote in a draft recollection. Besides, she was too busy helping in the coffee tent to see or hear much— unlike nineteen-year-old Alice Walker, who was sitting in a tree on the Mall trying to get a better view. She was skeptical about protesting in Washington, DC: the first time she'd been there, on a rare family vacation, the Lordes had been denied seating in a restaurant because of their race. But even she was moved in the end, when "we all joined hands with other Black and white strangers and bathed our feet in the Washington Monument Pool while the last gasp of brotherhood overcame us, and we shimmered like rainbows."

Feeling stronger and more purposeful as a parent, Audre now felt her life to be defined by a "poetic excitement" in which her motherhood, marriage, and political engagement were all at the forefront of her attention. For lack of time she wrote down images and phrases on scraps of paper that she stashed in Beth's diaper bag. The finished poems were published in collections of African American poetry and in the mainstream magazine *Negro Digest*. In 1964 the poet Langston Hughes included her in his anthology *New Negro Poets U.S.A.*, an important boost to her career, especially after *Time* magazine singled her out for praise.

Audre observed that it was "easier to deal with a poet, certainly with a Black woman poet, when you categorize her, narrow her so that she can fulfill your expectations. But I have always felt that I cannot be categorized." In literature as in her life, she never entirely fit into one group, whether it was the Black mainstream, the mixed-race Beat scene, white feminist academic circles, or the radical Black Arts Movement. Gwendolyn Brooks recommended her publisher, Black Arts–affiliated Broadside Press, and Audre would publish two books there, but she left over their reluctance to let her include a lesbian poem. Like many great writers, she would have to create through her work the audience she needed.

A group that she could belong to was her self-made community of mothers, and of friends who supported her motherhood. Audre surrounded herself with what sociologist Patricia Hill Collins calls "othermothers," the friends, neighbors, and kin who, especially in African American communities, help each other raise children. Blanche had wanted children, and had married briefly in hopes of having them. Though that didn't work out, she and her life partner, playwright Clare Coss, were fond godmothers who celebrated holidays with the family and in the summer went with Audre and the kids to the beach. Yolanda Ríos, a friend and lover who had married, had children, and moved in downstairs from the Lorde-Rollinses, shared childcare with Audre as well as sex and sympathy. Another neighbor, Elizabeth Maybank, was Audre's lifesaving babysitter, and sometimes her housekeeper when both she and Ed were working.

Audre would always cheer on her friends' child-raising, especially lesbian friends like the poet Pat Parker, who adopted a daughter with her partner. When the adoption was challenged on grounds that they wouldn't have enough "family support," the two women packed the courtroom with their whole community of lesbian othermothers. When Audre learned that her young Scottish poet friend Jackie Kay was having a child as a single mother, she urged her to enjoy her pregnancy and enclosed a small check in pounds she'd been sent by a British publisher, suggesting Jackie open an account for the baby.

Diane di Prima became an ally as both parent and poet. As Diane moved restlessly back and forth between New York and the West Coast, she and Audre exchanged letters, snapshots, and boxes of hand-me-down clothes, and Audre checked in on Diane's kids while they visited their grandparents back east. Diane nourished Audre's flower-power side, the woman who baked bread, collected beads, made jewelry, studied astrology and the *I Ching*. In the Seventies, responding to feminism, they exchanged the poems that became Diane's powerful goddess sequence, *Loba*, and Audre's sensual and spiritual invocations of West African female deities in *The Black Unicorn*.

In one year, 1968, Diane published Audre's first book and Audre helped Diane with the birth of her fourth child. As Audre told it, when Diane asked her to act as midwife she looked up "Home Delivery" in a medical handbook and read: "Not advised." Undeterred, when the time came she put on a silver amulet, drove downtown to the residential hotel where Diane, her partner, and her children were staying, and recalled what she'd learned from birth scenes in novels: "I know you don't really need boiled water and I know you really need sterile scissors, and I will play it by ear." Diane's labor went well, and the joy of being present for the first moments of Diane's daughter Tara made Audre feel connected to the deepest mysteries of life. "Babies, when they are born, are as if they are from another world . . . , aligned to human beings but not quite human. They are so beautiful and so completely themselves. It is a very wonderful thing to see and to be a part of, . . . mystic and spiritual and erotic and empowering."

THOUGH ED ENCOURAGED Audre's writing and was a devoted father, he turned out not to be the stable breadwinner she had hoped he would be. He was temperamental and susceptible to depression; Beth later thought he might have had undiagnosed bipolar disorder. The year he became a father, he lost his job in a law office, and though he turned to freelancing and worked constantly, his mood suffered. President Kennedy's assassination depressed him deeply. The day after Christmas 1963, he left a lit cigarette burning on the dresser in the baby's room while they went to visit Audre's mother, starting a fire that severely damaged their apartment. By the time they found a new place, Audre was pregnant again.

If you're caring for two small children and trying to write, there's not much room for anything—your partner's work, your child's health or your own—to go wrong. The Lorde-Rollinses' son, Jonathan, was born August 31, 1964, and they settled into an apartment on the twentieth floor of a new high-rise complex in Manhattan, at 140th and Riverside Drive. But the bad luck continued. When Jonathan was ten months old and Elizabeth was two, Audre suffered a neck injury in a minor car accident that affected her for months, keeping her even from picking up her children: Ed had to put them on her lap. After she recovered, Ed confessed that he wasn't earning enough to pay the bills. To support the family Audre took a job as a librarian at a nursing school, on the four-to-midnight shift.

Working evenings, running the household, maintaining her circle of friends and lovers, and helping her mother with the Lorde real estate business left her little time even for sleep. She used amphetamines to keep up. When she wrote, it was on sheer determination. Jonathan would cry whenever she went to work, filling Audre with "pain and fury" at having to leave him. She blamed Ed for his irresponsibility, but as Ed became less responsible, she became more controlling. She wanted him to talk about his feelings, but he didn't think a man should have to communicate. She wanted to know where he went in the evenings: she suspected he was picking up strangers instead of bringing his lovers home, as she did and thought he should do. She worried about him: he found it hard to accept being gay, and she urged him to seek therapy. But speed made her irritable, and she yelled at him and even hit him at times.

In 1967, when Audre was thirty-three, a student at City College asked her if he could interview her for a class assignment. In the finished paper he asked, "Why did this poet of such early promise stop writing?" His assumption made her sad, then angry, then ready to get her career back. She pulled herself together and started taking herself seriously as a writer. She got her children, ages four and three, into nursery school at the progressive New Lincoln School on the Upper East Side (where Susan Sontag's and Faith Ringgold's children were in high school). Diane gave her a desk, which Audre put in her bedroom, pleased by all the space it took up. Ed agreed to take the kids for three hours on weekends so she could write. She learned to work with the children playing nearby, too, tuning out their noise and savoring the "precious . . . moments of complete submersion into her work."

That winter Audre received a phone call from Diane, who had started a small press. She said she'd gotten a grant from a new government agency, the National Endowment for the Arts, and told Audre it was time to publish a book. In the collection Audre put together, *The First Cities*, she works through themes that she would return to throughout her career: her relationship to her parents and her children, her racial identity, and her pleasure in physical and romantic love. Like many African American writers—and science fiction writers—she thought of herself as writing in the future tense of hope and change.

> I think it is in our poetry . . . that we begin our inner vision, that we begin to create visions of what has never been before, that can possibly be. Poetry is not a luxury. Our poems and our dreams extend us, make our knowledge beyond where we can understand, begin to give shape to the chaos in a way that we can then attend to it. . . .
>
> What lies beyond is, I think, made real in our poetry, as it is in our dreams.

MOVING FROM THE private to the public sphere was not easy for Audre, who still felt shy and "inarticulate": "It was very frightening to me, the idea of someone responding to me as a poet." But when the chance came to her unexpectedly, she took it. The NEA had started funding writers-in-residence at historically Black colleges. Just after Audre sent her manuscript to Diane, in January 1968, she was offered a five-week residency, starting in a month, at Tougaloo, in Jackson, Mississippi.

Her first reaction was to think of the dangers. To her, Mississippi was Emmett Till; Medgar Evers shot dead outside his home in Jackson; Fannie Lou Hamer beaten nearly to death for trying to register to vote. On February 8, 1968, police in Orangeburg, South Carolina, fired on a civil rights demonstration at historically Black South Carolina State University, killing three students and injuring twenty-eight. Aside from her physical fear, teaching felt risky for her as a writer. To do it right, she thought, she would have to be at least partly open to her students about how she lived her life.

She was also reluctant to leave the children for so long; but Ed said he would care for them and urged Audre to take the chance. And since she already had to "walk out and hear [Jonathan] screaming in order to go down to the library and work every night," she decided she might as well do something she cared about.

In the poetry workshop she led at Tougaloo, all but one of her students were Black, and most were committed to the civil rights movement and Black Power. They were impressed with her short afro—they had never seen a teacher with natural hair—but weren't pleased about her interracial partnership, which they saw as disloyal. Even Audre was ambivalent, since she wasn't getting along with Ed. But when others weren't comfortable with her, she felt safest outing herself, and she wanted to claim, if not the relationship itself, the "right to examine it and try it." Withstanding their challenges showed her that she was strong enough to defend her choices in love.

For Audre as a poet, the workshop was a new encounter with herself. Teaching pushed her to think in formal terms about her work, and in return it gave her a sense of vocation that she called "the consciousness of poeting, of being a poet." It revealed to her that her writing was how she could cope with—and change—herself and the world, "that being a poet connected in all ways with everything that I was, all the different parts of me, and that it was work I had to do." It also taught her that "the best thing I have to give anyone has to come out of myself or it doesn't—you can pick it up on the street; you can pick it up in Woolworth's, unless it is anchored in the heaviest power I know, and that is me."

She came home full of ambition and eager to meet the moment. With her book now out—the first copies had arrived when she was at Tougaloo—she began to be asked for readings. She also got her first teaching job, giving lessons in grammar and composition at City College in its innovative, idealistic SEEK program, which helped first-generation students make the transition to college. From then on she taught in the City University system, ending up in the 1980s at Hunter College, her alma mater.

Teaching not only gave her an income and a public presence, it helped her work out her thoughts on race and difference, especially when she developed a class on institutional racism for police officers at the John Jay College of Criminal Justice. Through SEEK she got to know other writers, including Toni Cade Bambara, June Jordan, and Adrienne Rich. She became especially close to Adrienne, enlisting her as an ally, but also offering granola recipes and home remedies and writing that what she loved best in her friendships was "food, jokes, teasing, music, and joy."

The biggest change that came out of the trip to Tougaloo, though, was that Audre fell in love. Seeing visiting professor Frances Clayton in the mail line, perhaps she wondered what was behind her professional exterior, or maybe she was drawn by the dazzling smile that matched her own. One day she mentioned to Frances that she didn't know what to do about a girl in her class who seemed to have a crush on her. Frances answered, "I'm not the person to ask, because I share those feelings about you."

Frances was an experimental psychologist from Brown University, in Providence, Rhode Island, who was teaching that semester at Tougaloo. She was a white woman who had grown up poor and had made her way in the academic world. She was forty-one, single, committed to civil rights, and saw and cherished the person Audre was ready to become: a "Black, lesbian, feminist, mother, poet, warrior."

To Angela Carter 1968 felt like "Year One," when all the old social conventions were coming undone. Audre was old enough to know whose hard work had gone into the undoing, and something about the costs. The murder of Martin Luther King Jr. that spring gave her a new urgency, a sense that "life is very short, and what we have to do must be done in the now." She began to consider living in a partnership with Frances.

Ed wanted her to stay. Frances, in Providence, wanted a commitment. For two years, Audre went back and forth until she finally asked Ed to move out in the summer of 1970. The split was hard on everyone, especially Beth and Jonathan, who had had no warning, and Ed, who desperately missed his family. At first Audre stayed in their old apartment with the children, wanting time for herself, with babysitting help from Mrs. Maybank. Blanche recalled that in difficult times Audre didn't easily lose herself; instead "she regrouped, confronted her options, and understood life was about the struggle." When she did commit to living with Frances, she entered the years she later called "the most chaotic as well as the most creative of my life."

IN FAMILY PHOTOS from the 1970s, Audre and Frances are a radiant couple, with their sturdy figures, practical sweatshirts, beads for formal occasions. They posed with the children at holidays—Kwanzaa, Christmas, the solstice—or with their friends. They posed with each other, Frances gazing into Audre's eyes while she beamed back. They kept the photos on the coffee table in their new house: a tall, old, handsome home with bay windows, room for a garden in the back, and plenty of space for the four of them to be together.

They were living, literally, on an island. Frances had wanted space and a tree-lined street, so in 1972 they bought a house on Staten Island, the most suburban of New York's five boroughs, a ferry ride away from Manhattan.

The kitchen held a rock tumbler (Audre and Frances collected stones), a fridge with a list of chores (Frances liked things organized), and a telephone that Audre used to keep up with fellow writers and her many friends. She liked to start her day with coffee and the *New York Times*, a kiss with Frances if the kids weren't looking, then a call to Yolanda and one to Blanche, to check in. Support from her friends was how she coped with sexism, homophobia, and what she called "the daily trivializations of white racism." Blanche remembered, "Nothing would stop her, but that was costly. It took strength of character and emotional empowerment to face those situations head on."

She felt nourished by her home life, too, and she and Frances enjoyed making their queer family as normal as they could. Sometimes they acted so normal they annoyed their children. Audre remembered fifteen-year-old Beth complaining: "You think just because you're lesbians you're so different from the rest of them, but you're not, you're just like all the other parents." Beth recalled accusing Audre and Frances of being "hypocrites. The world thought they were revolutionaries; I knew they were Ozzie and Harriet. Or Harriet and Harriet."

In her late thirties and early forties, Audre, with Frances by her side, worked at shaping and tending the different aspects of her life: teaching, poetry, household, love. Looking back, in an essay on lesbian parenting, she wrote, "Raising two children together . . . balancing the intricacies of relationship within that four-person interracial family, taught me invaluable measurements for my self, my capacities, my real agendas. It gave me tangible and sometimes painful lessons about difference, about power, and about purpose."

Her children gave her connection, and they gave her joy. In a poem draft from 1973 she wrote

> If I remember me I remember
> the children out of my body
> bodies I have loved

She could be an exacting mother. A household has realities of meals and laundry that aren't easily remade, and Audre and Frances, as working parents, expected Beth and Jonathan to do more in the house than most of their friends, cleaning, vacuuming, mowing the lawn. She also wanted them to get good grades, speak proper English, keep a journal while they were traveling (work that she paid them for), and, on Thanksgiving, to think of children who had less. She encouraged them to be aware of their Black identity and not to let gender stereotypes define them. She wanted them to have what she felt she'd lacked: the knowledge and skills that would help them make their way in a racist, sexist world.

She was a physically affectionate mother, and her intuition and empathy made her a resourceful one: she loved being able to give her children the recognition and independence that she hadn't had. She still thought in lines of poems, Beth remembered: "When I was having problems with math, she quoted [Millay's] 'Euclid Alone Has Looked on Beauty Bare' . . . ; when I was in extremis over junior high girls teasing me, she looked at me over the top of her glasses and recited: 'I'm nobody! Who are you?'"

Beth recalled, "I think that one of the hardest things in parenting is to truly want your children to be free, . . . not to see them as an extension of yourself, but to see them as their own being, and to conduct yourself accordingly: that you are only stewarding them until they need no more stewarding, and giving them whatever you can. That was my mother's approach to parenthood from the get."

There were limits to how well Audre could negotiate all these projects at once, and sometimes writing and parenting got in each other's way, the two stories refusing to become one narrative. When Audre took her family to West Africa in 1974, the trip filled her with poetic inspiration and interpersonal irritation. On their five-week tour of Ghana, Togo, and Dahomey (now Benin), Audre searched for connection with her ancestors while encouraging her children to learn from their experience. As it turned out, the kids got bored in buses and hotel rooms, Frances nagged them to behave, and Audre, torn between their competing needs and her own, was short-tempered with everyone. For her poetic imagination, though, the trip was a revelation, especially Dahomey, whose king was once guarded by a legendary army of women warriors. In Ouidah Audre encountered a pantheon of Yoruba, Fon, and Dahomeyan deities that she incorporated into her spiritual practice and elaborated into an African American feminist mythology in her 1979 collection *The Black Unicorn*.

Families, especially blended families, have loose ends. One was Ed, who remained sporadically in his children's lives. At one point he threatened to sue Audre for custody on grounds that she was an unfit mother; fortunately, he didn't follow through. Instead Audre took him to court when he fell behind on his child support payments, after which he didn't call or see his children, then young teenagers, for about four years.

When Audre wrote about raising children in a lesbian partnership, she left Ed out of the story. Multiple parents, in more than one household, caring for children was an idea whose time hadn't yet come, and Audre evidently wasn't interested in making it come any faster. But the children had their own views and insisted on Ed's role, especially when sixteen-year-old Jonathan, after a fight with Frances and Audre, went to live with him for a year.

Ed had requested a custody agreement in which neither parent could reside out of state. That meant that Frances had had to move to New York to be with Audre, leaving behind her tenured position at Brown. She wasn't able to find a new position at her level, partly because she couldn't tell prospective employers she'd left to live with a woman, and it took a few years for her to find her footing again. Ultimately she gave up research to retrain as a therapist in private practice. An extraordinary and generous woman in her own right, she did groundbreaking work helping lesbians through the process of coming out.

She also devoted herself to Audre's career. Her care for the household gave Audre space to grow, as a poet, as a teacher, and as the public figure that successful artists and writers must eventually become. Though she'd never planned on having kids, she did more of the day-to-day mothering than Audre did, and she remained close to her stepchildren long after the relationship ended. Like Audre, Frances experienced her motherhood as one of the joys of her life.

It was a challenge for Audre not to bring home the stresses of her daily dealings with racism. She never disciplined her children physically, remembering her own mother's punishments, but she was strict with them and could get "toweringly angry," Beth recalled. "She cuddled intensely; she cooked and fed us intensely; and yes, she got pissed intensely."

Dealing frankly with her own anger was an important part of parenting for Audre and one she had in common with Adrienne Rich. In *Of Woman Born*, Rich wrote of the frustration and fury that erupted in her when she tried to do too much for others. Measuring herself against a maternal ideal of constant availability to her husband and three sons, she felt like "a monster—an anti-woman" when she wished her own needs, for once, didn't have to lose out. Rich included excerpts from her diaries from the 1950s in which she wrote of fighting to control her feelings: "How shall I learn to absorb the violence and make explicit only the caring?"

While Adrienne feared her anger as a violation of an ideal, Audre approached it as a known hazard. "Every Black woman in America lives her life somewhere along a wide curve of ancient and unexpressed angers," she wrote. "My Black woman's anger is a molten pond at the core of me, my most fiercely guarded secret." Her strategy was to use writing and political organizing to redirect her feelings outward, away from herself and her family: "It was not restraint I had to learn, but ways to use my rage to fuel actions."

She poured it into her poetry, too. Her sorrow and outrage at racism's human cost were ever present in her work in the years that she was raising children. One of her most celebrated poems and one she often read in public, "Power," was written after a white New York City police officer was acquitted of murder in the 1973 shooting of ten-year-old Clifford Glover. Audre drafted it in her car at the side of the road, where she'd pulled over in a sick fury after she heard the news on the radio. "A Woman/Dirge for Wasted Children" was another poem for Glover, who was only a year older than Jonathan. In it Audre challenged the cruel "futility of effort" (Alice Neel's phrase) for Black mothers under white supremacy:

> on murderous sidewalks
> I am bent
> forever
> wiping up blood
> that should be
> you.

Putting her emotions to work for change, Audre increasingly spoke and wrote about being Black and a lesbian, how they intersected, and how her position could be made visible. An early adopter of feminism, she pressed Black men to rethink their ideas about gender while pointing out to white, college-educated feminists their blind spots about race, class, and sexuality. Did their sisterhood extend to the women who cleaned their houses and cared for their children? Did women of color have equal voice in their organizations? Was her son welcome? (She and Frances once refused to attend a feminist event when the organizers said they couldn't bring eleven-year-old Jonathan.) Lorde was calling for an inclusive feminism when she made one of her most famous statements, "The master's tools will never dismantle the master's house." If intersectionality interrupts entrenched patterns of thought, Audre throughout her life was willing to look at what doesn't cohere and search for the liberating power in embracing difference.

As the Seventies went on Audre became involved with Black lesbian activists, going on retreats organized by Boston's Combahee River Collective, the Black feminist group named for Harriet Tubman's legendary Civil War raid. Along with the collective's cofounder, Barbara Smith, Audre helped found Kitchen Table: Women of Color Press, whose books included the renowned feminist anthologies *Home Girls* and *This Bridge Called My Back*.

Yet collective action, with the inevitable clashes of interests and personalities, didn't entirely suit her independent mind. (That she, Alice Neel, and Alice Walker were all Aquarians may or may not be a coincidence.) She felt most herself when she could be a mentor to younger women and a gadfly to her peers. In the 1980s, when Beth and Jonathan were in college, she began traveling regularly to Europe. There she made contact with feminists and lesbians from the African Diaspora in West Germany, the Netherlands, and Britain and found a role at which she excelled: inspiring and affirming others. Anthropologist and academic Gloria Wekker was part of a Dutch Black lesbian group who named themselves "Sister Outsider" after Lorde's influential book of essays. When Audre came to Amsterdam at their invitation, Wekker was amazed by her "intensity and focus" and by "how full of life and joy she was. . . . When she encountered someone, she gave that person the feeling that she really wanted to know her, without delay, as if she was saying, 'Tell me your story; there is no time to lose.'"

Jackie Kay, a member of the UK collective Sheba Feminist Press, was drawn to Audre's bold embrace of her identities, which made her feel less alone as a lesbian and poet. "Later, when we became good friends, she taught me that there is strength in embracing seeming contradictions, and not to be afraid of being different." Audre's belief in "a multiple and complex self" was liberating to Kay, who came from Glasgow and felt both Black and Scottish: Audre insisted that she didn't have to choose. Another member of the collective, Pratibha Parmar, recalled how they "devoured and were fed deeply by her honesty and radical will to empower women, especially lesbians of color."

Though Audre may not have needed to sleep around to keep from being claimed, she chose not to be monogamous with Frances. Seduction was still a way for her to feel valued and safe, and maybe, having put so much work into making the self and family she wanted, she felt confined by them, too. Frances had asked for monogamy and Audre had agreed, but she went on seeing Yolanda Ríos in secret and had affairs when she traveled for readings and conferences. Lovers brought new ideas: after she attended FESTAC, the legendary festival of Black arts and culture put on by the government of Nigeria in 1977, Audre had a long-distance relationship with another participant, the African American painter Mildred Thompson. Thompson, who based her abstract work on her interpretation of physics, mathematics, and cosmic forces, appreciated Audre's feeling for myth and the fantastic, while her thinking resonated with Audre as well. In one of her many romantic letters Thompson wrote, "You really are all the things I love and admire and want to be a part of, attached to, identified with."

Her partnership with Frances suffered, and after seventeen years together they separated in 1985. By then Audre was already seeing the woman who became her partner of her last years, Gloria Joseph, a Black, Caribbean-born academic with whom she made a home on Saint Croix, in the part of the world her mother had always longed for. Audre's life with Frances may have been partly a casualty of the children leaving home, as Beth went off to Harvard, then medical school, and Jonathan studied at Vassar, then became a naval intelligence officer. They had raised the children as a couple, and now they were losing their joint project. Audre picked a fight with Frances the summer Jonathan went to college, accusing her of wanting to put that part of their lives behind her, but that may have been Audre's way of expressing her own sorrow at the empty nest.

In any case, her sensuality was an inseparable part of her. Jackie Kay recalled that when she visited New York, Audre took her out into the back garden, where she and Frances had planted a black fig tree. She asked Kay if she had ever tasted one. "'No?' she said. 'Then you haven't lived.' And she peeled the fig and fed it to me, standing outside in her garden by the fig tree."

A LUMP IN HER RIGHT BREAST, found during a self-exam. It was 1977, and Audre was forty-three. When the biopsy came back benign, she was relieved. She was also furious at herself for believing it was cancer, at the doctors for alarming her, at the situation for confronting her with her own vulnerability. A year later, in September 1978, she found the second lump, the malignant one.

"Each woman responds to the crisis that breast cancer brings to her life out of a whole pattern, which is the design of who she is and how her life has been lived," she wrote. At a time when personal writing about illness was very new, she confronted her cancer and mastectomy by keeping a diary of her treatment, which she published as *The Cancer Journals*. She described the physical pain, the grief and depression that held her in their grip long afterward, and her fear that, "like the [bumble]bee that was never meant to fly . . . I am not supposed to exist."

At the same time she felt a furious need to do her work while she still could. Her writing felt to her like a "lifeline" and, anxious and depressed, she didn't feel she could share a house with two rebellious teenagers. With the summer approaching, she called in a favor. One morning she turned to sixteen-year-old Beth and said, "You're going to go to San Francisco. I've spoken with Diane and she said it will be fine if you stay with her."

Beth protested, complained, and finally flew out west, where Diane welcomed her to an apartment that felt a lot like her house, but with a different "mix of revolution and formality." It had a warm, familiar smell of incense and books, but clothing seemed to be optional and no one was getting yelled at for leaving dirty dishes in the sink. With Diane's help, Audre was giving Beth the gift of perspective.

That perspective allowed Beth to reencounter her mother and develop the relationship children need to their parent's work. Though she had helped Audre file papers in her office, and knew that "poetry was part of who my Mom was, and it was part of the mother she was, too," she had never appreciated her literary importance. Now, looking for something to read on Diane's shelves, Beth found Audre's books and devoured them. She began to realize why her mother had never packed her lunches, like other moms did, "why we weren't getting that kind of service at home. She had bigger fish to fry." She learned to accept her mother's vocation, saying: "Talent does what it can; genius does what it must."

One effect of cancer on Audre was to give her courage: in the face of death, she no longer had a reason to hide who she was. At the time of the first cancer scare she'd been scheduled to participate in an academic panel on lesbian writing, titled "The Transformation of Silence into Language and Action." Her talk, published under the same title, became one of her most quoted works.

"I have come to believe . . . that what is most important to me must be spoken . . . even at the risk of having it bruised or misunderstood. That the speaking profits me, beyond any other effect," she said. In facing her mortality, she said, "what I most regretted were my silences. . . . I was going to die, if not sooner then later, whether or not I had ever spoken myself. My silences had not protected me. Your silence will not protect you."

She observed that death, "the final silence," might be coming for her now, she said, "without regard for whether I had ever spoken what needed to be said, or had only betrayed myself into small silences, while I planned someday to speak, or waited for someone else's words." The only answer, she thought, was for her to be herself: "a Black woman warrior poet doing my work—come to ask you, are you doing yours?"

Around this time she drafted her great poem "A Litany for Survival," with its insistence that children's future must not require the death of their parents' dreams, and with its last lines:

> So it is better to speak
> remembering
> we were never meant to survive.

Talking about "A Litany for Survival" in a radio interview with Blanche, ten years before her death from cancer in 1992, at age fifty-eight, she added that by "survival" she did not mean mere existence. "Implicit in survival is joy, mobility, and effectiveness. And effectiveness is always relative. I mean, none of us are going to move the earth one millimeter from its axis. But if we do what we need to be doing, then we will leave something that continues beyond ourselves. And that is survival."

Susan Sontag and David Rieff waiting for the start of a custody hearing, New York City, 1964.

The Discomfort Zone

NOT BEING ALL THERE

◆

One of the great traps for the woman writer is the desire to be loved for oneself as well as admired for one's work, to be a Beautiful Person as well as a Great Artist. (ANGELA CARTER)

[Adults] possess a degree of power over the lives of children that we would find inconceivable and unspeakably tyrannical in any other context. Yet, we mostly wear this power as some divine right not to be questioned, not to be wrestled with as one would wrestle with an angel for the sake of one's soul. (JUNE JORDAN)

A lump in her left breast, found during a doctor's exam. It is 1975 and Susan Sontag, forty-two, is diagnosed with stage 4 cancer. After the mastectomy, she undergoes more operations, then thirty months of chemotherapy. Like Audre, she becomes a pioneer in writing about illness. Unlike Audre, she writes a whole book about cancer, *Illness as Metaphor*, without mentioning herself. Unlike Audre, she declares victory over death.

She doesn't see her mortality as demanding honesty of her, or complete selfhood. Instead she denies her vulnerability. This is the price her fear asks of her, and she pays it, over and over.

In February 1962, twenty-nine-year-old Susan arrives at a Manhattan court-room in her most demure and professional clothes: a dress that buttons high at the neck, lipstick, stockings, sensible heels. Her ex-husband has found out that Susan is in a relationship with a woman and has sued for full custody. She has dressed to persuade the court not to take away her nine-year-old son. She can't live as a lesbian and still be a mother; she has to choose.

The price for keeping her son is a piece of herself, and she pays it. To the end of her life she will lie about her love for women.

In 1962 Susan writes in her diary that she must choose between books and sex, ambition and love, because she can't devote her full energy to both. In 1978, speaking of her divorce, she tells an interviewer that "somewhere along the line, one has to choose between the Life and the Project." Yet Audre would have told her that the two together are possible. And anyone else might have said this was just a fancy way of saying "books versus babies," that founding lie of artistic exclusion.

At different ages, in many different transactions, Susan uses herself as currency. In 1939, the year she turns six, Susan's father dies. When she begins having terrifying asthma attacks, kneeling on her bed gasping for breath, her terrified mother leaves the room. To keep her mother with her, she denies her own illness and vulnerability.

It begins in childhood, one's negotiation with illness and death.

At eleven Susan makes a promise to herself: "I will be popular." She takes the necessary steps.

At fifteen she writes in her journal, "I feel that I have lesbian tendencies (how reluctantly I write this). . . . All I feel, most immediately, is the most anguished need for *physical love* and mental companionship." Shortly afterward she reads Radclyffe Hall's 1928 novel *The Well of Loneliness*, in which the queer, writer protagonist is advised stoicism, secrecy, and brilliance: "Work's your only weapon. Make the world respect you, as you can do through your work."

At twenty-six, in her journal, Susan echoes Hall's words: "My desire to write is connected with my homosexuality. I need the identity as a weapon, to match the weapon that society has against me. . . . I am just becoming aware of how guilty I feel being queer."

At seventeen, in her second year of college, Susan talks to her professor of sociology. He's skinny, balding, kind. She's afraid of her sexuality; she's starving for intellectual conversation; she wants out of her childhood. He tells her that she's the woman he wants to marry. She says yes, out of pure astonishment, "because no one had ever called me a woman before."

January 3, 1951, the day of her wedding, Susan writes in her journal: "I marry Philip in full consciousness + fear of my will toward self-destructiveness." Afterward, because they're in the suburbs of Los Angeles, the cultureless, storyless place she's trying to escape, she, her mother, stepfather, younger sister, and new husband go out for hamburgers. Her mother is proud that Susan is marrying a professor, even if he is twenty-eight and she is still only seventeen.

Several months later, contraceptive failure narrows Susan's choices. Lacking money or a doctor's address, she phones home to ask her mother for help. Mildred Sontag's own mother had died suddenly when Mildred was fourteen. The family maintained that it was food poisoning, but Susan's diaries suggest a connection between sex and her grandmother's death: An unwanted pregnancy? A deadly abortion? Was this the beginning of Mildred's habit of denial? (It took her six months to tell Susan her father was dead.) When Susan tells her why she needs the money, she puts down the phone and leaves the room.

The abortionist works without anesthetic and turns up the radio to drown out the screams. Within half a year Susan is pregnant again.

As a girl, Susan fantasizes about redoing her mother's motherhood, only better. "I would have a boy-child. . . . I would be a *real* mother. . . . This was a fantasy about getting out of childhood, attaining a real adulthood; freedom. . . . I was both myself as the mother (a *good* mother) and the beautiful gratified child."

In September 1952, after months of denial, nineteen-year-old Susan wakes up in the night with a stomachache and thinks she has wet the bed. Philip explains to her that her water has broken and that she's in labor. After the birth her childhood nanny, Rose McNulty, comes to help with the baby. "That's one of the reasons David and I resemble each other so much," Susan will say nearly fifty years later. "We had the same mother." David is put on a bottle: "It never occurred to me to nurse him."

Rose cares for David and Susan stays home for a year, trying to work out her motherhood. She loves David: a friend will later tell her biographer, Benjamin Moser, that her baby son is "the center of her life." She likes the intimacy of mother and infant. Like many parents, she will never stop having baby cravings. In her forties, cute kids will make her joke that she wants to kidnap them.

Her intellect also demands attention. In an autobiographical fragment, she describes a person whose energies are "concentrated in an attempt to evade the role into which she felt herself to be locked—that of a wife and mother—without ceasing to be that."

With David it seems she could have authentic feelings she couldn't have with anyone else, or at least that's one interpretation of a few much-debated lines in her journal: "I hardly ever dream of David, and don't think of him much. He has made few inroads on my fantasy-life. When I am with him, I adore him completely and without ambivalence. When I go away, as long as I know he's well taken-care-of, he dwindles very quickly. Of all the people I have loved, he's least of all a *mental* object of love, most intensely real."

This sounds like a healthy relationship for a mother-writer, a fire-escape relationship: better to save your energy to love him when he is there than worry about him when he isn't. She writes this, however, when she is away from him for a year, in Oxford and Paris. She visits the British Museum and notes in her journal, "Wrote a letter to David about the Elgin Marbles." He's five years old.

In January 1953, a few months after David's birth, Susan records in her journal a series of dreams about sex with women. They culminate in a vision of winning recognition for her genius, but also of being cherished for herself, of being adored by many and known and loved by one: "I stood at the side of the stage, in some kind of ceremonial dress. A great crowd awaited me, but still I dared carelessly to touch the side of my hand to hers."

In this dream she is an exception, a great woman, to whom the usual rules do not apply. In this dream she does not have to choose—between love and recognition, private and public, work and self.

The waking Susan, submitting to her married state, writes tearfully, "I struggle to be one—to set my heart under my hand."

Susan doesn't like the word "mother." Of her adult son she says, "I'd rather he see me as—oh, I don't know—his goofy big sister," and claims she thinks of him as "more like my brother" and "my best friend." These are terms that imply a close relationship, but one in which the adult isn't the more responsible or giving one. It suggests a relationship in which a mother doesn't have to choose between her son's needs and her own.

When David is almost two, Susan has a pregnancy scare. Now it's her turn to leave the room, letting Philip take the doctor's call while she hides in David's bed and covers her ears. The test is negative, but they stop making love. "P and I used to talk often about using double contraception + starting to have sex again. It never came close to happening—to our *doing* anything about it, it was just talk. We must have known."

Instead, she uses the marital bed to write on. Spinning straw into gold, she is turning a heap of Philip's notes into an important evaluation of Freud's thought. When she finally, guiltily, leaves Philip, she lets him put his name on their book, her intellectual firstborn.

In 1957, still married to Philip, she applies for a grant to study in England. In her journal: "If only I get the fellowship to Oxford! Then at least I'll know if I am anything outside the domestic stage, the feathered nest."

Philip plans to come with her to Oxford. But then he is offered a prestigious fellowship at Stanford. (Charles Le Guin will later hold the same fellowship.) He asks Susan to give up her grant and go with him, making her choose between her education and her motherhood. In September 1957, just before David's fifth birthday, Philip, Rose, and David go to California. Susan goes to Oxford.

Away from home, she can't escape what Maggie Nelson calls "the tired binary that places femininity, reproduction, and normativity on one side and . . . sexuality and queer resistance on the other."

One evening she invites a younger American student, Judith Grossman, to her room. Grossman believes she is looking for more than friendship. But after Susan shows her a photo of David and talks about missing him, she guesses Susan must be straight after all. "In any case a mother, to my understanding then, was sexually out of the question."

Judith leaves, and Susan writes to Philip: every evening another blue aerogram. In those days, she will say, "I didn't feel like a separate person." Unlike Audre, she doesn't like to define herself. Honesty feels to her like resignation, a "sense that things must be as they are."

Even to herself Susan sometimes feels sexually out of the question. From her journal:

> I can't give myself steadily (or at all) to sex, work, being a mother, etc. For if I did I would be naming myself an adult.
> But I wasn't ever really a child!

Nonetheless, in December 1957 she abandons Oxford for Paris, where she gets back together with a girlfriend from her teenage years, Harriet Sohmers. Harriet loves Susan less, is mean to her. Susan accepts it, isn't good at equal affection, never learned in childhood how to be both seen and loved. But Paris has a community of gay expatriate writers and intellectuals. Susan writes that it's "good to be home, as it were—to have women, instead of men, interested in me."

The next summer, she comes home and tells Philip she wants a divorce.

In January 1959 Susan gets off a plane in New York with David. Rose vanishes and is not mentioned again. Susan writes, "Like smoke evaporating, my failed marriage wasn't there anymore. And my unhappy childhood slipped away also, as though touched by magic."

She loves starting over, returning to the time before choice. David: "Always, there was a fresh beginning, a new first act."

In New York, she doesn't have to choose. Music, film, art, the first "happenings," lovers gay and straight: she takes speed, goes everywhere, does everything. She understands that freedom, intellectual and sexual, is the question of her times. She refuses to be the old-school critic as gatekeeper, defending high culture against bad taste. A favorite critical judgment of the 1950s was "vulgar," which excluded whole classes of experience—female, homosexual, maternal—as trashy, bodily, domestic, impure. In her early reviews, Susan lets it all in.

Within a few years Susan, in her early thirties, is celebrated as a cultural phenomenon: a photogenic, charismatic, star-quality woman of genius.

If liberation is the siren song of a generation, how to combine that freedom with responsible parenting is one of its dilemmas. Still, Susan and David give each other structure, the daily metronome of "eating, homework, bath, teeth, room, story, bed." In these years, mothering gives Susan security and warmth. Photographers who come to portray the glamorous Sontag like to include her equally photogenic young son, and she gazes at him in real affection.

Susan ignores the community of mothers. She takes David with her to parties, where he falls asleep on the coats.

The narrator of Susan's 1999 novel *In America* notices a "little boy curled up on another woman's lap, rubbing his eyes, instead of home tucked in his bed. He must be an only child, his mother must have wanted him near tonight, even if I hadn't seen her pay any attention to him for these last two hours at the table."

No longer an aspiring writer, she becomes, as the decade progresses, a literary celebrity. The stakes go up. She fears that the price of real genius is loneliness. Already she has "given up on human satisfactions (except for David)."

She writes, "I've experienced my *strength* (my mind, my eyes, my intellectual passions) as condemning me to perpetual isolation, separation from others." Yet her writing earns her the admiration of her fans. She fears that to be loved for herself, she must give up the love of the crowd. She is not willing to pay this price. She would rather keep the crowd.

In 1967:

> When did I give up hoping anyone would see me? . . . I must have started hiding, making sure they *couldn't* see me. . . . Always (?) this feeling of being "too much" for them—a creature from another planet—so I would try to scale myself down to size, so that I could be apprehend-able by (lovable by) them. . . . I gave up, first of all, my sexuality. . . . I gave up most of the ordinary range of access to myself, to my feelings. I gave up my self-confidence. . . . I gave up being at home in my body.

Unable to be her authentic self, she needs David more than ever, as "safety, refuge, wall."

At seventeen he is

—someone I can love unconditionally, trustingly—because I know the relationship is authentic (society guarantees it + I make it)—because I *chose* him, because he loves me (I've never doubted that)—: my one whole-hearted experience of love, of generosity, of caring—

—my guarantee of adulthood:—even when I experience my childishness, I know I'm an adult because I'm a mother. . . .

—order, a structure, a limit to any tendency to self-destructiveness.

—endless delight in his company—having a companion, a friend, a brother. (Bad side: a chaperone, a shield against the world)

When David leaves home, Susan goes to Europe, falls in love with a beautiful, empty-headed duchess, practices the art of losing.

Having given herself away to lovers and others, she will spend the rest of her life trying to get herself back from her son.

After the cancer, in the mid-Seventies, David lives with Susan. His girlfriend, Sigrid Nunez, also moves in. Susan and David fight; they make up. She gets him a job with her publisher, then she insists he become her editor. She yells at him when he makes mistakes. When he withdraws, she turns back into the adoring mother. She doesn't want him to leave. She doesn't like to be alone.

Speed makes Susan bad-tempered. Cancer makes her angry. Sigrid Nunez recalls her depression emerging as "darkest rage. . . . When she was unhappy with the world, she lashed out. . . . In her inner circle she always had at least one whipping boy, or girl, and she would strike and strike and strike."

Audre Lorde: "It is easier to be angry than to hurt. . . . It is easier to be furious than to be yearning."

She falls into a crippling depression and goes into therapy.

"Why did you try to make a father out of your son?" the therapist asks.

Nunez: "At first when she heard this, Susan said, she was shocked. She didn't know *where* the therapist could have come up with *that*! But then it hit her, she said: she *had* tried to do that. And we both started to cry."

Susan embraces feminism, then abandons it, frustrated by its insistence on writing from the personal. She argues about this with Adrienne Rich, in the letters column of the *New York Review of Books*: Is feminism limiting or necessary? Susan points out that feminism can be dogmatic. Adrienne (in the process of theorizing motherhood in *Of Woman Born*) says that critical thinking misses something when it gets separated from the conditions of one's own life.

Afterward they meet at Susan's apartment and make love.

In the 1980s Susan starts projects, isn't satisfied, doesn't finish them, can't find a new beginning. She enters the long midlife of people who suffer and don't change.

In an introduction to her 1993 play *Alice in Bed*, Susan writes of the "ego-centricity and aggressiveness" that creativity demands, but isn't this just setting boundaries and pushing back? Le Guin says she works by setting the self aside: "If I can keep myself, my ego . . . out of the way . . . the story tells itself." Even Susan doesn't really believe writing is ego. "It feels true only in a trivial sense to say I make my books. What I really feel is that they are made, through me, by literature."

In 1986, Mildred Sontag dies. In 1987, on her mother's birthday—"her first non-birthday"—Susan projects her loneliness onto her son:

> For decades, being D.'s mother made my identity bigger—I
> was an adult, I was strong, I was good, and I was loved
>   entirely positive . . .
>
> now it's negative:
> I feel stripped of my identity when I'm with him.
>   Not a writer—
>   Just his mother
>   And his rival
>   And I'm not loved

Susan's novels win awards, though they get mixed reviews. She will always be a genius, though her later essays feel more dogged. She befriends people who interest her, then drops them before they can make any claim on her. Some of her short stories are brilliant, funny, true. It's hard to sustain a novel when you are not all of yourself, but in stories an authentic self can, for a moment, let itself be seen.

The idea of Susan inspires many, but close up her admirers are often disappointed, or feel abandoned when she denies she's gay. In 1980, journalist Lindsy Van Gelder asks Susan directly if she's a lesbian. "She went through a spectacularly elaborate bit of horseshitterie about how she was looking for a man, maybe she should try the personal ads, yada yada. It was hypocritical on steroids. After she died I rolled my eyes at every obituary mention of her fearlessness and intellectual honesty."

Susan spends her last years in a relationship with a woman, the photographer Annie Leibovitz. Even when everyone knows they are a couple, even though it's much safer than it used to be, she denies it.

When Annie says she wants to have a baby, Susan is jealous. Annie has the baby anyway, in 2001, and lets her cut the cord. Susan, now sixty-eight, gets over herself and loves Annie's daughter. Looking at pictures she's taken of the two of them, Annie asks herself, "Which one is the child?"

When she was a young woman, one of Susan's favorite novels was *The Price of Salt*, by Patricia Highsmith, in which two women fall in love and go on the road. The price for their romance in full view is that one of the women, the divorcée Carol, loses custody of her child. Yet Highsmith believed that in concealing desire, one conceals one's "humanity and natural warmth of heart as well."

When Susan is again diagnosed with cancer, in 2004, she refuses to believe she is dying. To the very end, she speaks of new beginnings: when she leaves the hospital she will meet new people, she'll write differently. Because she won't admit she's dying, David can't talk to her about it, and so they never say goodbye to each other, even though he's with her to the last.

In 1977, confronting her own mortality, Audre writes: "Most of all, I think, we fear the visibility without which we cannot truly live."

Alice Walker with Robert Allen and Rebecca, 1989.

Freedom

ALICE WALKER (1944–)

◆

I have looked and looked for the Black woman who would really be my mother—who could tell me how the lies we swallowed in the tenderest winters could be toughened and explored and thrown away, who would name me hers. . . . Who would recognize me as both proud and loving. (AUDRE LORDE)

What kind of love is this, which means always to be for others, never for ourselves? (ADRIENNE RICH)

When everything one represents and looks like is strategically disparaged or exploited by the dominant culture, how does one live a heroic life? (CAROL COOPER)

IN AN ORDINARY HOUSE in Jackson, Mississippi, in 1970, a young writer sits alone in a room, courting her muse. The room is her own, and she's decorated it to please herself, hanging handwoven fabrics and artworks and placing fresh flowers on her desk. She's made the space beautiful to remind herself that her work is serious, to keep depression at bay, and to shut out the requirements of the world.

Her writing is flowing on the current of her talent and ambition. She's energized by the successes of the civil rights movement, and she's encouraged, after a few years in the urban North, by her homecoming to her native South. She feels full of poems, short stories, and ideas for a second novel, all arising from her experience as a southern Black woman. Writing is self-care for her, helping her to heal childhood's wounds.

Other creative mothers have worked in provisional spaces: Neel in her living room, Le Guin in the attic, Lorde in the bedroom, Sontag on the bed. But Alice Walker is not good at writing in short bursts or early-morning moments. To reveal her own experience to herself, to write the books that she yearns to read, she needs long, private hours to contemplate and dream. Right now, she and her husband can afford a sitter only three afternoons a week. He adores their new baby as much as she does, but he goes every day to his job as a civil rights lawyer, leaving her behind, not free.

Not every interruption of her writing is from the baby. Her husband's work, her writing, and their existence as an interracial couple all challenge the status quo, and she's in an embattled place. If the phone rings while she's at the typewriter, she might hear a friend's voice or an anonymous caller threatening violence. The mailbox holds correspondence from publishers, notes from friends, and abuse from strangers. Every time Mel travels for his work, she worries he might not come home. Sometimes after he leaves the house in the morning, despair takes over and she starts to cry.

"I found it very hard to be that suddenly split person," Alice said of her first year of mothering. At twenty-six, she was already a published poet, essayist, and novelist, full of talent and assurance. But it took her a long time after the birth of her daughter Rebecca, in November 1969, to be able to recollect herself. She felt like she wrote nothing that year "that didn't sound as though a baby were screaming right through the middle of it."

Two decades later, when Alice had become a literary celebrity, the outspoken and beloved author of *The Color Purple* and *The Temple of My Familiar*, others saw and admired her wisdom and joy. Describing her at forty-five, Alexis De Veaux wrote, "She does not walk into a room. She glides in, glowing like a goddess. Laden with the wisdom of history and tribal stories. Exuding a seductive, earthy bliss."

That bliss was hard-won. Born on February 9, 1944, a decade after Sontag and Lorde, she grew up in a rapidly changing world and did everything she could to encourage that change. Where Audre moved cautiously and watched her back, Alice was never afraid to go out on a limb—even though that's not the easiest place to be a mother.

IN 1949, a five-year-old girl goes with her older brothers and sisters to the fair in Eatonton, Georgia. As it gets dark they get ready to head for home when they realize she isn't with them. Frantic, they search the fairgrounds until the eldest brother looks up and sees his baby sister alone at the top of the Ferris wheel. She's persuaded the white operator to let her on without a ticket and she's swinging her legs back and forth, enjoying the view.

"Be nobody's darling," Alice once wrote, but as a girl she was everyone's darling. Her seven older siblings adored her; her childhood friend Doris Reid recalled that she "could charm a rock." She was also, as she once wrote of Zora Neale Hurston, "made of some of the universe's most naturally free stuff." She was determined from the start to be the heroine of her own life, the one who lived by Camus's existentialist advice: "The only way to deal with an unfree world is to become so absolutely free that your very existence is an act of rebellion."

A refusal to accept limitations was a hard position to stick to under segregation, in a place and time when Black parents seldom got enough support, or their children enough love. Alice's sensitive father, Willie Lee Walker, worked as a tenant farmer, moving his family from tumbledown cabin to dilapidated shack, fighting to get ahead in a sharecropping system designed to hold him back. Her mother, Minnie Lou Grant Walker, was another example to Alice of resourcefulness and strength, but it was strength in endurance more than in loving connection. Like so many African American women, Mrs. Walker was capable, hardworking, community minded. She cooked and cleaned in a white household, performing the double shift that, in poor families, often constitutes mother love. When Mrs. Walker left her children home alone, Alice "dared not complain. And yet I missed her with every fiber of my being."

What the Black residents of Eatonton did have was a close-knit community of othermothers, women who made Alice feel recognized and who encouraged her to learn. She remembered, "You just need one person to *notice* that you're doing something and to say, 'My goodness, that's wonderful, that's different, that's whatever,' but at least they notice." But her brilliance set her apart from her parents, neither of whom had gone to school beyond fifth grade. "I used to think I had just been dropped into my family, and I didn't know by whom or what. I think I started writing just to keep from being so lonely, from being so much the outsider."

Though Alice loved belonging to the culturally rich Black community of Eatonton, she sometimes found it limiting. Audre could roam New York, trying on new selves, but Alice had nowhere else to go and less sense of permission. As a child, she wrote, she "rarely saw individualistic behavior, and when I did see it, for a long time I could understand it only as rejection of community, rather than the self-affirmation it very often was."

Her sense of difference also stemmed from two acts of violence she suffered when she was eight. While she was playing unsupervised with her two older brothers, who had BB guns, a pellet hit her in the eye. As she lay in shock and pain her father walked out to the road, hoping to flag down a car to take her to the hospital. A white driver stopped, but then, hearing it was a Black girl who had been injured, drove off.

This double pattern of domestic and racist harm was all too common in Alice's world, as was the toll it took on Black bodies. Alice lay on the porch and watched as her vision was blotted out. The accident left a mass of white scar tissue in a "wandering" eye that would give her years of shyness and shame at her appearance.

Later her parents took her to a doctor who accepted their borrowed money, then brusquely told them he could do nothing for her. He also said casually that if one eye was blind, she would probably lose sight in the other, a callous remark that terrified Alice—and made her distrust doctors. When she was teased and bullied in a new school, her parents sent her to stay with her grandparents, but that made her feel rejected by her father. To keep away her suicidal thoughts she sought beauty and solitude in the woods around Eatonton, and she read and wrote, especially poetry.

Later Alice found healing in her daughter's words. In an essay on beauty, Alice wrote of the first time three-year-old Rebecca noticed the scar about which she was so self-conscious. She had been watching the educational TV program *Big Blue Marble*, which began with a photo of the earth seen from space. Looking at her mother, she saw what she thought was the same image and looked at it closely. "She . . . holds my face maternally between her dimpled little hands. . . . 'Mommy, there's a *world* in your eye.'"

Alice was delighted when her daughter redefined her injury as something whole and valuable. At the same time, her use of the word "maternal" for her daughter's touch suggests a wish that Rebecca could make up for what her own parents hadn't had in their power to give.

THE SUMMER AFTER her sophomore year of college found Alice literally out on a limb. At the 1963 March on Washington she climbed a tree to watch Martin Luther King Jr. as his Georgia-inflected voice rolled out across the nation's capital. While Audre poured coffee, Alice felt her soul lift, hearing him call for justice on the red soil of Georgia and for freedom to ring "from every hill and molehill of Mississippi and every mountainside." Alice felt like he was giving her back her birthplace, the South, with all the rights of a citizen.

In the Sixties, in both Britain and America, doors began to open to those who'd been excluded from an education, including Angela Carter and Lorna Sage. In the South, though, there were many who tried to keep them closed. In January 1961, Alice watched on the Walkers' television as two Black students, Hamilton Holmes and Charlayne Hunter, arrived at the University of Georgia. In response, over a thousand white Georgians rioted, hurling bricks and bottles at Hunter's dormitory window. At seventeen, Alice wasn't so physically brave—for one thing, she was afraid of losing the sight in her one good eye—but she was thrilled to see Black students on the news, singing, praying, and marching for civil rights. That fall, with a scholarship, she boarded a bus to start her own education at Spelman, the historically Black women's college in Atlanta.

She took with her the typewriter her mother had bought her with her maid's wages, and as the bus drove away she saw her father standing sorrowfully by the side of the road with his hat in his hands, watching her go. When the driver told her to move to the back, she did, but it reminded her why she had to leave. That bus journey took her into the place where she would have to invent herself as a writer and a young mother: a field of tension between home and away, belonging and change, love and freedom.

Arriving at the college in a skirt and sweater, with her hair in a bouffant, Alice looked the part of a fresh-faced student and quickly made friends among her classmates. She also found admirers at Morehouse, the neighboring men's college. But her independent mind put her at odds with Spelman's administration. At the time, Spelman was a cautious institution that took an even more narrow view of gender roles than Radcliffe had a decade earlier. Founded by and dependent on wealthy white benefactors, it had educated a long list of impressive women but saw its primary role as preparing its students for a middle-class marriage in the segregated South. Civil rights lawyer Marian Wright Edelman, who graduated from Spelman the year before Alice arrived, recalled it as a "staid" institution for turning out "safe young women who married Morehouse men, helped raise a family, and never kicked up dust." It had not only a dress code and curfew, like Radcliffe, but compulsory chapel six times a week and a "lights out" policy that got Alice reprimanded for staying up past bedtime reading poetry. The cognitive dissonance of living with these restrictions while students were demonstrating for civil rights—and being beaten and jailed by Atlanta police—was hard for Alice to bear.

Spelman was the first stage of leaving home for Alice, and like some early marriages, it promised more freedom than it delivered. As a would-be writer, Alice needed other Black writers to show her her past, and political thinkers to point the way to her future. But here, too, Spelman was on the defensive, steering its students toward Hemingway, Austen, Dickens. She loved Tolstoy and Doris Lessing, but she didn't feel she could put Keats or Millay at her service the way Audre had. Though she liked French classes, she turned down a fellowship to study in France, saying she couldn't live happily abroad until she could live freely in the American South.

Alice soon recognized the curfew and the high wall around the campus as signs of women's second-class citizenship, especially after the older member of the campus community who hired her as an assistant started groping and harassing her. "Perhaps this was one of many births of my feminism," she later commented. Ultimately, Spelman felt to her like a "limitation on [the] imagination. . . . I could think as far as the window, but I didn't dare think about opening the window and going out there."

In her sophomore year, Alice stood on the grass at nearby Atlanta University, listening to fellow students John Lewis and Julian Bond speak on civil rights, then singing "We Shall Overcome" for the first time in her life while the demonstrators held hands to feel brave. The professor who mentored her and praised her writing, the young leftist historian Howard Zinn, supported the protesters, and that summer Spelman fired him for it. Alice wrote him when she heard the news, saying she was so upset she could barely finish her letter. She added, "I shall write again when I have 'gotten myself together' (smile—chin up, chest out!)."

One way for Alice to cope with anger and disappointment was to hold it in, not to let it show. Another, a little like Alice Neel's, was to disrupt everyone's expectations. She spent the summer of 1963 in Boston, living with her brother Bill and his family, working in Jordan Marsh department store, and dating a white northerner, David DeMoss, who had come to Morehouse on an exchange. At the end of the summer David went with her to the March on Washington, and afterward she brought him home to Eatonton, where they horrified everyone by walking together down the main street, past the courthouse and the Confederate memorial, holding hands. The Walkers were upset, Alice's friends were shocked, and as

Bill Walker recalled, "the whole town was blown away. . . . Eatonton was not ready to give Blacks the kind of freedom and acceptance Alice was demanding. So, I guess she rubbed it in their face."

In Atlanta in 1963, Ursula Le Guin wrote of having "nowhere to go but in." To "go in," to live in books and stay out of trouble, was what Alice's teachers wanted her to do, but she refused. That winter she transferred to Sarah Lawrence, the women's college near New York City that Audre had so badly wanted to attend.

Here Alice started getting the distance she needed to think her own thoughts. At Sarah Lawrence she was an exception, a stranger in a cold land—she didn't even own a winter coat when she arrived in January—but she found there what she needed: "freedom to come and go, to read leisurely, to go my own way, dress my own way, and conduct my personal life as I saw fit."

Pure freedom seldom lasts long, especially in maternal lives, and Alice's liberty was briefly but dramatically threatened when she got pregnant. She spent the summer of her senior year volunteering in Kenya, and there met up unexpectedly, and a little too joyously, with David DeMoss. Back at Sarah Lawrence, when she realized what had happened, she became despondent. When she wasn't throwing up she lay in bed in her dorm room, unable to sleep, unable to get up, not knowing what to do. Her eldest sister, Mamie, told her on the phone she was a "slut." Her other sister, Ruth, unable to have children, pleaded with Alice to give her the baby to raise. David proposed marriage. Alice, feeling that "it was me or it," started making plans for suicide.

Finally a friend found an abortion doctor for her, with a fee to match his Upper East Side address: $2,000. Her friends tapped their emergency funds; so did David. When she woke up from the anesthetic, the white friend who had gone with her was standing over her, holding a red rose. Twenty-one-year-old Alice felt like she was handing her back her existence.

Like Audre, Alice experienced her abortion as a turning point, a statement of her own self-worth. In her short story "The Abortion," a woman who ends a pregnancy in college says that the event bore "all the marks of a supreme coming of age and a seizing of the direction of her own life." Being alive, when she could have been dead, brought a new sense of urgency and vocation. She wrote constantly that fall. When she graduated in January 1966, stockbrokerage heir Charles Merrill, funder of the travel grant that she had turned down at Spelman, gave her a private grant of $2,000 so she could write. Not long afterward, she had her first book of poetry accepted for publication.

Sarah Lawrence had given Alice her freedom, but in her first published personal essay, in 1967, she wrote that the civil rights movement had given her an equally fundamental belief in her own humanity. Her parents' invisibility in a white world would not be hers. Since she first saw King on the family TV as a teenager, she wrote, "I have fought and kicked and fasted and prayed and cursed and cried myself to the point of existing. It has been like being born again."

THE RIGHT BALANCE of time and support is never easy to come by, especially for women, especially in marriage. For a while, though, it seemed like Alice had found the ideal man. She met Mel Leventhal in the summer of 1966, when she went to Mississippi to volunteer for civil rights. On one of her first assignments for the NAACP Legal Defense Fund she was sent along with Mel, a Jewish law student from Brooklyn, to interview people who had been evicted from their homes for trying to vote. Alice was skeptical of white activists fresh from the North, whose shock at first witnessing open racism seemed to her naive. On the other hand, she thought he was cute. After white locals threatened them, they ended up sharing a motel room for safety, in separate beds, with Mel reading out loud from the Song of Solomon in the bedside Bible in the middle of a thunderstorm.

Mel, who shared both Alice's political passion and her feeling for literature, became her first great love. She showed him the poems that would become her first book, and he later said, "I was smitten by Alice the first day I saw her, but I fell in love with her when I read *Once.*" That fall he went back to finish law school in New York and she went with him, sharing his tiny apartment on Washington Square, setting up her typewriter on a table covered with a bedspread. Mel taught her how to drive and also how to swim, making up for her childhood exclusion from Eatonton's public pool.

Friends who saw them together worried that love might distract Alice from her writing. Instead, with Mel's affirmation and companionship, she wrote more intensely than ever. Mel critiqued and praised her work, and when she was accepted at the MacDowell writers' colony in New Hampshire that winter, he drove up every weekend to be with her. At her readings he sat in the audience with "the biggest glow of all on [his] face. I had never experienced such faith before."

When he graduated in the spring of 1967, they went back together to Jackson. But Alice didn't want to go South as Mel's girlfriend, another Black woman living as a white man's mistress. Anyway, their marriage would be a satisfying challenge to segregation: interracial coupledom was still illegal throughout the South. Out of love, high spirits, and a sense of adventure and possibility, Alice proposed. Mel said yes. They talked of starting a family, but for now they were a chosen community of two.

Big statements upend small worlds: Alice's parents were anxious and afraid for her, knowing white people only as a threat, while Mel's mother said she never wanted to see him again. Still, they went back to Jackson full of hope, and Alice felt ready to be among southerners again: "The first two years passed in a fever to get everything down—in poems, stories, the novel I was writing, essays. . . . It was a period of constant revelation, when mysteries not understood during my Southern childhood came naked to me to be embraced. I grew to adulthood in Mississippi."

She audited a course on African American literature at Jackson State University, taught by the poet Margaret Walker, where she discovered literary ancestors: Jean Toomer, Ralph Ellison, James Baldwin. A little later she went in search of Black women writers for a class she developed at

Wellesley College. There she taught works by Nella Larsen, Ann Petry, and Paule Marshall, as well as Brooks's *Maud Martha* and *The Bluest Eye*, Toni Morrison's 1970 debut. Zora Neale Hurston, forgotten until Alice popularized her work, would become especially important for her when she looked for ways to celebrate the African American South, and to bear witness to joy as well as grief.

Jackson was then a city of about 150,000 people, one-third of them Black. Alice found her community there in the civil rights movement, where she stayed involved by teaching Black history to teachers in the Head Start program. She enjoyed shocking the locals by going out with Mel, her hair in a tall afro, her back to the rude stares. Even walking down the street or going to the movies with him felt like a statement of hope, answering violence with a public demonstration of love.

Their choice to have a baby was made from love, too, but in the two years it took for Alice to get pregnant with their daughter, Rebecca, her mood turned. On April 4, 1968, a year after Alice arrived in Jackson, Martin Luther King Jr. was murdered at age thirty-nine. In New York, Audre heard the news at Carnegie Hall, at a fundraising concert with Duke Ellington and the Tougaloo choir. In the audience and onstage, everyone wept. In Jackson, Alice, newly pregnant, felt "as if the last light in my world had gone out." She went with Mel to Atlanta to walk in King's funeral procession, and when she had a miscarriage a week later her anger and despair were complete. "I did not even care. It seemed to me, at the time, that if [King] must die no one deserved to live, not even my own child."

Alice spent most of a year trying to conceive again and writing to keep her feelings at bay. King's assassination made her question the value of nonviolent resistance. "When I didn't write I thought of making bombs and throwing them. Of shooting racists. Of doing away . . . with myself," she wrote. Her motherhood wasn't entirely chosen: she was desperate to have a baby because it would exempt Mel from the draft and Vietnam. At the same time she worried that her writing wouldn't survive. "I feared being fractured by the experience if not overwhelmed. I thought the quality of my writing would be considerably diminished by motherhood—that nothing that was good for my writing could come out of having children."

When she finally did get pregnant, she suffered miserably from nausea and depression. Mel sold their red VW Beetle to pay for a trip to Mexico, but it didn't cheer her up the way they'd hoped. The experiences of pregnancy and childbirth—your body doing things outside your control; health-care providers ignoring your wishes and dismissing your worries; all the indignities, the fears—can feel like threats to a hard-won autonomy. It helped that Alice managed, three days before she went into labor, to finish the manuscript of her first novel.

Worries like these seem reflected in the bleak view of childbearing and mothering that characterizes Alice's fiction debut, *The Third Life of Grange Copeland*. Pregnancy can also be a time for looking back at one's own family: Who raised you? What gifts did or didn't they give you to survive the changes that are about to hit your life? *The Third Life of Grange Copeland* describes rural Georgia in Alice's parents' generation as a time and place in which oppression, poverty, and domestic violence combine to make mothers vulnerable.

The novel grew in part out of another scene of violence from Alice's childhood. When she was a young teenager her older sister Ruth took her to the funeral home where she worked to view the body of a woman who had been shot and killed by her husband. She was the mother of one of Alice's schoolmates, a Black woman who had worked hard, suffered, and been "strong." And now she was lying on a table with a shattered face that Alice couldn't bear to look at. Instead her gaze moved downward to the woman's shoe, still stuffed with newspaper to patch a worn-out sole.

The title character of the novel is a tenant farmer whose labor is exploited and sense of self eroded by the sharecropping system. Frustrated, ashamed, and afraid of the landowners he works for, he vents his feelings on his wife and child, then deserts them in a desperate flight to the North. His wife commits suicide and his abandoned son grows up to become a man as bitter as his father. Walker shows how the men's violence has its origins in oppression and despair, but she also makes it clear that the target of their meanness is women and children—making motherhood a deadly trap.

Unchosen maternity is a theme Alice dealt with in all her first three novels, including *The Color Purple*. Grange's son, Brownfield Copeland, enters into an abusive marriage with a woman named Mem, and pregnancy is the tool he uses to destroy her pride.

> The first early morning heavings were a good sign. Her body would do to her what he could not. . . . She could not hold out against him with nausea, aching feet and teeth, swollen legs, bursting veins and head; or the grim and dizzying reality of her trapped self and her children's despair. He could bring her back to lowness she had not even guessed at before.

In another scene a pregnant white woman refuses the rescuing brown hand Grange offers her and subsequently drowns, "her big belly her own tomb."

Though Brownfield kills Mem, Alice still turned the novel toward hope. Brownfield and Mem's daughter Ruth is rescued and brought up by a wiser Grange Copeland, in his "third life" of the title, when he has come home to take responsibility for his own actions. Caring for Ruth helps him "thaw the numbness" in himself, and she finds agency and purpose in the civil rights movement, with its commitment to nonviolence. There's hope that it will be safe for Ruth to become a mother, because she is learning the self-love that will help her resist racism's assault on the soul.

LIKE HER NEW LIFE after her abortion, Alice's life as a mother began with red roses, an enormous bouquet of them that Mel brought to her hospital room after Rebecca was born. Mel's gift surprised the medical staff of the recently desegregated hospital. In the experience of Jackson, Mississippi, in 1969, a white man might father a baby with a Black woman, but he didn't do it beaming in delight, with flowers in his arms.

Under other circumstances Alice might have enjoyed making a statement. But her labor had been frightening. Alice later remembered seeing Black women "screaming in the hallways, each encased in her own private hell." Her white woman obstetrician acted "chilly and abrupt," apparently disapproving of her marriage to the white man who had raced home from arguing a case in New Orleans to be with her for the birth.

Alice was delighted with Rebecca, her baby daughter, whose eyes seemed to be those not of a stranger but of "an old acquaintance re-entering a room we happened to be in." But she also remembered still wondering whether she could create and procreate. "Curled around my baby, feeling more anger and protectiveness than love," she concluded that what she needed was "the courage to believe that experience"—the life of a mother-writer—"may simply be different, unique even, rather than 'greater' or 'lesser.'"

In a 2013 documentary by Pratibha Parmar, Alice said, "I loved being a mother. We were so pleasantly surprised, [Mel] and I, at how much we loved it. . . . I spent [the first] year completely devoted to Rebecca." Still, it seems to have been hard for her to shape a maternal identity that didn't make her feel she was losing herself. Her life didn't look like her mother's, nor could she use the traditional middle-class housewife model. The ideal of an intellectual marriage with two working parents, both getting their needs met—a writing marriage—hadn't yet reached Mississippi. Mrs. Walker was unsympathetic: how could one baby be a distraction? Alice's Black neighbors disapproved of her: they could understand a mother working outside the home, but not one who needed a babysitter just to occupy a desk chair. Mel went out every day "to slay the dragons of racism and ignorance," leaving Alice to climb the Himalayas alone.

New fathers also search for their identity, and sometimes their choices lead them away from care. On behalf of his wife and daughter, Mel redoubled his devotion to civil rights, often working late into the night on important cases. But that left Alice feeling lonely—and guilty for wanting his attention. She wasn't getting the right combination of solitude and companionship—at that point she had too little of both—and the relative isolation and lack of mobility of new motherhood felt not only like cabin fever but like "solitary confinement. . . . Between 'projects,' my books, there were days that contained only a scream into the silence." The trouble was, other people depended on Mel. "More than I did, I sometimes thought. How could I say I also needed him?"

If Mel had shared more in the child care, Alice might have felt less isolated. If America had been less racist, she might have been less depressed. As it was, she felt "the old conflict resurfacing between loyalty to 'other' and loyalty to myself."

In the beginning there were roses, but maybe there could never be roses enough.

THE MOTHER OF a baby reencounters her body, newly powerful but also newly at risk, and a social order that may not be on her side or her child's. Camus said that the response to social repression was personal freedom, but how can a parent be "absolutely free"? Alice wrote frankly about this conflict in her much-reprinted, groundbreakingly frank essay on her motherhood, "*One* Child of One's Own." She writes of her joy and pride as a mother, and of her pleasure at this "meaningful—some might say *necessary*—digression within the work(s)." She also foregrounds her intense ambivalence about motherhood in a society that does not value her or her child—as she famously put it, one that is "badly arranged for children to be taken into happy account."

Every woman who has a child harbors a special animus against at least one person who, around pregnancy, birth, or care, judged her, ignored her, or refused her the help she needed. In a central scene of "One Child,"

Alice and two-year-old Rebecca are both sick in a strange northern city. Alone and miserable, Alice calls the phone number a friend has given her for a prominent pediatrician. It turns out to be his home phone, and he answers her rudely. The next day in his office, he remains distant. Her history has given her little reason to trust doctors, and now the white physician's indifference to her distress—and her double vulnerability to racism through her own and her daughter's needs—makes her furious.

Further, Alice describes a fruitless search for solidarity from white feminists who are blind to Black women's interests and obstacles, and from Black nationalists who deny feminism a place in their politics. Even her mother's advice to hurry up and have a second child feels hurtful: it's like a visit from the motherhood police. (The title of the essay is Alice's answer.) "One Child" becomes a manifesto on intersectionality, in which forms of oppression meet in motherhood, denying women of color the wherewithal to nurture both their families and themselves.

"For me, there has been conflict, struggle, occasional defeat—not only in affirming the life of my own child . . . , but also in seeing in that affirmation a fond acceptance and confirmation of myself in a world that would deny me the untrampled blossoming of my own existence," she states. With enough resources, mothering can be a protected space, a shelter from the intensities of a creative life. But for Alice, creative life *was* the shelter. Writing was her act of resistance and her means of healing. If the interruptions of mothering kept her from writing, how would she go on?

She found the validation she needed partly in her connection to Rebecca, claiming her this time not as maternal figure but as ally. In "One Child," written when Rebecca was nine, she declared proudly, "We are together, my child and I. Mother and child, yes, but *sisters* really, against whatever denies us all that we are."

THE LONGER ALICE STAYED in Mississippi, the more depressed she became. In May 1970, during Rebecca's newborn year and just after the shootings at Kent State, two students at Jackson State, where Alice had studied and taught with Margaret Walker, were killed and another twelve injured by police who opened fire on a demonstration. During her Jackson years, Alice later wrote, "I never knew a single Movement person (and I include myself) who wasn't damaged in some way from having to put her or his life, principles, children on the line." It was often Black women who gave solace and reassurance to all the others, carrying an extra burden of emotional labor on top of their own troubles.

As the peaceful, inclusive civil rights movement gave way to the militant Black Power movement, Alice also felt increasing pressure to conform to what was then called "correct" thought. Originality pisses people off; when it's intersectional, it seems to piss people off in all directions. Audre Lorde wrote that in this difficult time she "often felt like I was working and raising my children in a vacuum, and that it was my own fault. . . . Either I denied or chose between various aspects of my identity, or my work and my Blackness would be unacceptable."

Alice too felt excluded from community, especially since all her communities now seemed to be making a problem out of her closest ally, her husband. Even when she and Mel had first married, some of Alice's friends had accused her of "putting down the Black man" or sleeping with the enemy. Now, it seemed like the whole movement opposed her marriage to a white man. The Black Arts–allied poet Nikki Giovanni came to visit Alice and Mel in Jackson, bringing her small son, who was Rebecca's age. Instead of offering a fruitful mother-writer connection, Giovanni wounded Alice by asking her, as Alice remembered it, how she could go to bed with someone she wanted to kill.

Mel stopped going to Alice's readings because his presence made audiences frosty. When Alice was invited to speak at Sarah Lawrence in 1970, June Jordan recalled that the Black student group nearly boycotted the event. As usual, Alice reacted to disapproval by refusing to do what was expected. Where Jordan, who was teaching at the college, wore militant chic—"I had a huge Afro and wore a trench coat, boots, and dark sunglasses, day or night"—Alice gave her talk in a "nice, plain, ordinary dress." She gently advised her listeners to aim their anger well. Two years later, she told another group of students that "no person is your friend (or kin) who demands your silence."

Alice soon started writing a new novel, *Meridian*, about the psychic toll of the civil rights movement on a woman activist. Change doesn't take time, resistance takes time, a wise feminist once said; and Alice was starting to burn out from the struggle. Sometimes she hated it that she couldn't do enough. Other times, as deeply committed as she was to thinking and writing about Black experience, she felt "worn out by the prison of race. I just got sick of race being at the center of everything. My spirit resisted being limited or defined exclusively on those terms."

When Doris Lessing speculated in her memoirs about the person she might have been if she had stayed in her first marriage in benighted Salisbury, she concluded, "I would not have survived. A nervous breakdown would have been the least of it. . . . I would have had to live at odds with myself, riven, hating what I was part of, for years." Alice began having similar visions about equally provincial Jackson. She wrote a friend in the summer of 1971 that Mel wanted to stay. "I know, however, that if I continue here without doing the things I want to do I'll become a thin-lipped, disgruntled harridan." In September 1971, reluctantly leaving Mel behind, she accepted a fellowship at Radcliffe and took Rebecca with her to spend a year in Cambridge.

THE FELLOWSHIP YEAR became two, and with more financial security, less stress, and more creative community, plus day care, Alice acquired more agency and saw her career blossom. Black women's art and writing was flourishing in the early Seventies, and so was the movement that Alice would soon dub "womanism," a feminism rooted in Black experience.

Alice used her time at Radcliffe partly to explore and teach Black women's writing. She wrote poetry, which was published in her 1974 collection, *Revolutionary Petunias*, and most of the short stories that became her second work of fiction, *In Love & Trouble* (1973). It was at Radcliffe, in 1973, that Alice gave as a talk her essay "In Search of Our Mothers' Gardens," in which she claimed a heritage of Black, female, individual artistic agency in the beauty of her mother's flowers.

Magazine editor Marcia Ann Gillespie, who was in the audience, told biographer Evelyn C. White, "It was as if she'd brought forth all the ancestors and allowed us to collectively grieve what Black women had never been able to achieve. . . . By the time Alice finished, you could hear sisters sobbing all over the room." But it was partly because of her children that Minnie Lou Walker had not had a chance to use her gifts, another part of Alice's complicated maternal yearning. In her short story "Everyday Use" Alice wrote about a woman who leaves home to get an education and becomes cut off from her mother's traditions. Coming from rich cultural backgrounds but not learned ones, Walker and Carter both found that self-transformation brought losses as well as gains.

After Radcliffe Alice briefly returned to Mississippi, but when Gloria Steinem offered her a job editing fiction and poetry at *Ms.* magazine in 1974, she persuaded Mel to move to New York. There she again found community among fellow writers. Just before she arrived, *Revolutionary Petunias* was nominated for the National Book Award for poetry. Among the eleven nominees were three other women, including Adrienne Rich and Audre Lorde. Rich, the most likely winner of the four, phoned the others and proposed that if one of them won the award, all should accept it. Audre and Alice agreed; the fourth, Eleanor Lerman, opted out. On April 18, the prize was awarded jointly to Allen Ginsberg and to Rich, for *Diving into the Wreck*. Walker wasn't there, but Rich and Lorde took the stage, where Rich read a powerful statement the three had written together, "refusing the terms of patriarchal competition" and accepting the award "in the name of all the women whose voices have gone and still go unheard."

"To this day," Walker writes, "I feel this means we all won."

At *Ms.*, like everywhere else, Alice was willing to take risky positions. In 1975 she wrote a favorable review of *Loving Her*, Ann Allen Shockley's novel of an interracial lesbian relationship. Some mainstream feminists, most notoriously Betty Friedan, saw lesbian organizing as a threat to their relatively cautious, establishment goals. It would be another fifteen years before Alice came out publicly as bisexual, but she was using her growing influence on behalf of Black lesbians.

Mel had been Alice's creative partner, the man who understood. Now Alice found solidarity and understanding among women. In New York, Alice and June Jordan, the single mother of a teenage son, organized a support group of writers, who met informally at Jordan's home in Brooklyn. Calling themselves the Sisterhood, they included Toni Morrison, playwright Ntozake Shange, and food writer Verta Mae Grosvenor, among others. Looking back in 1985, Morrison praised the community of Black women,

> how many of us are battered and how many are champions. I note the strides that have replaced the tiptoe; I watch the new configurations we have given to personal relationships. . . . When you say "No" or "Yes" or "This and not that," change itself changes. . . . And all along the way you had the best of company—others, we others, just like you.

Alice might have queried the "just like you," but the new understanding that feminism brought, both of female community and of permission to draw boundaries in close relationships, was real. Solidarity among women was not emphasized in *Grange Copeland*, but a few years later, it would be the joyous central theme of *The Color Purple*.

"CARING FOR MYSELF is not self-indulgence, it is self-preservation, and that is an act of political warfare," Audre argued. In the 1970s, the words "intersectionality," "self-care," and "emotional labor" had not yet been coined, but all three of them are the subject of Alice's intensely felt second novel, *Meridian*, published in 1976. Like Lessing's Martha Quest novels, *Meridian* follows the political awakening of a woman who defines herself by her activism. And like *The Golden Notebook*, it considers the relationship for women between political and personal change, as well as what happens to organizers when a movement falls apart.

As a teenager, Meridian Hill, like Martha Quest, sleepwalks into pregnancy and marriage, then, fearing that the work of mothering will "shatter her . . . emerging self" as it had her own mother's, leaves her husband and son. Unlike Martha, who sees her motherhood as a private, psychological problem, Meridian looks at it in the context of her racial history: she says she is rejecting "the horror, the narrowing of perspective, for mother and for child" that for Black women this institution "had invariably meant." Yet she feels like a traitor to the generations of enslaved women who had longed in vain for the right to keep and raise their children. Wracked with guilt, she thinks of her own bitter, self-sacrificing mother as being "worthy of this maternal history, and of herself as belonging to an unworthy minority, for which there was no precedent and of which she was, as far as she knew, the only member."

Later in her journey out of motherhood, she has an abortion without anesthesia and, when the doctor offers to follow up with a tubal ligation in exchange for sex, answers in anger and distress, "Burn 'em out by the roots for all I care." It's as if she wants to refuse the whole idea of mothering until it can become more generative. Afterward, Meridian's lover, Truman, marries her white friend Lynne, and both turn to Meridian for emotional support in coping with their interracial union. When Truman accuses Meridian of taking Lynne's side, she exclaims, "Her side? I'm sure she's already taken it. I'm trying to make the acquaintance of my side in all this. What side *is* mine?"

Meridian deals with the price paid, in body and soul, by Black women activists who gave all their energy for the cause, witnessed too much injustice they couldn't remedy, and couldn't rely on either Black men or white women for solidarity. In a climactic scene, Meridian carries the body of a five-year-old boy who has drowned in a reservoir—he wasn't allowed to swim in the public pool—to city hall, where she lays his decomposing remains on the mayor's desk. This is now her maternal work; but by this time she is alone and reeling from survivor's guilt. Devotion to a cause can be another form of female self-sacrifice, and in writing the novel Alice was almost certainly grappling with those feelings in herself. Reluctantly, Meridian chooses her own side, concluding that "the respect she owed her life was to continue, against whatever obstacles, to live it, and not to give up any particle of it without a fight to the death, preferably *not* her own."

Meridian helped pave the way for Alice's third novel, *The Color Purple*, with its celebration of Black pleasure as well as pain. But like *Meridian*, Alice now needed time alone. At first, in their fixer-upper house in Brooklyn, Mel and Alice were hip young parents, raising their daughter on gender-neutral Erector sets and books, encouraging her to be anything she wanted. Their marriage, however, was starved of time and attention, and in 1976 it ended.

The criticism from all sides, including their families, had put a strain on the marriage, and so had Mel's habit of hard work. Rebecca remembered a fight her parents had had one weekend when Mel said he was too tired to go with Alice to the Botanic Garden, one of the borough's few oases of green. Stressed by the city's crowds and lack of space, Alice began having anxiety attacks on the way to the *Ms.* office.

Roberta Flack's hit "Killing Me Softly" became the soundtrack to their breakup. Alice wrote a friend that she felt torn apart. "Frankly, I think I'm unsuited for marriage. . . . The problem is that Mel is magnificent and leaving him will take just about every ounce of gumption I can muster. And there is the pull of Rebecca, her happiness and so on." In her grief Alice turned to six-year-old Rebecca: in the bed the two now shared, she cried every night while her daughter put her arms around her.

She moved with Rebecca to an apartment of her own, where one night, Rebecca recalled, she started giving instructions for her funeral.

"There should be a party," Alice suggested. "Lots of people dancing. . . . And don't let them put me in a big ugly coffin." Rebecca wrote carefully on a legal pad, "N-o u-g-l-y c-o-f-f-i-n." Later she said, "I felt proud that my mother trusted me, you know, to take care of business. But it was terrifying to hear her talk about dying. I kept thinking, 'What about me?'"

Like Susan Sontag, Alice needed support and sought it from her child, telling Rebecca that they were more like siblings than mother and daughter. Rebecca would recall that this emotional reliance had been both a source of pride and a burden to her. "I feel strong when she says those things, like I am much older and wiser than I really am. It's just that the strength doesn't allow for weakness."

Feminist psychoanalyst Rozsika Parker suggests that mothers who have had to set aside their own needs may react ambivalently to their daughters' longings, relating to them "as inconsistently as they relate to their own neediness." At nineteen, to Alexis De Veaux, Rebecca described their relationship almost the way Alice had her own mother's absence: "I put pressure on myself to be very well adjusted, for my mother, so she could work, and I wouldn't bother her all the time."

Meanwhile Alice and Mel discussed a new childcare arrangement, joint custody. In the past, one parent had either vanished after a divorce or been more or less banished from the scene. But in the 1970s, as divorce rates in the US and Europe rose, more parents living separately chose to bring their children up together.

The question was where and how to do it. Mel began a relationship with an old flame, a white, Jewish woman, and took a job in Washington, DC. Alice cautiously began seeing an old friend from college, Morehouse graduate and magazine editor Robert Allen, who lived in California. Since Alice was thinking of joining him there, they decided that Rebecca would live the coming two years with Mel and her stepmother in Washington, then change every two years until she finished high school. "Our intention was for Rebecca to grow up with both of us and to have as much stability as possible," Alice later said. "The decision was made out of total love."

Still, it must have been traumatic for Alice: "*One* Child of One's Own," with its cry of maternal pain as well as anger, was published in *Ms.* in August 1979, when she was separated from her daughter. Rebecca too found it hard to cope. Instead of a mixed-race household where both of her identities were present, she now lived first with two white parents, then on the opposite coast with two Black ones, Alice and Robert. This left her feeling "fragmented . . . like slivers from a mirror." In her 2001 memoir *Black, White and Jewish: Autobiography of a Shifting Self,* she wrote that in Washington she missed her mother, her physical affection, her brown skin affirming Rebecca's own color. Without her two parents "blocking out the world" with their love, as Mel put it, their biracial child felt like a failed experiment in racial reconciliation.

Part of love for Alice was setting her child free—not from her as a mother, but from the narrowness of possibility that her own life had offered. To Rebecca, though, that freedom sometimes felt "overwhelming" and unsafe. She writes, "My parents did not hold me tight, but encouraged me to go. They did not buffer, protect, watch out for, or look after me. I was watered, fed, admired, stroked, and expected to grow. I was mostly left alone to discover the world and my place in it." At thirteen, recently moved from her father's house to her mother's and seeking security, she slept with her boyfriend for the first time. At fourteen she got pregnant, despite the Pill. Alice helped her get an abortion, then took her to the movies, but Rebecca portrays Alice as failing to recognize the loneliness that had led her to have sex early.

During her separation from Rebecca, in the two years after she moved to San Francisco in 1978, Alice grew as a writer. With a Guggenheim grant to live on, she found an apartment in the city and a house in remote Boonville, California, where she spent a fallow year resting, thinking, talking to her characters, and waiting for her new novel to ripen. She wanted to tell the hero's journey of a southern woman who, at first powerless, sexually abused, trapped in a forced marriage, falls in love with her husband's mistress and learns to claim herself.

It's possible that she needed Rebecca with her to write the novel, though, because she didn't feel ready to start until her daughter came to live with her at the beginning of a new school year. After that she wrote furiously, finishing the book the day that Rebecca left for camp the next summer. She thought of the characters, Celie, Shug, and Mister, as communicating not only to her but to her child. "Rebecca gave [Celie] courage (which she *always* gives me)—and Celie grew to like her so much she would wait until three-thirty to visit me. So, just when Rebecca would arrive home needing her mother and a hug, there'd be Celie, trying to give her both."

Her hardest narrative problem, Alice writes, was figuring out how to bring Celie's own lost children back to her. But once Celie learns, with Shug's help, to value her body and her talents—to become her full creative and sensual self—her children are restored to her, as if she is finally ready then to be a mother.

"It is my happiest book," Alice said when it came out. "I had to do all the other writing to get to this point" of giving her characters hope, pleasure, and maternal joy.

FROM A CANVAS FOLDING CHAIR, a mother watches as her daughter assists on a film shoot. At fifteen, her child strides across the set with her dreadlocks flying, megaphone in hand, walkie-talkie at her belt. She's proud of her confidence, her independence, the extraordinary opportunities she can give her. When she can't be there, Oprah Winfrey watches out for her daughter.

The writer also serves as an unofficial dialogue coach and script doctor and, from a growing mysticism, gives tarot readings to the cast and crew. When she is frustrated, she now meditates to ease the stress.

On the film set of *The Color Purple*, Alice recalled, Rebecca amazed her "with her beauty and competence. . . . I like her tallness, her directness, her characteristic cheerful and no-shit attitude. I know she would

not like to get along without me, but she could. She is already herself."
This portrait is an admiring one, but it also recalls Alice Neel, painting
Isabetta as a girl with no need for a mother.

The Color Purple made Alice a literary star. It became a bestseller, selling at least six million copies since its publication, received the National
Book Award, and won the Pulitzer Prize for fiction, making Alice only
the second Black woman to win a Pulitzer in any category. Gwendolyn
Brooks commented that she was glad to have company.

Having a public persona is one thing, being a celebrity another. Thirty-
eight when the book was published, charismatic Alice took up her fame
like the "goddess" De Veaux saw her as. At the same time, De Veaux
wrote, the success of *The Color Purple*, the book and especially the 1985
film version, "drew battle lines in Black communities that cut as deeply as
civil war." Alice was again accused of disloyalty. "It was said that I hated
men, Black men in particular," she wrote, and "that my ideas of equality
and tolerance were harmful, even destructive to the Black community."
When the movie, directed by Steven Spielberg, came out, African American groups boycotted it. Though she stayed strong in public, Alice was
wounded by the attacks.

At the same time she was suffering from the effects of Lyme disease and
grieving her own mother, now bedridden from a series of strokes, leaving
Alice to try to be "the strong one." Robert, feeling jealous and neglected,
had an affair that contributed to their breakup in 1990, with Alice writing
that their bond was "complicated" by his troubles with alcohol and "by
my need to live in my own space most of the time, by my periods of creative and/or depression-driven moodiness." Their relationship, she wrote,
"lost its numinousness, especially sexually: without a sense of the sacred
in our physical connections I began to slowly starve." Alice went on to
have relationships with both men and women, some of them celebrities
in their own right, such as Tracy Chapman. She never remarried or lived
long-term with a partner.

While Alice continued her successes with the wide-ranging fantasy *The Temple of My Familiar* (reviewing it, Ursula Le Guin called it thematically rich, "amazing, overwhelming. A hundred themes and subjects spin through it . . . a whirl of times and places"), Rebecca left home to study at Yale. At twenty-two, in an article for *Ms.*, she proclaimed a new "third wave" of feminism, and she went on to be one of its leaders, an acclaimed writer, lecturer, and activist for gender, racial, and economic justice. Continuing her mother's legacy of openness about her personal life, she has also written memoirs about her childhood and her own motherhood.

As she entered adulthood, Rebecca became more ambivalent toward her mother's vocation, feeling—and saying in public—that she had been too low on Alice's priority list. The bonds between parent and daughter grew strained when Rebecca, at thirty-four, became pregnant. In *Baby Love: Choosing Motherhood after a Lifetime of Ambivalence*, she writes that it was hard for her to enter into motherhood purposefully, in the midst of a successful career. Women her age were asking the questions Alice had: "Can I survive having a baby? Will I lose myself—my body, my mind, my *options*—and be left trapped, resentful, and irretrievably overwhelmed?"

Rebecca's fears were belied by the transformative joy she felt in mothering her infant son—and her pleasure in joining the maternal collective, which she called "the first club I've unequivocally belonged to." Motherhood rearranged her bonds of love and friendship in ways that empowered her to step into the center of her life. She explained, "The idea of my vulnerable, defenseless child seeing his mother destabilized by any kind of relationship forced me to stick up for myself in a way I hadn't been able to." But this "final and dramatic departure from daughterhood" led to a rupture in which mother and daughter, though they later reconciled, didn't speak to each other for several years.

In "*One* Child of One's Own" Alice wrote that Rebecca's birth had "joined me to a body of experience and a depth of commitment to my own life hard to comprehend otherwise. Her birth was the incomparable gift of seeing the world at quite a different angle than before, and judging it by standards that would apply far beyond my natural life."

To get to this place she had had to reject the obscuring myths about motherhood, she wrote, and added (her italics), *"Distance is required, even now."*

The Baby on the Writing Desk;
or, Two Things at Once

A change in physical relations and conditions changes mental and emotional states beyond what even the most revolutionary of reformers can begin to foresee. (DORIS LESSING)

To destroy the institution [of motherhood] is not to abolish motherhood. It is to release the creation and sustenance of life into the same realm of decision, struggle, surprise, imagination, and conscious intelligence, as any other difficult, but freely chosen work. (ADRIENNE RICH)

IN SHROPSHIRE, ENGLAND, in May 1960, seventeen-year-old grammar school student Lorna Sage staged a jailbreak from a maternity ward to study for her A levels. The nurses wouldn't let her read—"We don't feed our babies on books," they said—so Lorna handed her newborn daughter to her own mother and took her exams, leaking milk and thinking Latin, "caught up in a kind of euphoria, scribbling for my life."

The headmistress of her grammar school told her no university would take her, a person of low morals, no matter how good her results. But in her brilliant memoir of her lower-class childhood, *Bad Blood*, Lorna wrote that adults' disapproval taught her her own value: it "fueled my conviction that I must *mean* something."

Mother-writers who came of age around 1960 in Britain staged private rebellions, refusing to choose between books and babies, declining their mothers' burdens of masochism and guilt, rewriting the motherhood plot.

They looked for support where they could find it: from husbands, from sympathetic teachers, eventually from the women's movement that would bring them together. "It was a lot easier to have a baby than to be delivered of the mythological baggage that went with it," Lorna Sage observed, bracing herself for a fight against all those who thought that a teenage mother of the lower classes should know her place. "From now on I was making my way against most people's assumptions, I'd have to count my friends and fight back."

The same year, 1960, twenty-three-year-old Antonia Susan Byatt had her hands full with a baby and a novel. What she wanted was education and children, brains and love, and so she had gone to see her graduate-thesis supervisor, the Oxford don Helen Gardner, to say she was getting married. Gardner had informed her that not only would marriage ruin her mind, it would cost her her income. As a married woman she would lose her research grant, though a married man would have his increased.

So Antonia went off in a rage and married her economist boyfriend. Like Le Guin, she was not sorry to abandon her thesis: "I truly would rather have been a writer than an academic, and I needed to be forced into making that decision." But she was terrified of losing herself like her own mother, who after graduating from Cambridge had married, had four children, and ended up haunting her own house as a depressed, embittered *femme maison.* Byatt said she and her sisters all shared the determination "not to get stuck in the kitchen because you could see it had destroyed . . . something essential in our mother."

Matrophobia (Adrienne Rich's term for the fear of becoming one's mother), plus a strong sense of vocation, carried Byatt through her early motherhood, when she had two children in two years. "The first baby was a total accident," she later said. "When she was born, I did think, for a very short time—well, I called her Antonia because I thought, she'd better have the name, because now I won't write a book. . . . And then after a bit I just went back to writing a book. . . . I wrote with a baby on the desk, in one of those little plastic chairs. What you have to learn to do is pay complete attention to two things at once."

As a student Byatt heard it said that Cambridge professor Elizabeth Anscombe, who was a philosopher, authority on Wittgenstein, and mother of seven children, was once so lost in thought while changing trains that she left her sleeping baby on the platform at Bletchley. It was permission-giving, the knowledge that it was possible to forget one's children. Like the baby on the fire escape, the baby at Bletchley station is a more drastic version of the baby on the writing desk: the state of presence and forgetting that allows the work to get done.

Babies eat books, as happens literally in *The Millstone*, Margaret Drabble's 1965 novel about a woman choosing single motherhood. The baby crawls into the mother's roommate's room and chews up several pages of her novel in progress. (Tape and retyping rescue the manuscript, though they can't do anything for the bad reviews.) But babies create books too: *The Millstone* brought maternity back from its ghostly status by revealing it as a hero's journey and a tale worth telling. Buchi Emecheta's 1974 *Second Class Citizen* did the same: its autobiographical protagonist refuses to play the roles she's offered (loyal wife, submissive immigrant) and instead incorporates her motherhood into her writing. Emecheta was determined to become someone for her five kids, causing Alice Walker to call her admiringly "a writer because of, not in spite of, her children."

If motherhood can make a writer fall silent, so can the pain of losing a child. In 1972, Byatt's son, Charles, the second of her four children, was walking home from the park when he was hit by a drunk driver whose car jumped the curb. He had just turned eleven. A few days before, she had felt his warm breath on her cheek as he slept on her shoulder in the bus, and now he was gone.

Byatt was pregnant with her youngest and had just taken a job teaching at University College London to pay for her son's school fees. She stayed on for the next eleven years, writing little. In her short story "The

July Ghost," a mother feels too rational to see apparitions, yet she longs to be haunted by her child, because it would be less unbearable than his absence. "After he died, the best hope I had, it sounds silly, was that I would go mad enough so that instead of waiting every day for him to come home from school and rattle the letter-box I might actually have the illusion of seeing or hearing him come in. [When] they said, he is dead, [I thought] *is* dead, that will go on and on and on till the end of time."

Lorna got into university despite her headmistress's warnings. When she discovered she was pregnant, she and her boyfriend, Victor Sage, had gotten married and spent the next months living at Lorna's parents' house, studying together for their exams, two teenagers supporting each other in their improbable determination to live a life of the mind. At her school's speech day, the headmistress pointedly took as her theme "Be good, sweet maid, and let who will be clever," but when Lorna crossed the stage to receive a prize her fellow pupils cheered.

Lorna and Vic applied to university together, and Lorna, because she had a husband, was promptly rejected by all the Oxbridge women's colleges. She could have waited until she was twenty-three, when a married woman could be accepted as a "mature student," but she was afraid that if she waited that long, she'd forget she'd ever intended to be a scholar. Finally Durham University, moving with the changing times, dropped its prohibition on married students to admit them. They left their daughter, Sharon, with Lorna's parents during the term, and accepted their status as "freaks" in the other students' eyes. When they graduated together with firsts in English, they were such a novelty that the *Daily Mail* printed their picture, with four-year-old Sharon pouting in their arms. They both got teaching positions at the new University of East Anglia and were able to bring Sharon to live with them full-time.

Though their sex lives never recovered from the shock of the unplanned pregnancy and they eventually separated as friends, they nurtured each other's careers as Lorna became a brilliant academic and feminist critic. Unstoppable in her eagerness to work and live, Sharon recalled, she was the kind of young mother who shows up to a parent-teacher conference dressed in full Swinging London mode. But she was also "very much in [my] corner, always."

All these women befriended, supported, or paved the way for Angela Carter, who had her baby at forty-three, in 1983. When she did, in the wake of the sexual and feminist revolutions, a community of mothers and others gathered around her. Some had never married; some had same-sex partners; some had married but hadn't had children; some had chosen single motherhood. They enjoyed showing Angela how it was done, the burping and the baby talk, and were pleased with themselves and with her, all together raising children, or not, on their own terms.

Angela Carter at home, surrounded by toys and birds, South London, late 1980s.

Her Own Version

ANGELA CARTER (1940–1992)

◆

All times are changing times, but ours is one of massive, rapid
moral and mental transformation. Archetypes turn into millstones,
large simplicities get complicated, chaos becomes elegant, and what
everybody knows is true turns out to be what some people used to
think. (URSULA K. LE GUIN)

AFTER ANGELA CARTER DIED in 1992, at age fifty-one, her friend
Lorna Sage said of her that she had lived her life "in the (conventionally) wrong order." Instead of marrying, having children, and then
starting a career, she had married, published novels, won prizes, left her
husband to live with a lover in Japan, returned home, begun a relationship
with a younger man, and had her only child at forty-three. Sage added,
"The shape a woman's life takes now is a lot less determined than once it
was. Or: the determinations are more subtle, you're *sentenced* to assemble
your own version."

But for Carter, coming of age in the 1960s, self-invention was her
challenge and her good fortune, and she made the most of it. Her novels
and short stories are full of theatricality, audacity, and play, often at the
service of imagining how women and men could live. After all, it had
taken more than one generation of ardent self-transformation to get her

family out of the working classes; she once claimed that it was only "an accident of the twentieth century" that she could read and write.

She did sometimes worry about what people thought of her, a gray-haired writer who was raising a baby with a partner fifteen years younger. While she was pregnant with her son, Alex, she had generally let her friends assume it had been an accident, not wanting to own up to her maternal desire. Sometimes she defiantly emphasized the contradictions of the mother-writer. When one journalist turned up at her house in South London for a naptime interview, she came to the front door wearing high black leather boots and a black jumpsuit, then pointed out that she had spots down her front from Alex's lunch. She bristled at London bus drivers who saw her with Alex and called her "Mum," reducing her to "a common noun" and denying her her individuality. Her battles against her obstetrician's disapproval became the subject of one of her many brilliant essays. She never wanted to be only one thing.

Because she was able to become a mother on her own terms, she enjoyed it, to her surprise. "The beauty of children is a conspiracy to which I have only recently become a party," she wrote in her journal. She had an intense sense of difference and need to become more than people had told her she was. For a long time she thought it wasn't possible for her to combine that with an ordinary domestic life, until she managed, together with her partner, to define motherhood for herself.

WHETHER OR NOT to have a baby was a question that Angela thought about and, for many years, put off. It turns up in her private writing, sometimes as longing, sometimes as distaste (especially for dull mothers); and in the year she turned forty it was very much on her mind. Not that she had any definite plans. If anything, she seemed to be making a bid for independence when she left London for Providence, Rhode Island, where she had accepted a year-long teaching position at Brown University.

She had taken the job to pay the mortgage on the house where she lived with her partner, Mark Pearce, but though they were happy together, she doesn't seem to have been quite ready to commit.

For years, ever since she left a confining first marriage, travel had been a way for her to set boundaries and refuse a conventional life. She had been to Bangkok, Tashkent, and Warsaw, seen Russia from the Trans-Siberian Railway, and crossed the US by Greyhound bus in 1969 at the height of the counterculture. (Visiting a California commune, she proclaimed it not edgy enough: too many goats, not enough sex.) The two years she had spent in Japan in her early thirties had been generative for her, giving her a place where she could liberate herself from her marriage, get some perspective on men and women, and get happily out of her comfort zone.

But when she went to Japan, it had been to throw away the life she'd had, and now her inclinations—as described in her first letters home— were more domestic. Her correspondence with Mark gives the impression that she had underestimated, until Providence, how much she wanted to share her life with him. In some ways she was glad he wasn't there, because it left her free to work at night, which he hated and she loved. But she complained that he hadn't written, and as soon as she bought a telephone ("the saleslady tried to sell me a kitchen, bathroom and bedroom exten-sion. . . . I was briefly tempted by a Mickey Mouse phone"), she started running up her bill. "You know I am not good at writing it down or say-ing it in crowded kitchens full of interested and sympathetic people like on the 'phone on Monday but I *do* love you and I do think, in a sense, I am always with you and you with me," she wrote to him. A month later: "I am often consumed by sexual longing. Yes? Yes. Nobody else will do."

Meanwhile she was suspicious of America's commerciality and its freeways (she didn't drive). She was scandalized by Brown's high tuition, $6,000 a year, and did not plan to be bossed around by such privileged children. Sensitive and thin-skinned, like Alice Neel, she had learned to protect herself and assert authority by acting outrageous. On her first day she arrived in the classroom in her current antifashion look: Doc Martens, unruly gray hair. According to one of the students, the later novelist Rick Moody, she

> was charged with reducing the number of would-be participants in her class to fourteen. Maybe thirty people were in the room, and she simply stood before us and tried to take questions. Some young guy in the back, rather too full of himself, raised his hand and, with a sort of withering skepticism, asked, "Well, what's your work like?"
>
> . . . Before she replied, she cocked her head and said "um" once or twice. Then she said, "My work cuts like a steel blade at the base of a man's penis."
>
> The room emptied out at the break, and I'm not sure a quorum of fourteen returned. Maybe only eleven or twelve.

Humorous shock effects were a specialty of hers. Her writer friend Robert Coover, who had invited her to teach at Brown, recalled that if she felt challenged "she could say these things that just draw a line under any further comment." Later in the semester, when Moody went to hear Carter read on campus, the room was packed with young women sitting at her feet. Her acclaimed book of short stories on fairy tale themes, *The Bloody Chamber*, had appeared the year before. She had gone through a period of struggle and change as a writer and was just coming into her own.

As a prospective mother she wasn't sure, and in her letters to Mark she kept circling the question. That fall, for a magazine assignment, she took the train to New York City to interview the older novelist and critic Elizabeth Hardwick. Hardwick, charming and persuasive, explained that she had had her only child when she was forty and formed half of a literary couple with the poet Robert Lowell. Though she tended toward the old school of women's suffering for love, she evidently convinced Angela that having a child was possible and that it wasn't too late.

Reporting this to Mark, two weeks later, Angela worried. Her period had come early, and "of course I thought: it's the Change! it's the first sign of the Change!" She added that she had consulted a "lady biologist at the Uni" who assured her she was too young for menopause. "Not that this consoles me. . . . I don't think you'll stop loving me or anything like that. . . . But there is indeed an inexorable quality about the Change in a woman's life, dear, and I don't want to be hurried into it." In her next letter she was still stewing, now about her desirability: "I will be a little old lady by the time you see me again and you will sod off with a blonde, probably with Sharon" —Sharon Sage, Lorna's twenty-year-old daughter.

Age was one of the differences between Mark and Angela. When they first met she was thirty-four and had published six novels; he was nineteen and was renovating the house across the street. She asked him to look at a broken pipe. A year later she wrote to her friend Fleur Adcock, "He came to help me with the house, painting and so on, allegedly for a fortnight, this time last year and just never went away." She tended to be evasive about their relationship, even with close friends, although Lorna had recently married a younger man. By the time she went to Providence she and Mark had been seeing each other for six years, yet she wrote an editor that her "caretaker"— presumably meaning Mark—was dealing with her mail.

At Christmas, though, when Mark came to Providence, Robert Coover saw how happy Angela was. They rented a car, traveled together, bought matching overcoats at a military-surplus store, and something changed between them, he sensed, or was resolved. "From that time on, they were a pair." They would go on to wear the matching coats around London, an ironic but also genuine statement of their affection. Together they found a balance that allowed Angela to work and mother, despite her well-earned distrust of the whole idea of home.

ANGELA GREW UP in between worlds, the child of a "rootless, upward, downward, sideways socially mobile family" who, like Maude and Michael Tayler, were occupied with a somewhat dysfunctional reinvention of their own lives. Angela Olive Stalker was born on May 7, 1940, at the start of the Second World War, and shortly afterward evacuated—with her mother, her brother, who was eleven years older, and her maternal grandmother— from London to the gritty South Yorkshire coal-mining village her grand- mother had left years before. They lived there in a terrace house out of a D. H. Lawrence novel, with a privy at the far end of the garden and cham- ber pots at night. "When did the queen reign over China?" her mother liked to joke, introducing her daughter to "the wonderful world of verbal transformations." Her grandmother, who loved to tell fairy tales, would pounce on and tickle her as the wolf in "Little Red Riding Hood," giving Angela a first clue to the possibilities of role-playing and self-reinvention.

At the end of the war they returned to the family home in Balham, South London, a "predictable," "seedily proper," unimaginative bit of nowhere on the wrong side of the Thames. Angela's Scottish father, Hugh Stalker, had come to London after serving in World War I and had taken a job as an editor on Fleet Street. Her mother, Olive Farthing, had been raised in South London, in rough, colorful, working-class Battersea, and had worked as a shopgirl before her marriage. When Hugh and Olive married in 1927 they chose Balham for its convenient Tube stop: Hugh worked the three-to-midnight shift and trains ran later on the Northern Line. Angela describes the Stalkers as living in their own world, on her father's hours. When she came home from school, she wrote, "the dream- time engulfed me, a perpetual Sunday afternoon in which you could never trust the clocks."

In an essay on her father Angela portrayed him as an eccentric who valued extravagant gestures in a banal world. She recalled him bringing home from Woolworth's a plastic parakeet, which he attached to an old gas fitting on the kitchen ceiling while her Shakespeare-loving mother watched and quoted sourly, "Age cannot wither nor custom stale your infinite variety."

Later, when she owned her own house in South London, she kept real birds and let them fly through the house, their vivid plumage harmonizing with the purple, yellow, and scarlet walls. They became a symbol to her of imaginative freedom, of sensual pleasure, of everything that Britain in general and Balham in particular had lacked in the hard, dry years after the war. Fleur Adcock wrote in her diary about going with Angela in the early 1970s to a North London pub where they sat outside on the grass "watching the flora and fauna—chestnut tree, children. Angela thought there should be birds, too, walking birds, toucans. 'Not only is your service lousy but there are no fucking toucans.'"

Angela's mother wanted more for her daughter than she had had herself, and expressed this in possessiveness about Angela's body and mind. Her brothers had gone to university and she was bright enough to have done more, but she had married instead, becoming one of the midcentury mothers that Lorna Sage called "women girlified, exiled and isolated in domesticity." On one hand, Olive encouraged Angela's precocity: "The fact that I had been scribbling away . . . since almost as soon as I could write, my mother regarded as a perfectly normal activity for a child." On the other, she was overprotective. Until Angela was well into her teens, she made her bathe with the door open, lest she slip in the tub and drown. She fussed about her clothes and her health, especially after Angela's brother Hugh left home to go to Oxford. She showed her love with chocolate and ice cream, and Angela was stigmatized at school for her size.

"I thought they wanted my blood," she later said of both her parents. "I didn't know what they wanted of me, nor did I know what I wanted for myself." At seventeen, when her mother was busy warning her against a male attention that she longed for and didn't have, Angela decided to lose weight. Much later, when the first books on anorexia were published, she recognized herself in the estrangement from one's body that is both the cause and the effect of extreme dieting. She became dangerously thin before she recovered, and since she took up smoking to keep the weight off, in a sense she never recovered from using her body as a battleground.

Still taller than average, she dressed to emphasize her difference and began wearing sexy, outrageous outfits that were part beatnik fashion, part parody of feminine style. She had rebelled against her mother by becoming conventionally attractive, but that meant exchanging one set of expectations about her body for another, and irony and theatricality were part of her attempt to make her body her own. She saw her clothes as "a more or less conscious form of social affront or visual insult," a hostile refusal of conformity that made a space where she could think about who she wanted to be. In her first novel, *Shadow Dance*, she took revenge on traditional standards of beauty by making the female central character into an image of impossible feminine prettiness, then turning her into a monster, then killing her off.

Rebelling in other ways, she became the kind of daughter who pauses Christmas dinner by exclaiming, "Oh good, here comes the fucking turkey." But as it had been for Doris, the biggest casualty in Angela's war with her mother, aside from their love for each other, was her education. Under new laws that broadened educational access, Angela, like Lorna, had gone on scholarship to an academically challenging girls' grammar school, and her teachers there had encouraged her to go to Oxford. Olive approved, but announced that if Angela got in she would move there too. In self-defense, Angela refused to apply.

Instead, with her father's help, she became a reporter for South London's *Croydon Advertiser*. In the newsroom her style, tall and elbowy, in black stockings and a floppy hat, was met with amused tolerance and she was allowed to write record reviews. One coworker said she dressed "like a cross between Quentin Crisp and the Wicked Witch of the West." When she met Paul Carter, her first husband, a year later, her style became both an escape from South London and a way to preserve her selfhood against the demands of marriage.

ANGELA AND PAUL found each other in a hole-in-the-wall record store where he worked weekends; he was a twenty-seven-year-old jazz and folk music fan who had a day job as an industrial chemist. In the summer of

1959 they spent their weekends exploring the city and discovering each other, "kissing for hours in the shop with the sun creeping through the venetian blinds." Angela described their groping sessions as having "a desperate quality, as if taking place at midnight, on a cliff, with thunder & lightning & the end of the world at hand." Her one disappointment was that Paul wouldn't actually sleep with her unless they got engaged.

Paul was quiet, even shyer than she, but his interests were an exciting change from Balham. They went to hear bands and see French films, and together they joined the three-day Aldermaston marches against nuclear arms, which were co-organized by Doris in her post-Communist years. The marches were linked to the folk music revival, which was Paul's passion. Later he recorded traditional singers and musicians and ran pub nights, with visiting musicians often sleeping on the Carters' floor.

At twenty, over her parents' objections, Angela married Paul. But almost as soon as they moved in together, Paul left or lost his day job. Resilience doesn't seem to have been among his gifts, and he sank into depression, while Angela supported them both with her paycheck from the *Advertiser*. She'd already started work on a novel; friends remembered seeing pages of it in her typewriter at the couple's apartment in Croydon. But Paul was too gloomy to encourage her writing, particularly when it interfered with her housekeeping. She alternated between concern for him and irritation, but female pity for the male ego won out and she spent most of the marriage trying to make him feel better. It was the same old discovery that wives have no more autonomy than daughters, other than their complicity in their own disappointment. It was, she said in her journal, "one of my typical burn-all-bridges-but-one acts; flight from a closed room into another one."

After Paul found work as a lecturer in chemistry at Bristol Technical College, Angela left her newspaper job and in the summer of 1961 the couple moved to Bristol. Around then she missed a period. It turned out to be a false alarm, the first of several "phantom pregnancies" she experienced over the years at times of stressful change—a move, a breakup, a finished novel. If, as she once wrote, menstruation is the uterine clock that strikes once a month, then a late period might be the body's resetting of the time.

If Paul had wanted children, Angela might have had them without thinking. But he didn't, and throughout their marriage Angela used contraception, with mixed feelings. She wanted children most at moments when she felt maternal and protective toward him, or unloved by him, at one point writing in her journal, "If only he would let me have babies. If only." At the same time, she thought young mothers were boring and resented the aura of social approval that surrounded them. At twenty-two she wrote disdainfully, "To have lots and lots of kids amidst roars of applause is really the ultimate in backing out of Laïfe, I suppose."

GETTING OUT OF South London—seeing herself in another context—helped Angela clarify her vocation as a writer. She started a journal when she moved to Bristol, the first of a series of notebooks combining excerpts from her voracious reading with close observations of people and places. Exploring Bristol, she noted the effects of mist and light in its steep streets and practiced describing its occupants, from tramps to a young man whose unformed face seemed "like barely congealed wax, as though pressure would leave a thumbprint." She wrote about her body, too, whether she had a cold or was making love to Paul with the light on. Along with places, bodies and bodily sensations—pleasures and aches, smells and effluvia, including those of pregnancy—were among her favorite subjects in her journal, as if there too she needed to explore and claim residency. She was gathering her material, exercising her gift for metaphor, learning to own her perspective.

In Bristol she ended up going to university after all. At first, having been rejected for reporting jobs by the local newspapers, she stayed home and wrote fiction. But she wasn't satisfied with her progress, and after she'd been in Bristol for several months her mother's brother, an archi-

tectural historian, came to visit, sized up the situation, and suggested she
apply to the University of Bristol.

For the next three years she read constantly and eclectically, studying
medieval literature—she wrote her thesis on its connections to folk music—
and finding inspiration in eighteenth-century satirists such as Pope and
Swift; twentieth-century writers such as Dinesen, Firbank, and the French
surrealists; and philosophy and literary criticism. Not surprisingly she had
an affinity with fantasists, dandies, performers, anyone who was willing to
rewrite the rules of belonging. She had what she later called "an element of
the male impersonator" in her early writing and often chose male points of
view. But fired by new possibilities, she started writing fiction again as soon
as she got her degree and at twenty-six published her first novel.

At a time when most Bristol students—and American ones, like Alice
Walker, just arrived at Spelman—wore neat skirts and sweaters, Angela
now began dressing in Goreyesque outfits featuring jeans, high-tops, and
a ratty, secondhand fur coat, her latest way of walking around in irony
quotes. She hennaed her hair, left her legs unshaven, and, when she lost
a front tooth, took her time getting it replaced. People who knew her
in Bristol remembered her "holding court" over pots of tea in a student
café, blowing cigarette smoke and talking politics and gossip, her cack-
ling laugh echoing across the room. Her way of talking was, as one friend
put it, "an odd mixture of hesitancy and point-blank self-assurance," of
awkwardness and confidence in her talents. In a short story she wrote a
few years later, the autobiographical character muses, "I was always rum-
maging in the dressing-up box of the heart for suitable appearances to
adopt. . . . That was the way I maintained my defenses for, at that time,
I always used to suffer a great deal if I let myself get too close to reality."

At home, though, she was mired in the realities of domestic life. The
Carters' apartment—two large rooms, plus a small one for Angela to work
in, in the Georgian neighborhood of Clifton—shared a bathroom with
the neighbors and had no hot water. For heating there was a coal fire,
which required hauling coal and taking out ashes, tasks Angela particu-

larly resented. Yet Paul expected her to do them, and complained when she was too caught up in writing to clean house. Like Audre, Angela made a point of taking up space, noting in her journal, "My lovely monster desk in position. He hates it because it is not baroque. Also he is angry because I have filled the dresser with books. Too bad. The books will stay."

Doris Lessing wrote of herself in her first marriage, "Women's instinct to please confuses men, but it confuses women too." Angela loved Paul, cared about him, and enjoyed making love to him (although later, after she'd had other lovers to compare with, she recalled in her journal that his "desire" had often been "in need of cosseting and attention"). She intuited only obscurely that she was growing out of her marriage. Paul reacted to her independence with what Angela called "massive infantile sulks," which she greeted with tears and (in the privacy of her notebook) annoyance. At one point the neighbors complained to Paul that Angela had left drips on the shared toilet seat. Angela thought it was unfair—female bodies drip—but his silence and shame made her wail, "I'm unhappy enough to die. I want to go home."

At this point in our story, we know where this marriage is going. It wasn't that Angela couldn't write and be married: during the nine years she lived with Paul, she got her degree and published four novels. Her powers of concentration were immense, she had her own room to work in, and her time was mostly her own. But the emotional labor she was putting into the relationship was not reciprocated. On the contrary: Paul suffered from her growing success. As she began to find friends in college, he fell into a severe depression. When her first book, *Shadow Dance*, appeared in 1966, he apparently sulked for weeks.

Angela felt that he had settled into a life that satisfied him, while she was still searching and growing. "Oh dear, why did I marry?" she wrote in her journal. "I want to move on. Not from Paul; with him, but he is not footloose like me." It dawned on her that she was complicit in their emotional inequality: "As I try & grow, as I submit myself to change, to help him, as I make allowances & act tenderly & do all the things a good wife should, my fucking understanding, my kind heart, so I am building a better & stronger cage for myself every day & in every way."

Despite her ambition and confidence in her writing, there's a streak of female masochism in the story of Angela's marriage. Her resentment of it came out in her fiction, in which family and femininity tended to meet violent ends. In the best of her early novels, the wonderfully strange *Magic Toyshop* (1967), she created a vision of a family as a patriarchal puppet show, with a mute mother and an angry father pulling the strings. Then she set her teenage heroine free by burning it all down.

It was in the hippie summer of 1968, Angela later wrote, that she first became conscious that her life had been shaped by social fictions about womanhood and class, and that they could be reshaped if she chose. A year later, she won the Somerset Maugham Prize, which came with money to be used for travel. At a time when kids in Britain were hitchhiking to India or sleeping in parks in Amsterdam, Angela had never left the British Isles. She decided to go around the world.

Getting ready for the trip, she copied into her journal for 1969 a quote from the Victorian explorer Isabella Bird: "Travelers are privileged to do the most improper things with perfect propriety."

IN THE FALL OF 1969 Angela was sitting in a coffee house in Tokyo, reading a book and observing the local scene. She had been in Japan for three weeks of a planned six-week stay and was enjoying the international atmosphere of the café, the Fugetsudo, where European backpackers came to write letters, rinse their underthings in the lavatories, and mix with Japanese hippies in bell-bottoms and tie-dyed tops. Later on, after she came to live in Tokyo, she met a "prim" businessman there in a crisp white shirt who handed her a note reading, "I am a masochist. Please make me your willing slave. Thanking you in advance for your kindness." It can be satisfying to look as singular as you feel, and here, in unfamiliar surroundings where her height and skin color marked her unmistakably as a foreigner, Angela felt at home.

On this particular day she was waiting for something to happen when a young Japanese man named Sozo Araki approached her table wearing, as she recalled it, "the great international seducer's smile." He told her he was twenty-four and had just dropped out of college to write fiction. After a while they went to a "love hotel" to spend the night. Their first try was awkward, but their sex the next morning was a revelation to Angela. By the time she left Tokyo, two weeks later, she had made up her mind to come back. She needed a plan to leave her marriage, and she was infatuated with Sozo, with Japan, and with the idea of herself as a person who would move halfway across the world for love.

It took her six months to get back to Tokyo. First she traveled home via Hong Kong and Thailand, breaking up by letter with Paul on the way. He was devastated—he hadn't seen it coming—and never got over what he saw as her abandonment of him. She longed to comfort him, and her pity made her ruthless: she refused to see him.

Angela's mother was furious, on the logic that having made a foolish marriage Angela ought to endure it. Then she collapsed with a pulmonary embolism and was rushed to the hospital. Angela went to see her, offering peace, but her mother turned her face to the wall. She died shortly afterward, at sixty-four. For a few months Angela stayed with her father in Balham, keeping him company and getting to know herself as a person without a mother. In any case, while she waited for her visa to Japan she had nowhere else to live. Self-pityingly, she wrote, "Home is where you go when nobody else will have you." But she was getting ready to step into the center of her own life. To a friend she reported that she'd made an "interesting Freudian slip" in a letter to Sozo. "I wrote: 'I feel I belong to you.' When I read it back, however, I realized I had, in fact, written: 'I feel I belong to me.'"

In April 1970 Angela finally flew to Tokyo, where she more or less fell straight into bed with Sozo. She wrote in her journal: "Sustained by passion only, we walk the tightrope of desire and acrobatically perform the double somersault of love without a safety net." The sexual pleasure she had with Sozo was intense, though she also wrote in her journal and her letters of him coming home drunk at five in the morning or with another woman's lipstick on his underpants. Hurt by his infidelity, she accepted it for the usual reasons: partly out of self-denial, partly because it gave her her independence. It gave her room to explore love as a stance, to play at love and also mean it, to put behind her the obligation to live a domestic female life.

With some difficulty Sozo and Angela found an apartment whose landlord was willing to rent to a foreigner. It was in a street of small wooden houses and little privacy: the walls were "so thin we can hear our neighbor belch and listen to his supper-time fish sizzling in the frying pan." They were an odd couple there, "living in a room furnished only by passion amongst homes of the most astounding respectability." The other residents viewed Angela in particular with suspicion, and she found it "a painful and enlightening experience to be regarded as a colored person."

Within her privilege, her foreignness helped her step out of English categories of class and femininity and reencounter herself. Outside of the disaffected, international hippie crowd that hung around Shinjuku, she could not even think of fitting in. Fascinated by the distancing effect of Sozo's racializing gaze, she described herself in orientalist terms: "I had never been so absolutely the mysterious other. I had become a kind of phoenix, a fabulous beast; I was an outlandish jewel. He found me, I think, inexpressibly exotic. But I often felt like a female impersonator." The small sizes of Japanese women's clothes made her feel "as gross as Glumdalclitch," but she was learning to embrace her physicality. She also took a close look at the male chauvinist aspects of Japanese culture, which, being new to her, were easier to see than the familiar sexism of her own. She read Foucault and Barthes and began to intuit that bodies aren't as natural as they seem, that "our flesh arrives to us out of history." She was finding her way to feminism, partly by seeing with new eyes the ambitions and appetites that had once seemed alien to her about herself.

At the end of her first year in Tokyo she and Sozo went to spend the winter in a house on the beach, where they both devoted themselves to writing and shared the housework, a partnership of equals that gave them their happiest months together. The greatest lesson that she learned from Sozo, though, came not during their relationship but at its unforeseen end. In April 1971 Angela went to England to do publicity for her fifth novel, *Love.* She returned in July, flying via Moscow to Khabarovsk, taking the Trans-Siberian Railway to Nakhodka, then embarking on a ferry for a two-day trip to Yokohama. Though she had written to say when she was coming, Sozo didn't meet her at the dock.

Angela caught the train to Tokyo but couldn't find him. Shattered, she wandered through the streets crying, suffering, but also embarrassed to see herself playing the role of abandoned woman. Describing the scene in a short story, "Flesh and the Mirror," she depicted herself not as romantic victim but as "my own heroine . . . walking through the city in the third person singular." She saw herself in a drama of tormented love like Smart's *By Grand Central Station*, believing that heartache was the price she had to pay for her life—until a young stranger fell in beside her and suggested that if she couldn't find her lover she might as well go to bed with him. In the story, she goes with him, has great sex beneath the mirrored ceiling of a hotel room, then looks at herself in the mirror and suddenly laughs, claiming pleasure and refusing self-sacrifice.

As painful as the loss of Sozo was, it showed her that she, not her lover, was the source of her feelings. She began to suspect that she had "created him solely in relation to myself, like a work of romantic art, an object corresponding to the ghost inside me." Rejecting the moral high ground of suffering, she set out to discover what she actually wanted, and what it meant for a woman to want. A few years later, in her revision of "Little Red Riding Hood," the girl would climb into bed with the wolf for a night of pleasure: "She knew she was nobody's meat."

She stayed in Japan on her own, feeling "a need to establish myself existentially . . . the way I should have done when I was 19," and within a few months, through an English friend, found a new relationship in which she took the initiative and the starring role. Mansu Kō was nineteen to her thirty-one and admitted to her that he suffered from "mental instability." But she loved his gentleness, and after he moved in with her and began keeping house, she wrote a friend that he had brought out something maternal in her—as well as, "equally obviously, a need to be in control." She also pointed out—truthfully, in that era—that if she were a man her age dating "a girl . . . as bright and freaky and pretty" as Kō, no one would disapprove.

This time she didn't mean for love to last. In January 1972, when she thought she was pregnant, she looked into getting an abortion—which hurt Kō's feelings—before realizing it was another false alarm. Not long afterward, with her visa running out, she decided to go back to England. She still had to work out the details, but she went home with some of the self-possession that later informed her writing, her relationship with Mark, and her sense that she could become a mother without losing herself.

WHEN ANGELA ACTUALLY ARRIVED back in England, however, she felt lost, alone, and overwhelmed by the prospect of rebuilding her career. She had gone to Japan an acclaimed writer, and two and a half years later she was broke and had lost her momentum. The surrealist novel she had written in Japan, *The Infernal Desire Machines of Doctor Hoffman*, had been her bid for serious literary status. It was published in the UK to warm reviews, but not only did it not reach a wide audience, it initially failed to find a US publisher, a financial disaster for Angela. She wrote a friend, "It really means I can no longer hope to make a living from writing. This is back at square one with a vengeance."

Living in a rented room at the North London home of the poet Fleur Adcock, who she'd met at a party, she got involved with an old friend from Bristol. He was a man she could talk to about writing, she said, "one of the few people I ever met who took fiction seriously, as a mode of truth." But he also had a violent temper, once throwing a typewriter in her direction in a fit of anger. To get away from him she went to stay with a gay friend in Bath, a post-hippie oasis of health foods and New Age bookstores that must have seemed like a safe place for another reinvention.

With help from her father she ended up buying a small house there where she lived alone, working on short stories and a new novel. At times she could barely afford the heating bill, let alone the "ravaging" stress of keeping up with the mortgage. To make money she wrote for magazines, turning out book reviews, travel pieces, and witty, sharp-eyed takes on culture and politics, developing a feeling for the zeitgeist that made her a sophisticated interpreter of her times.

Meanwhile the second wave of feminism was gathering momentum, and her situation as a self-supporting single woman combined with her disaffection with gender roles to make her a convert. In 1973, her first year in Bath, she wrote several articles for the new British feminist magazine *Spare Rib*. The first was on the British artist Evelyn Williams, whose grotesque wax dolls Angela said conveyed "the loneliness of the child, the loneliness of the mother, the loneliness of the mother-and-child as a self-enclosed unit."

Through *Spare Rib* editor Rosie Boycott she met Carmen Callil, then setting up the feminist publishing house Virago. She signed with a new agent, Deborah Rogers, who sold her unfinished novel to the editor Liz Calder at Gollancz; all these women became friends and allies. So did Lorna, who shared Angela's analytic genius and love of irreverent laughter. Angela's closest friends were often upwardly or internationally mobile and, like her, self-created and self-imagined. They included Adcock, who had grown up in New Zealand, Callil, who was Lebanese Australian, and her later writer friends Salman Rushdie, Kazuo Ishiguro, and Caryl Phillips. Her American friend Robert Coover had the impression that in general "she relished a certain outsiderness. She was pleased to feel that she had not been absorbed."

Her fiction up to that point had been confrontational, but also ironic and self-concealing. For the next several years she worked to put her thoughts on women and bodies into words, wrestling with feminism's demands on her muse. She'd written ironic critiques of sexist fantasies, but the next step, imagining alternatives, was harder. Still battling with the demon of selflessness, she wrote, "All the mythic versions of women, from the myth of the redeeming purity of the virgin to that of the healing, reconciling mother, are consolatory nonsenses . . . obscuring the real conditions of life."

She published a slim book of short stories, *Fireworks*, combining autobiographical narratives of her time in Japan with Gothic tales that foreshadowed the revelations of *The Bloody Chamber*. And she worked hard at her next novel, *The Passion of New Eve* (1977), a postapocalyptic satire on gender roles in which male and female are constructs that can be chosen or discarded. This book seems to have cleared a path for her: on the far side of it, she abandoned both the male impersonations of her earlier novels and her fear of female difference.

Starting with her next work of fiction, *The Bloody Chamber*, she drew on her sense that she and her generation were new women in the history of the world, with more power over their sexuality and fate. She rewrote fairy tales to draw out their latent sexual content—all those devouring wolves and erotic metamorphoses between human and beast—while making girls and women active, desiring heroines. In the title story she used the Bluebeard myth to emphasize the dangers of female innocence, then let the teenage wife be saved not by her brothers but by her mother, hair flying, pistol waving, riding to the rescue. In "The Tiger's Bride," the girl married to the predator discovers that she herself is more carnivore than lamb, in a sexual partnership in which "his appetite need not be my extinction."

For a while she and Fleur, comparing notes, were in agreement that living with a man was not worth the bother. Nonetheless, in the summer of 1974, after a one-night stand with a casual acquaintance ("the furry Welsh animal from over the road," she wrote in her journal), she discovered that for the first time she really was pregnant, at thirty-four. She had an abortion—legal in Great Britain since 1967—but was fascinated by the physical and emotional experience of pregnancy. She described in her journal a feeling of

> extraordinary solitude. . . . The magic of ambiguous states—I felt I was not my self, or myself; I felt estranged from myself but also enhanced. Against my will, I was slowed down. I felt myself in a state of dreamy slowness, it was like walking under water, an intense lethargy, and the focus of this lethargy was the thing in my belly, the thing—or being—so undeniably, even implacably there, that had lodged there so casually, like a blown seed. Hazard. Fecundated at hazard, I had become the instrument of nature, of processes now entirely beyond my control, that changed me into this passive container, my belly into a waiting room, things were happening inside me, under this thick, warm snow-fall of calm—which I didn't want, I was involuntarily tranquillized—immense amounts of secret activity were taking place. I felt most strange, I felt possessed. And sometimes I adored being pregnant, I loved my own slowness and the changes I could see in my body.

She was also alarmed by how "in need of protection" she felt, and wrote, "If all it takes is a fresh infusion of hormones in my metabolism to make me start inventing invisible companions, like a lonely child, then who am I? Isn't the identity fragile?"

Justly wary of the layers of sentiment and control around motherhood, she added, "It is always difficult to explore areas where so much mystification conceals a true mystery."

A FEW MONTHS LATER, as she put in long hours at her desk, a builder started working on the house opposite hers. Seeing her through the window, he was fascinated by her self-sufficiency and concentration. One day she came over to ask for his help with the plumbing. Soon she and Mark were sleeping together.

Earlier that year Angela had been back to Japan and had found Kō embittered and very much changed by their breakup two years before. Mark was the same age Kō had been, and she was cautious about getting too involved with him. When they made love for the second time, she wrote in her journal, she blurted out in a moment of tenderness that she loved him. "When I recovered myself, I said, 'I didn't mean to say that.' 'Why?' I hid my face a few times before I managed to say, 'Because it isn't true.'"

If it wasn't true then, it became so, though she downplayed the relationship to her friends, perhaps partly because Mark's creativity and originality didn't fit the standard intellectual mold. (Neither did hers, of course, which must have been part of their bond.) Fleur, who visited Angela in Bath several months later, observed only that Mark was painting her front door. "It never occurred to me that he was anything but just a helpful young neighbor, with perhaps a crush on her, which presumably he had." Angela's friend Christine Downton thought that Angela's evasiveness was her way of avoiding a sensitive subject. She had a "style of appearing slightly surprised and confused about life," Christine said, that was both part of her appetite for the dramatic and a kind of defense, "a flag for areas where you didn't want to go." In fact, she thought, Angela and Mark's relationship was a stable and satisfying one from the beginning.

The first test of their commitment came when Angela decided to move to London. Christine, a lecturer in economics at the University of Bath, had taken a new job in the capital and in 1976 the two women agreed to buy a house together. They found one in Clapham, not far from Balham in South London, and Angela took the upper and Christine the lower two floors. It needed work, which gave Angela an excuse to invite Mark to come with her. He began putting sweat equity into the Clapham house, while Angela, now with an even bigger mortgage, supported them both financially. In 1976 she took her first job in a creative writing program, one of several teaching gigs she would do over the years to make money for Mark and Alex, her "boys."

She had to make up her mind what Mark meant to her, or what she wanted him to mean. When she first met him and still thought they were just having a fling, she had quoted in her journal a friend's love advice: "One has to work out how long a relationship will do, whether for a night, or a week, for a year, or a lifetime."

Four years later, in Providence, she and Mark made their choice, and at forty-one Angela got pregnant. In March 1982, on a visit to Amsterdam, she mixed her notes on the city ("whiff of sour herring; solid, handsome, loose-jointed men") with another vivid description of the changes she felt: the nausea, the alterations to her body's shape and odor, her worry, her hope. "To travel hopefully is better than to arrive," she wrote. "Experience of pregnancy; the state is one of grace; but what happens, after?"

A month later she noted, "We did not arrive." In the midst of spring, with the lilacs coming out "mauve as genitalia," the pregnancy had ended at about twelve weeks. Ten days afterward she reported "recurrence of backache, nausea, odd gouts of black blood," then added, "[Mark] has never seemed more beautiful and beloved to me; I am breathless and as if shocked with love, appalled at the idea I might have lost him."

The next spring she was pregnant again. This time she took no notes, but the pregnancy held. Elliptical as ever, she told Fleur only that she was having minor health trouble. "'It's uterine,' she said. And I thought, oh, well, one of these menstrual problems, or something. I didn't like to ask. But what was in the uterus was a baby."

She didn't tell Christine Downton at all, until Christine, who by then had a house of her own, came by one day to see her friend. Angela opened the door a crack and "peeked round it, which was weird, not very Angela. And then she sort of crept out," leading with her enormous belly. "She was laughing and embarrassed, but also perfectly comfortable really with what she'd done." She was getting ready to start a family where she could star in all her swearing, exotic-bird-keeping glory.

For every mother celebrating her difference, there's an agent of the motherhood police ready to let her know she's out of line. When Angela was thirty-eight weeks pregnant, she had a particularly unpleasant run-in with an obstetrician acting as the border patrol. It was November 1983. Her novel *Nights at the Circus* was being readied for publication. *The Company of Wolves*, a film that she and director Neil Jordan had written together, was in production. She had just served as a judge for the Booker Prize. The day after the gala ceremony, suffering from high blood pressure, she had been admitted to South London Hospital for Women.

There she made the mistake of making a joke. Tired of saying "fine" when the doctor asked how she felt, she answered, "A bit apprehensive. Not so much about the birth itself as about the next twenty or thirty years."

With Angela "flat on [her] back, dress pulled up, knickers down, vulnerable, helpless, undignified," the doctor informed her that it was not too late to change her mind about the baby. "She pressed down on my belly so I couldn't move and said, 'Of course you've done absolutely the right thing by *not* having an abortion but now is the time to contemplate adoption and I urge you to think about it very seriously.'" She should discuss it with Mark, she advised, though, "I know he's only your common-law husband."

After she was gone Angela wept and raged. As if she and Mark weren't the most committed couple she knew; as if she hadn't spent half her life considering motherhood. "Each time I think about it, the adrenalin surges through my veins," she wrote Lorna from her bed in the maternity ward. "I want to *kill* this woman. . . . I want to rip out her insides." And she was in a situation of relative privilege, she observed. "If she delivers this kind of unsolicited advice to the white middle-class . . . then what manner of abuse does she feel free to dish out to the black proletariat?"

Adding injury to insult, the hospital gave her a case of puerperal fever, the bacterial infection from unwashed hands that had killed so many women in the past. She recovered, but felt like she'd endured a childbirth "more like that of a 19th century literary lady than that of a twentieth century one." A few weeks later she got her own back by writing about it, in a piece called "Notes from a Maternity Ward." By then she claimed to have a whole "post-partural hit-list" of people who made irritating assumptions about mothers and childbirth. ("Isn't one allowed a year's justifiable homicide after the event?") Welcome to the land of maternal rage, but Angela's entitlement to her negative feelings around the birth is one of the changes that came with feminism, which gave women like her permission to begin their motherhood by talking back.

AFTER THE YEARS of working her way up to it, Angela's motherhood seems almost an anticlimax in this story. Predictably, for someone who loved love, she fell hard for her baby, though she did her best to treat motherhood as yet another slightly ironic identity. All that came more easily to Angela, by then, than actually caring for something so tiny and fragile: Christine recalled that she seemed afraid of breaking her newborn son. She gave up breastfeeding fairly quickly, partly so that Mark could be more involved in Alex's care, and "bond with the baby" was a phrase that irritated her: "More like bondage," she snarked. Although she and Mark were infatuated parents who stood over Alex's crib watching him until he went to sleep, she was quick to get back to work: when Alex was three and a half months old they all went to Australia, where she spent two months as writer-in-residence at the University of Adelaide. While she wrote in an office on campus, Mark was a full-time dad, wheeling his son around the botanical garden before meeting Angela for lunch.

Later they settled into a routine in which Angela cooked, a cleaner helped with the housework, and Mark did most of the day-to-day care. (Angela had no patience for the notion that men who changed babies weren't sexy and claimed to "find *nothing* more erotic than the spectacle of a man up to his elbows in the sink.") She also relied on her maternal tribe:

some of her flustered behavior around tiny Alex may have been a way of getting more experienced friends, like Fleur and Lorna, to take over.

Her friends, in turn, enjoyed showing off their expertise, though Fleur was also struck by Angela's ability to put space between herself and the everyday business of child-raising. When Alex learned to speak late, a speech therapist told Angela she hadn't been talking to him enough. Reporting this, she added, "What do you *say* to babies?"

"Well, we all know what you say to a baby," Fleur observed. "You say, 'Come on now, time to get up, and put your foot in here, and here we go, and here's your dinner,' and blah blah blah. You just babble to them. And she obviously thought, babies are perfectly intelligent people, they don't need all this running commentary. She probably just didn't think of addressing him as a sort of inferior species, because as far as she was concerned he was an equal."

On an imaginative level, however, Angela seems to have had trouble putting her baby on the fire escape. She had always drawn in her fiction on her prevailing emotional states—anger, attraction, alienation—and had never been afraid to be dark or murderous. But maternal bliss was hard material for her to work with. Her friend Fay Weldon recalls Angela telling her that she'd started holding back. "It seemed so frightening; or she felt it was in some way damaging to the baby, to let your mind dwell on these things," Weldon thought. "I absolutely understood: it seemed bad luck." Her later fiction "didn't have that cold power which the early writing did."

Her friend Margaret Atwood said Angela had never discussed this with her, but that if she felt that way, at least temporarily, it wouldn't surprise her: "Most women feel like that right after they have babies." In some ways those years of Angela's career feel like a pause, a waiting to recollect herself. She had periods of depression, got restless in her partnership, and when she went into perimenopause in her mid-forties, with hot flashes and night waking, recorded in her journal feelings of "intense miserable isolation, of unlovedness, of quite blinding self-pity." Her notes on bodily states suggest a new sense of monstrousness as she perceived the signs of age. In 1988 she ended a notebook by calling it "a journal of my off-color years." Maybe, like Audre, she had worked so hard to become who she was that she felt restless, limited, trapped in the beautiful palace of herself.

Her journalism remained barbed and politically astute. She stood with her friend Salman Rushdie when religious fundamentalists threatened his life, along with Sontag, who defended him in New York, and Lessing, who helpfully let him know that she was on his side even though she didn't like the book. At the start of the first Gulf War in 1991, she left a three-minute message on her friend Susannah Clapp's answering machine consisting entirely of swearing. Atwood said she had the air of a "fairy godmother," but Sage called her "a wolf in Granny's clothing to the end."

There might have been more transformations to come, but Angela ran out of time. Before she became pregnant with Alex she had smoked heavily, so much so that one housemate recalled wisps escaping from the keyhole of her room while she was writing. In childhood she had breathed the polluted air of industrial Yorkshire and the last of the deadly London fogs. She developed a cough in September 1990 and a few months later was diagnosed with lung cancer. She died in February 1992, leaving behind her husband—they'd married at the end, to make sure Mark had parental rights—and seven-year-old son.

Her last novel was *Wise Children*, published the year before her death. It is a fantastic, theatrical comedy of Shakespearean twins, fathers who don't recognize their children, and an othermother, Grandma Chance, who takes in foundlings and puts together a joyous chosen family. "Mother is as mother does" is the family motto: it's not about bodies, biology, or social convention, but about showing up for the job.

During the no-holds-barred birthday party that ends the novel, Nora Chance pairs up with an old love who then gives her, along with her twin sister Dora, a miraculous gift: a pair of twins of their own to raise. The Chance sisters have just turned seventy-five, but never mind: as they leave the party, they make plans to live at least another twenty years to do a proper job of their late motherhood.

The work of care alters time, linking humans to the past and future, tying us to the present, insisting on simultaneity, allowing moments of selfhood, committing us to nostalgia and futurity. Carter's novel closes as Nora Chance, heading off to the all-night chemists' to buy bottles and formula for her new beginning, concludes: "Truthfully, these glorious pauses do, sometimes, occur in the discordant but complementary narratives of our lives and if you choose to stop the story there, at such a pause, and refuse to take it any further, then you can call it a happy ending."

Time and the Story

F IND A SUPPORTIVE PARTNER. Do it on your own. Have children, then build a career. Build a career, then have children. Have money. Live on public assistance. Have one child, or three, or seven. Write behind a closed door; paint in the living room; work with your baby on the desk next to you.

To the question "How can I have children without sacrificing my vocation, my perspective, my independence, my mind?" there's no single answer. On the evidence of the women in this book, a certain amount of "outlaw mothering" is helpful, as well as friends to do it with.

There were two things, though, that the women in this book absolutely had to have. One of them, of course, was time. They needed hours to work; a fair division of days; a way to game capitalism's cruel time-money equations. They lived for moments of insight; learned from moments of undoing; watched the clock that holds maternity and creativity in a productive tension.

Maternal time is the time of Alice Neel's and Angela Carter's "late" motherhood. It is Le Guin's simultaneous existences as writer and mother, Byatt's present continuous of grief, Lorde's future tense of change. It is the exploitive time poverty that kept Alice Walker's mother from her children and her garden. The temporal undertow of a stalled career. The sped-up hours of amphetamines. The unraveling time of children leaving home.

It is Barbara Hepworth's half an hour a day, "so that the images grow in one's mind." It is Lorde's scraps of poetry in her diaper bag and di Prima's "curtain of days" parting to reveal a moment for oneself. It is Penelope Fitzgerald's patience and Alice Neel's persistence. It's the time that the Art Project gave Neel and the year that a Guggenheim grant gave Walker, so she could get to know the characters in *The Color Purple*. It's Toni Morrison, getting up to write before her children woke, and Le Guin, who didn't bother, because her children always woke up too. It is Hettie Jones, her emotions too tangled to write, quoting the poet Marina Tsvetaeva: "It's precisely for feeling that one needs time, and not for thought."

THE SECOND THING a creative mother must have, along with time, is self. She requires boundaries and the conviction that she has the right to make her art. She needs not to give away too many pieces of her being.

The writer Claire Dederer, playing devil's advocate, calls creative work a series of "small selfishnesses. The selfishness of shutting the door against your family. . . . The selfishness of forgetting the real world to create a new one. . . . The selfishness of saving the best of yourself for that blank-faced anonymous paramour, the reader. The selfishness that comes from simply saying what you have to say."

What she's describing, though, is moments of self and other held in suspension, the times when the baby is on the fire escape.

For a while, one shape I gave in my mind to the maternal self came from Hepworth's art, especially a series of small stone sculptures she titled *Two Forms*. One of them, made in 1937, the year her triplets turned three, consists of two upright pieces of white marble, one slightly larger than the other. Perfectly smooth, pristinely self-contained, these forms stand next to each other and do not touch. They seem filled with a human longing to be intimate with another person and still be enclosed in a cool, rounded solitude.

I thought of each form as containing a necessary emptiness, the "void" that Adrienne Rich called "the creatrix, the matrix" of art. Le Guin pictured that space as potential, a container that could hold truth the way a pot carries water. Some of Hepworth's most beautiful sculptures are rounded, hollow shapes strung with taut wires, which also seem to me maternal, speaking of intense emotionality, intense control, and an almost unbearable availability, despite all other loves, to one's art.

On the way to the Hepworth show, my friend Nynke talked about not reading her mother's diaries, although they are all of her she has left. "I think my mother always kept a part of herself private. The diaries were for the part of her that didn't belong to us."

At other times I thought of mothering as so broad, so full of different experiences, that it seemed not self-contained but like a container full of stories. In her essay "The Carrier Bag Theory of Fiction," Le Guin writes that the archetypal hero is Man the Hunter, following the "narrative arc" like an arrow toward its goal. This is the story of creative lives: learning one's craft, overcoming obstacles, try, fail, succeed, all taking place in the time of fate and change that the Greeks called *kairos*, the time of the arrow's flight.

Left out of this narrative is Person the Gatherer, who finds useful bits and employs that much more ancient invention, the bag or net, to bring them home. The carrier bag might be the shape of a maternal story, happening in *chronos*, chronic time, the time that breeds unconnected musings—about bodies, and sex, and selves, and time itself. As I went along gathering anecdotes, observations, everything useful that caught my eye, I tried to make this book into a bag of maternal thought and experience, joy and suffering, self-loss and self-making.

In the end, though, I think neither the sculpted self nor the big sack of stuff is quite right. Even mother stories need *kairos*, need movement, need a heroine.

When I first started thinking about motherhood as a hero's journey, I wondered if anyone had written mothers as heroines—as people navigating the odyssey (or fighting the wars) of their own lives, mothering in the fateful time of growth and change.

Then I realized I knew some very old stories with mothers at the center. I had thought they were stories about adolescence and marriage until I looked again at the second part, the one that follows "happily ever after."

Here's one of them:

> *Given an impossible task to complete, the miller's daughter makes a bargain, saves her own life, and marries the king. But in her husband's castle, she'll need to be strong not to lose herself. A year after the wedding, the little man who helped her comes back demanding his payment: her firstborn. Resourceful, she goes into the woods, learns his name, and uses her knowledge to claim her child and her motherhood.*

The miller's daughter in "Rumpelstiltskin" is Neel, Lessing, Sontag, women who made straw marriages imagining they were gold, and who had children before they were strong enough to possess both their child and their vocation. They first had to leave home and gain more understanding—of the world, themselves, the shadow side of their marriage bargain. For Neel and Lessing, self-possession came too late for them to reclaim their firstborn children.

The girl escapes from her wicked stepmother, overcomes obstacles, and marries the king. But after she gives birth to a child the stepmother, disguised as a nurse, comes to the palace and murders her, putting her one-eyed stepsister in her place. As a ghost the young mother wanders the castle, nursing her baby at night, until the king sees her and recognizes her. When he names her as the true queen, she returns to life.

The girl in "Brother and Sister" is Elizabeth Smart and Shirley Jackson, undermined by their mothers, and Sontag and Walker, unrecognized by mothers who were themselves undermined. (Ellen Steiber, in an excellent essay, reads the stepsister as a figure for internalized childhood trauma, the "half-blind impostor self" that takes the real self's place in the world.) These women looked for partners to recognize them and help them not to lose themselves in motherhood, but as Walker and Angela Carter learned, to come back from that spectral state you have to recognize yourself.

The girl's father has cut off her hands. (A pact with the devil, incest: the reason varies with the telling.) She leaves home and wanders in the forest until she finds her way into the royal orchard. There the prince finds her eating fruit off the ground like a wild animal. Recognizing her beauty, he marries her, and she has a baby.

Then her husband goes on a journey and his family is tricked into sending her away. With the infant tied to her back, the woman with no arms returns to the forest. This time as she finds her way her hands regrow. In some versions an angel restores them; in others, her baby falls into the water and they appear when she reaches in to catch it. When her husband, after a long search, finds her and brings her home, she has come into her motherhood and her power.

"The Armless Maiden" is a story for every mother-writer or mother-artist. At some point each woman in this book got lost in the woods and had to learn to reclaim her potential, whether it was by caring for a child or welcoming her muse. The Armless Maiden's child can symbolize a woman's creativity, Midori Snyder writes: the talent she learns to use, the vocation she accepts. But it seems to me it can stand for both that and her mothering, which she learns to do without losing herself. The mother's retreat into the forest is one that can be repeated again and again, whenever she is in crisis, needs artistic inspiration, or wishes to recollect herself. It is the mother-hero's journey of gaining agency, authority, and selfhood—and then regaining it, each time she comes out of the woods with her child on her back and her life in her hands.

THIS BOOK TOOK too much time. I started thinking about it when my children were in elementary school, and as I finish they are both in college, living in and out of the house as their plans change or are changed by the long, slow pandemic time. They don't outgrow their clothes anymore, though their bodies' temporal progress still shows in a vertical clock of pencil marks on our kitchen wall.

Recently my daughter asked, "How long were you in labor with me?" I didn't know how to answer. Twelve hours? Eleven hours of waiting, plus one hour when temporality broke along with my water and everything happened at once? Why is labor measured in hours and not, say, chapters in a narrative? Should I tell her about the cliffhanger when, overwhelmed, I put my knees together and refused to go on with it?

I don't believe in giving birth as a metaphor for writing books. I refuse to think that the two are equivalent, even though I did swear at my husband in a fit of stress the night before I turned my manuscript in, the same way I yelled when labor ran me over. Still, it feels right to end on a beginning; and after all, they did both happen in my life, baby and book, both well past their due date, over my last-minute doubts, this book coming now to a close and my daughter born on a rainy Tuesday afternoon as the midwife called gently to her father, "Come here, it's time."

Acknowledgments

This book is a collective work, enriched by all the thought and creativity of this vital and fascinating conversation around mothering. I think everyone who tries to shift the motherhood discussion discovers how much that thing weighs and ends up moving it about two inches. My hope is that the experience and wisdom gathered here will give you heart in your own heavy lifting sessions with parenting and your muse.

During the long work of writing, I've been lucky to have a community of friends—mothers and others—who gave me advice, told me stories, read drafts, let me bend their ears, and helped keep me going. I'm grateful to Nynke Hendriks, Manjit Kaur, Liva Luyat, Carol Cooper, Margaret Sundell, Ann Maher, Rachelle Meyer, Elaine Showalter, Lynn Chandhok, Carrol Clarkson, Eloe Kingma, Eileen Gunn, L. Timmel Duchamp, Sally Eckhoff, Jann Ruyters, Leonie Breebaart, Nina Siegal, Amal Chatterjee, and Patricia Paludanus.

For space to write, thank you to Sonia Sin, Ellen Kushner and Delia Sherman, and Anton and Jantine Oskamp of the Writersblockhut. For opening their house in Portland to me so many times, Ingrid and Dick Spies.

Thank you to Hedgebrook for a transformative writers' retreat on the cusp of a pandemic, and to my Hedgebrook sisters for their ongoing encouragement and wisdom: Heidi Durrow, Roja Heydarpour, Jael Humphrey, Wendy Johnson, Michelle Ruiz Keil, Elizabeth de Souza, and Diana Xin. My deepest gratitude to the Whiting Foundation for the grant that allowed me to finish this book.

Thanks to my fellow biographers Benjamin Moser and Evelyn C. White for their help and friendship.

The staff at Atria, Amsterdam's feminist archive, provided many, many books. Aaliyah Hudson contributed her sharp eye. Janneke Patberg and David Bisschop Boele gave wise advice. Andrew Solomon kindly sent me his thesis. Jane O'Reilly told me the story about the children breathing under the door.

My beloved agent, Melissa Flashman, helped come up with the idea for this book after I said, "I want to do a book about women writers who leave their children but that would be too depressing." My invaluable editor, Jill Bialosky, believed in it from the start, and the tireless Drew Elizabeth Weitman kept me on deadline.

For support, research help, and for giving me the great good fortune to be a mother-writer, I'm deeply grateful to my husband, Jan van Houten, and Eise and Jooske, our children.

Notes

THE MIND-BABY PROBLEM

1 **"The maternal subject":** Lisa Baraitser, "Communality across Time: Responding to Encounters with *Maternal Encounters: The Ethics of Interruption*," *Studies in Gender and Sexuality* 13, no. 2 (2012): 117, https://doi.org/10.1080/15240657.2012.682932.

1 **"I insist":** Ruhl, "'Little Labors,' by Rivka Galchen," *New York Times Book Review*, May 15, 2016.

1 **"creative work":** Mary Oliver, "On Power and Time," in *Upstream: Selected Essays* (New York: Penguin Press, 2016), epub.

2 **"It takes":** Stein, quoted in Showalter, *A Jury of Her Peers*, 251.

2 **"the discontinuity":** Rich, "When We Dead Awaken: Writing as Re-Vision" (1971), in *On Lies, Secrets, and Silence*, 43.

2 **"the lonely sucking":** Walker, "*One* Child of One's Own," 381.

2 **"sacrifice all":** quoted in Tillie Olsen, *Silences* (New York: Delta, 1979), 30.

2 **"In the twenty years":** Ibid., 19.

2 **"The obligation to be":** Susan Sontag, *Alice in Bed* (New York: Farrar, Straus & Giroux, 1993), 113.

3 **"I had always":** Neel, in *Alice Neel*, directed by Andrew Neel, 2007.

3 **"not because":** Mary Catherine Bateson, *Composing a Life* (New York: Atlantic Monthly Press, 1989), 168.

3 **"The love you feel":** Megan O'Grady, "Scenes from a Marriage: Jenny Offill on Modern Motherhood," *Vogue*, January 28, 2014.

3 **"part-time, part-self":** Olsen, *Silences*, 19.

4 **"intractable problem":** Baraitser, "Book Review: The Theorist's Mother," *Feminist Review* 108, no. 1 (2014): e10, https://doi.org/10.1057/fr.2014.25.

5 **"Both essentialism":** Baraitser, *Maternal Encounters*, 93. In *Feminism, Psychoanalysis, and Maternal Subjectivity* (New York: Routledge, 2012), Alison Stone argues that maternal subjectivity originates in the body and in a mother's physical relationship with her own mother. "This subject-position rests on the mother's placing herself back within the maternal body relations of her past, so that she strives to integrate these relations into narrative and make them meaningful" (147). I found this too narrow and too stuck in the child's point of view to account for maternal creativity.

5 **"has taken up":** quoted in Philip Rieff, *Freud: The Mind of the Moralist* (New York: Anchor, 1961), 192. Rieff or Sontag has no patience for this, adding that Freud's "concession that 'an individual woman may be a human being apart from [her sexual function]' speaks for itself."

5   **"the interests of"**: quoted in Solomon, *Transition to Motherhood*, 6.

6   **"the impossible subject"**: Baraitser, *Maternal Encounters*, 4. For a useful discussion of the limitations of psychoanalysis in thinking about maternal discourse, see Hirsch, *The Mother-Daughter Plot*, 167–76. Winnicott does restore to mothers the possibility of an inner life beyond their motherhood, but really that's no more than conceding that they're human.

6   **"quarantining of"**: Nelson, *Argonauts*, 52.

6   **"He is born"**: Ibid., 45.

6   **"the experience . . . view"**: Ruhl, *100 Essays I Don't Have Time to Write*, 154–55.

6   **"the experience of"**: Cusk, *A Life's Work*, 3.

7   **"Is it possible"**: Manguso, *Ongoingness*, Scribd.

7   **"escape from"**: Kristeva, "Stabat Mater," 145.

7   **"a catastrophe . . . body"**: Kristeva, "Stabat Mater," 134. Baraitser observes that the critic Jacqueline Rose, commenting on Kristeva's essay, "describes the catastrophe as the simple fact that there is an unconscious, that is, there is a limit to knowledge, and that the name that we give this limit is the mother." To think about mothers is "to do violence then to what remains resistant to knowledge." Baraitser, *Maternal Encounters*, 5.

7   **"a nobody"**: Le Guin, "Earthsea Revisioned" (1992), in *The Books of Earthsea: The Complete Illustrated Edition* (New York: Saga Press, 2018), 987.

8   **"live and work . . . self-erasure"**: Erdrich, *The Blue Jay's Dance*, 4.

8   **"split in two"**: Cusk, *A Life's Work*, 56.

8   **"like a bomb"**: O'Grady, "Scenes from a Marriage."

8   **"call my soul"**: Brooks, quoted in Jackson, *A Surprised Queenhood in the New Black Sun*, 69.

8   **"the constant attack"**: Baraitser, *Maternal Encounters*, 15.

8   **"budge up"**: Ibid., 49.

8   **"felt chained to . . . subject"**: Ibid., 154.

9   **"stuff . . . navigation"**: Ibid., 157.

9   **"capture this new"**: O'Grady, "Scenes from a Marriage."

9   **"an assemblage"**: Manguso, *Ongoingness*, Scribd.

9   **"There was a time"**: Ruhl, *100 Essays*, 4.

10   **"There must be"**: Rich, "When We Dead Awaken."

11   **"great systole"**: Ruhl, *100 Essays*, 153.

11   **"little sips of selfhood"**: @NatashaRandall, Twitter, May 24, 2021, https://www.twitter .com/NatashaRandall/status/1396767423441907717.

11   **childless friend . . . rug**: correspondence of Le Guin and James Tiptree Jr. (Alice Sheldon), Tiptree and Le Guin Papers, both University of Oregon Special Collections and University Archives.

12   **"found a place before"**: Enright, *Making Babies*, 47.

13   **"If we merely"**: McClain, "As a Black Mother, My Parenting Is Always Political," *Nation*, April 15, 2019.

13   **"the illusory solution"**: Jill Johnston, *Lesbian Nation* (New York: Touchstone, 1974), 70. Johnston continues, "To tell the truth I just picked the first handsome intelligent sounding male that came along after I knew there was nothing else to do. . . . Four years and two kids later I might as well've made a cross atlantic solo flight in a balloon for all my marriage meant as a solution to anything whatever."

13   **"I had no idea"**: Rich, *Of Woman Born*, 5.

13   **"the most liberating"**: Bill Moyers, "A Conversation with Toni Morrison," 1989, in Danille

Taylor-Guthrie, ed., *Conversations with Toni Morrison* (Jackson: University Press of Mississippi, 1994), 270–71.

13 **"The radical"**: Gumbs, "m/other ourselves," in Gumbs et al., *Revolutionary Mothering*, 21.

14 **"A brown mother's"**: Eriksen, "My Son Runs in Riots," in Gumbs et al., *Revolutionary Mothering*, 79.

14 **"I was somebody's"**: Gloria Naylor, "A Conversation: Gloria Naylor and Toni Morrison" (1985), in Taylor-Guthrie, *Conversations with Toni Morrison*, 198.

14 **"Babies demand"**: Enright, *Making Babies*, 177–78.

15 **"must often hold"**: Erdrich, *The Blue Jay's Dance*, 143.

15 **"was always . . . paint"**: Nemser, *Art Talk*, 125.

15 **"the pit of"**: Ellen Willis, "Coming Down Again" (1989), in *No More Nice Girls: Countercultural Essays* (Middletown, CT: Wesleyan University Press, 1992), 256.

16 **"overwhelming, unacceptable"**: Rich, *Of Woman Born*, 224.

16 **"being face-to-face"**: Lamott, *Operating Instructions* (New York: Ballantine, 1993), 37.

16 **"Motherhood is"**: Solomon, *Transition to Motherhood*, 53.

16 **"It is to moments"**: Baraitser, *Maternal Encounters*, 3.

17 **"unique and unrepeatable"**: Cavarero, *Relating Narratives*, 71.

18 **"The notion of"**: Carter, *The Sadeian Woman*, 12.

18 **"On the subject"**: Rich, "Motherhood: The Contemporary Emergency and the Quantum Leap" (1978), in *On Lies, Secrets, and Silence*, 259.

18 **"The institution"**: Rich, *Of Woman Born*, 223.

18 **"Mothering and"**: Ibid., 257.

18 **"Any woman . . . place to be"**: Fowler, "The Motherhood Statement," 28.

18 **"the fantasy"**: Parker, *Mother Love, Mother Hate: The Power of Maternal Ambivalence*, 30.

18 **"It's because"**: Ellen Willis, "Feminism's Big Idea," *Women's Review of Books* 24, no. 2 (March–April 2007): 4.

18 **"pathological"**: Jennifer C. Nash, "The Political Life of Black Motherhood," *Feminist Studies* 44, no. 3 (2018): 701. Gumbs comments that white supremacy "targets poor and racialized mothers as the pathological cause of the very poverty and racism they experience and frames them as scapegoats for a global scarcity which justifies the expendability of Black life." Gumbs, *"We Can Learn to Mother Ourselves,"* 186, https://dukespace.lib.duke.edu/dspace/handle/10161/2398

19 **"I believe she"**: Barbara Weekley Barr, quoted in Janet Byrne, *A Genius for Living: A Biography of Frieda Lawrence* (New York: Bloomsbury, 1995), 393.

19 **"I wrote a list"**: Morrison to Kim Echlin, in Echlin, *Elizabeth Smart: A Fugue Essay on Women and Creativity*, 206.

19 **"listen to"**: White, *Alice Walker*, 372.

"THE PRESIDING GENIUS OF HER OWN BODY"

21 **"I simply could not"**: Carter, "Notes from the Front Line" (1983), in *Shaking a Leg*, 40.

21 **"We need to imagine"**: Rich, *Of Woman Born*, 292.

22 **expelled from university**: This happened to the literary critic William Empson, who not only lost his fellowship at Cambridge but was banished from the city.

22 **"utterly important"**: Mitchison, *You May Well Ask*, 70.

22 **"The orgasm focuses"**: Sontag, *Reborn*, 218, 11/19/59. More recently, the artist Cecily Brown has said of experiencing herself as a painter, "Desire itself was my driving force. Desire drives

painting too. Sex was the closest thing to painting in the real world." Rachel Cusk, "Can a Woman Who Is an Artist Ever Just Be an Artist?," *New York Times*, November 7, 2019.

23   **"She took out":** Lessing, *Under My Skin*, 249.

23   **"two-dimensional":** Sullivan, *By Heart*, 217.

24   **letter, countersigned:** Rich, *Of Woman Born*, 10.

24   **"Now that you're . . . eat it":** Sage, *Bad Blood*, 270.

24   **"What do you want":** Le Guin, interview with JP, April 2010.

24   **"six months after":** Weldon, *Mantrapped* (New York: Grove Press, 2004), 137.

24   **"In the beginning":** Hills, *Alice Neel*, 21.

ALICE NEEL

Indispensable sources for this chapter were Phoebe Hoban's biography *Alice Neel: The Art of Not Sitting Pretty* and Patricia Hills's *Alice Neel*. Ginny Neel generously contributed her memories of Alice; unless otherwise noted, her quotes come from our conversations. Alix Kates Shulman spoke to me about Alice's involvement with feminism. Details on the Federal Art Project come from Jed Perl, *New Art City: Manhattan at Mid-Century* (New York: Vintage, 2007). Background on the Village comes from Ross Wetzsteon's excellent *Republic of Dreams: Greenwich Village: The American Bohemia, 1910–1960* (New York: Simon & Schuster, 2002).

27   **"Be nobody's darling":** Walker, "Be Nobody's Darling," in *Her Blue Body Everything We Know*, 193.

27   **"You have to have":** Billops, in Lynda Jones, "Dream On, Dreamer," *Village Voice*, September 6, 1994. Quoted in Terri Francis, "Thinking through Camille Billops," Another Gaze, October 4, 2019.

27   **"eyes underneath":** Enid Nemy, "On a Night for Artists, Glitter Bows to Talent," *New York Times*, December 9, 1977.

27   **"auntie-hero":** Jerry Saltz, "Where Are All the Women?," *New York*, November 5, 2007.

28   **"I wondered how":** Hills, *Alice Neel*, 23.

28   **"in a polka-dot":** Sally Eckhoff, *F*ck Art (Let's Dance)* (New York: Water Street Press, 2013), 71.

29   **"How in the":** Ibid., 251.

29   **"really wasn't":** Hoban, *Alice Neel*, 15.

29   **"Other people":** Munro, *Originals*, 121.

29   **"She was so superior":** Hoban, *Alice Neel*, 15, from Munro interview transcript.

29   **"The minute I sat":** Hills, *Alice Neel*, 11.

29   **"was my only real life":** Hoban, *Alice Neel*, 13.

29   **"It was utterly beautiful":** Hills, *Alice Neel*, 12.

30   **"I didn't see life":** Ibid., 13.

30   **"Paint what you feel":** Hoban, *Alice Neel*, 24.

30   **"He used to give":** Ibid., 28. Women artists could be very cynical about their financial dependence on men. To biographer Laurie Lisle, Alice told a story about running into the sculptor Louise Nevelson one day in the 1930s. Nevelson was separated from her husband, and like Alice she was employed by the Federal Art Project. She had accepted a gift of clothes from a man, and when Alice asked how she managed to dress so well, she answered, "Fucking, dear, fucking." Lisle, *Louise Nevelson* (New York: Washington Square, 1990), 126.

31   **"the most repressed":** Hills, *Alice Neel*, 17.

31   **"Well I couldn't help it":** Hoban, *Alice Neel*, 38.

31   **"100 percent against":** Hills, *Alice Neel*, 21.

32   **"eight hours of agony":** Munro, *Originals*, 125.

32   **"After Santillana's death":** Hills, *Alice Neel*, 21.

33   **"Into it went":** Munro, *Originals*, 125.

33   **"consumed by . . . anything":** Hoban, *Alice Neel*, 65.

33   **"I lay in bed":** Ibid., 65.

33   **"My house is beside":** Ibid., 68.

34   **Having heard . . . fabrication:** Ginny Neel, interview with JP, October 2021. See Hoban, *Alice Neel*, 72.

34   **"I always . . . paint":** Hills, *Alice Neel*, 29.

35   **"The nights . . . life":** Hoban, *Alice Neel*, 71.

35   **"bohemian life":** Munro, *Originals*, 125.

35   **"now is the great":** Hills, *Alice Neel*, 41.

36   **"I'm not sure . . . systems":** Nemser, *Art Talk*, 123.

36   **"hypersensitivity . . . about you":** Nemser, *Art Talk*, 117.

37   **"Orphans":** Anatole Broyard, "Growing Up Irrational," *New York Times*, April 19, 1979, quoted in Henry Louis Gates Jr., "White Like Me," *New Yorker*, June 17, 1996.

37   **"Needle in":** Nancy Milford, *Savage Beauty: The Life of Edna St. Vincent Millay* (New York: Random House, 2002), 163.

38   **"She showed":** Eckhoff, *F*ck Art*, 71.

38   **"revolutionary paintings":** Hills, *Alice Neel*, 53.

39   **Alice was paid:** Hoban, *Alice Neel*, 106–7. According to the US Bureau of Labor Statistics, the median income for a family in New York City was $1,700 a year during the Depression. "100 Years of U.S. Consumer Spending," Report 991, May 2006, https://stats.bls.gov/opub/uscs/1934-36.pdf.

39   **Alice knew how easy:** In March 1933, Alice's work was singled out for praise at a group show in Philadelphia along with that of Elsie Driggs, another painter at the start of a promising career. A little later, Driggs married a fellow artist and had a daughter. She devoted herself to his career and for three decades barely showed her own work.

40   **"a rat who":** Hoban, *Alice Neel*, 136.

42   **"Dear mother":** Ibid., 356.

42   **"outlaws":** Rich, *Of Woman Born*, 193.

43   **"If you decide":** Nemser, *Art Talk*, 125.

43   **"worked out":** Hoban, *Alice Neel*, 227–28.

43   **turkey in the sink:** When the Museum of Modern Art published an *Artists' Cookbook* in 1977, Alice contributed her stuffing recipe.

44   **"If she . . . nothing":** Hartley Neel, in *Alice Neel*, directed by Andrew Neel, 2007.

44   **"Every single one":** Hoban, *Alice Neel*, 167.

44   **interest and empathy:** In *The Black Boys* (1967), for example, Alice painted two brothers, Jeff and Toby Neal, as preteens both responding to her observing eye and waiting for their lives to begin. Seeing the painting again years later, Jeff Neal observed that she was "looking at two ghetto children from uptown and bringing out the beauty in us." John Leland, "Two Brothers Posed for a Portrait. One Lived to See It in the Met," *New York Times*, April 2, 2021.

45   **"like an untenanted":** Hills, Alice Neel, 152.

45 **Hartley recalled:** Ginny Neel, interview with JP, June 2021.

45 **"He would terrorize":** Hoban, *Alice Neel*, 166.

45 **"Of course . . . understood":** Ibid., 248.

45 **"If things were . . . plenty of it":** Ibid., 208.

46 **"She enjoyed":** Ibid.

46 **"Out of the chaos":** Ibid., 162.

47 **"It was just":** Ibid., 315.

47 **stayed committed to portraiture:** It might also be that realism gave Neel structure and solidity in her work, while the extreme freedom of abstract expressionism, on the evidence, was hard on those who practiced it. Among abstract expressionists, the incidence of alcoholism (Pollock, Willem and Elaine de Kooning, Franz Kline, Joan Mitchell) and depression (Mitchell, Mark Rothko, Arshile Gorky) seems to have been high even by painters' standards.

48 **"She said":** Hoban, *Alice Neel*, 225. One of the FBI's sources, Hoban writes, was a person "they believed was either her sister or sister-in-law."

48 **"I hate like . . . 'Sam'":** Ibid., 220.

48 **"I doubt":** Munro, *Originals*, 121.

48 **"At first":** Hoban, *Alice Neel*, 221.

49 **"became famous":** Ginny Neel, in *Alice Neel*, directed by Andrew Neel, 2007.

50 **"wide-eyed":** Carter, in Lorna Sage, "The Savage Sideshow," *New Review*, July 1977, 54.

50 **stood by to light:** Nunez, *Sempre Susan*, 104.

50 **"I try to . . . paint":** Hoban, *Alice Neel*, 391.

51 **"We were both":** Ibid., 283.

51 **"respect you":** Ibid., 282.

52 **"grisly prenatal odalisque":** Ibid., 284.

53 **"I feel":** Hills, *Alice Neel*, 162.

53 **"observed that":** Hoban, *Alice Neel*, 269.

53 **"Alice looked":** Hilton Als, "Alice Neel's Eye." *New Yorker*, July 3, 2000, 27.

54 **"She was . . . unbelievable":** Marisa Diaz, in Hoban, *Alice Neel*, 358.

54 **"closer to the bone":** Le Guin, interview with JP, May 2010.

55 **"What will they":** Hoban, *Alice Neel*, 318.

ART MONSTERS AND MAINTENANCE WORK

57 **"There *is* a heroic":** Le Guin, "The Fisherwoman's Daughter," in *Dancing at the Edge of the World*, 224.

57 **"Maintenance is":** Mierle Laderman Ukeles, *Manifesto for Maintenance Art, 1969! Proposal for an Exhibition: "CARE,"* (October 1969), https://feldmangallery.com/exhibition/manifesto-for-maintenance-art-1969.

57 **"Manliness in art":** Pater, *Plato and Platonism* (Project Gutenberg, 2003; first published 1910).

58 **"lived a life":** Nemser, *Art Talk*, 14.

58 **"A woman artist":** Fiona MacCarthy, "Touchy Feely," *Guardian*, May 17, 2003.

58 **"If I was in . . . or you're not":** Nemser, *Art Talk*, 14–15.

58 **"My painting had been":** Stella Bowen, *Drawn from Life* (1941), quoted in Germaine Greer, *The Obstacle Race: The Fortunes of Women Painters and Their Work* (New York: Farrar, Straus & Giroux, 1979), 53.

59 **"My son bitterly"**: Nemser, *Art Talk*, 153.

60 **"She took up space"**: Sasha Bonét, "The Artist Who Gave Up Her Daughter," Topic, May 2019.

60 **"Men become"**: Collins, *Notes from a Black Woman's Diary*, 47.

60 **"No other creative"**: Michelle Elligott, "Faith Ringgold's Long Fight," MoMA Magazine, June 30, 2020.

60 **"Painting is"**: Ringgold, *We Flew Over the Bridge*, 196.

60 **"has two subjects . . . real artist"**: Mary Gabriel, *Ninth Street Women* (Boston: Little, Brown, 2018), 526.

61 **"To achieve"**: Randy Rosen and Catherine C. Brawer, *Making Their Mark: Women Artists Move into the Mainstream, 1970–85* (New York: Abbeville Press, 1989), 14.

61 **"I had a huge"**: "Mierle Laderman Ukeles Talks about Maintenance Art," *Artforum*, September 19, 2016, https://www.artforum.com/video/mierle-laderman-ukeles-talks-about-maintenance -art-63533.

SEX AND LOVE

For Naomi Mitchison I'm indebted to Jenni Calder's biography *The Burning Glass* and Lesley A. Hall's study *Naomi Mitchison*. Alexis Pauline Gumbs's dissertation *"We Can Learn to Mother Ourselves"* pointed me toward June Jordan.

65 **"Lovers make"**: Kate Moses, "A Mother's Body," in *Mothers Who Think: Tales of Real-Life Parenthood*, ed. Camille Peri and Kate Moses (New York: Washington Square, 2000), 176–77.

66 **"joy of the physical"**: Erdrich, *The Blue Jay's Dance*, 64.

66 **"beneficent"**: Rich, *Of Woman Born*, 15.

66 **"Do not wear . . . power"**: Jordan, "A New Politics of Sexuality" (1991), in *Technical Difficulties: Selected Political Essays* (London: Virago, 1992), 155–56.

67 **"I got . . . temperature"**: Mitchison, *You May Well Ask*, 69.

67 **"If the books"**: Ibid., 168.

67 **"temporary or"**: Hall, *Naomi Mitchison*, 54.

68 **"the essence"**: Lessing, *Walking in the Shade*, 126–27.

68 **"deep heartache"**: Mitchison, *You May Well Ask*, 73.

68 **"Perhaps we were"**: Ibid., 71.

68 **"turn[ed] the mills . . . uncensured"**: Ibid., 73.

68 **"sharpened"**: Ibid., 74.

69 **"had its own . . . long"**: Di Prima, *Recollections of My Life as a Woman*, 156.

69 **"No one, I vowed"**: Ibid., 157.

69 **"the pragmatism"**: Ibid., 207.

69 **"Di Prima . . . throughout"**: Ibid., 202. The Beats weren't all like that: Diane's daughter Dominique remembers Allen Ginsberg volunteering to babysit her so Diane could give readings. "Beat Poet Diane di Prima Taught Her Kids to Question Authority and Believe in Their Own Creativity," *As It Happens*, CBC Radio, October 27, 2020.

70 **"cool" about it:** Jones, *How I Became Hettie Jones* (Boston: Dutton, 1990). In this fine memoir, Jones writes of becoming mired in the family life that di Prima was trying to stay clear of. "I didn't *mind* my household life, I just couldn't do a damn thing with it. How did it translate to words, this holding pattern of call and response, clean and dirty, sick, well, asleep, awake.

Its only allure was need, and need was just a swamp behind the hothouse of desire—how could you want what you had to have?" (182)

70   **"I knew that"**: Di Prima, interview with David Meltzer (1999), *San Francisco Beat: Talking with the Poets*, ed. David Meltzer (San Francisco: City Lights Books, 2001), 12.

70   **"waiting for"**: Di Prima to Lorde, undated, Box 2 f39, Audre Lorde Papers, Spelman College Archives.

70   **"available"**: Di Prima, *Recollections*, 226.

70   **"Our erotic"**: Lorde, "Uses of the Erotic: The Erotic as Power" (1978), in *Sister Outsider*, 57.

70   **"that power which"**: Ibid., 53.

71   **"The aim of each"**: Ibid., 55.

71   **"When we . . . self-negation"**: Ibid., 58.

DORIS LESSING

In writing about Lessing's childhood and her parents, I drew primarily on her memoirs *Under My Skin* and *Alfred and Emily*. She wrote about her years in London in *Walking in the Shade*. The Whitehorn letters are held in the Doris Lessing Archive, British Archive for Contemporary Writing (BACW), at the University of East Anglia. Many thanks to archivist Bridget Gillies.

73   **"If you look"**: Sage, "Death of the Author," 238.

73   **"A woman who"**: Rich, *Of Woman Born*, 155.

75   **"get bored . . . admit"**: Lessing to Coll MacDonald, November 21, 1945, Doris Lessing Archive.

75   **"We use our"**: Lessing, "My Father" (1963), in *A Small Personal Voice: Essays, Reviews, Interviews* (New York: Vintage, 1975), 83.

75   **"one should"**: Lessing, *In Pursuit of the English* (Hertfordshire, UK: Granada, 1981; first published 1960), 6.

77   **"the mother who"**: Rebecca Solnit, *The Faraway Nearby* (New York: Penguin, 2013), 20.

77   **"how all her"**: Lessing, *Under My Skin*, 30.

77   **Doris told another story**: Lessing to Whitehorn, January 24, 1945.

78   **her father's gift**: Lorna Sage, a perceptive critic of Lessing as well as Angela Carter, writes of her life and fiction: "When the old male adventure story turns to 'dream' (leaving women to cope . . . with daily living and planning), a new and problematic imaginative horizon opens up for a daughter." Sage, *Doris Lessing* (London: Methuen, 1983), 22.

78   **"as far away"**: Lessing, *Under My Skin*, 203.

78   **"pure extract of *Zeitgeist*"**: Ibid., 188.

78   **"I will not"**: Ibid., 120.

79   **"raw young"**: Lessing, interview by Sue Lawley, *Desert Island Discs*, BBC Radio 4, November 21, 1993, https://www.bbc.co.uk/programmes/p0093wn3.

79   **"yearning and longing"**: Ibid.

79   **"locate the cause . . . History"**: Claudia Roth Pierpont, *Passionate Minds* (New York: Vintage, 2001), 229–30. Lessing's unauthorized biographer, Carole Klein, also takes this view.

80   **"claimed to despise"**: Lessing, *Under My Skin*, 403.

80   **"I seemed . . . helpless"**: Lessing, *Walking in the Shade*, 286.

80   **"There is an"**: Lessing, *Under My Skin*, 206–7.

80   **"He had been"**: Ibid., 211.

81 **"captivity . . . confined":** Lessing to Whitehorn, October 10, 1947.

81 **"the best":** Lessing, *Under My Skin*, 262.

81 **"the exuberant":** Ibid., 239.

81 **"Himalayas":** Ibid., 185.

82 **"I was bored":** Ibid., 233. Julia Kristeva offers one possible explanation for this craving: motherhood's "fundamental challenge to identity is . . . accompanied by a fantasy of totality—narcissistic completeness—a sort of instituted, socialized, natural psychosis." Kristeva, 1986, quoted in Solomon, *Transition to Motherhood*.

82 **"Eighteen":** Ibid., 229.

82 **"the disease of women":** Lessing, *Golden Notebook*, 318.

83 **"she, Martha . . . force":** Lessing, *A Proper Marriage*, 148.

83 **"keep brightly":** Ibid., 168.

83 **"rich, pleasurable":** Lessing, *Under My Skin*, 185.

83 **grim silences:** Lessing to Whitehorn, February 21, 1945.

83 **full custody:** When the writer Muriel Spark divorced her husband in Southern Rhodesia during the war, he was awarded custody of their son even though he was mentally ill and could not care for him. Eventually Spark was able to take her child with her to Scotland, where she left him with her parents to raise; that mother-son relationship is another story.

83 **"I was protecting":** Lessing, *Under My Skin*, 261.

83 **thought it was madness:** In *A Proper Marriage* Martha tells her young daughter as she leaves, "I'm setting you free" (70). But in a later novel, *Landlocked* (1965), Martha looks back on this statement and wonders what on earth she was thinking: "How could she have said it, thought it, felt it?" In *The Four-Gated City* (1969), Martha makes the same confession: "I was mad. . . . It was such nonsense, when I think of it now." And she starts to cry. The guilt feelings that Lessing left out of her memoirs are not hard to find in her fiction.

84 **"then flung aside":** Lessing to Whitehorn, September 29, 1947.

84 **that they could see:** Ironically, it was their conviction of their difference that made them susceptible to Communist propaganda: they saw it as a mark of their superiority that they could see what others couldn't, even when it wasn't there. After she lost her faith in Communism, she found in Laingian psychology and Sufi mysticism similar sources of superior knowledge.

85 **"an identity":** Lessing, *Under My Skin*, 401–2. Toni Morrison said something similar after her own divorce: "I knew that I would not deliver to my children a parent that was of no use to them." Gloria Naylor, "A Conversation: Gloria Naylor and Toni Morrison" (1985), in *Conversations with Toni Morrison*, ed. Danille Taylor-Guthrie (Jackson: University Press of Mississippi, 1994), 198.

85 **"full of . . . happen":** Lessing, *Under My Skin*, 297–98.

85 **"men who find":** Ibid., 298.

85 **get the sex to work:** In *Under My Skin* Doris called Gottfried "puritanical and inhibited" (303). To John Whitehorn (April 4, 1945), she wrote that she was the one who was too shy. In 1947 she wrote her gay RAF friend Leonard Smith, presumably based on her experience, that married sex was liable to leave the woman feeling either "like a recalcitrant car on a cold morning," if the man had been reading sex manuals, or "like a cup of tea that it is usual to drink before going to sleep." March 1947, quoted in Feigel, *Free Woman*, 162.

86 **"the dimwits":** Lessing to Whitehorn, February 7, 1945.

86 **"prevailing fog":** Lessing to MacDonald, August 30, 1945.

86 **"spending all":** Ibid.

87 **"I have been":** Lessing to Whitehorn, November 22, 1944.

88 **"In this most bloody":** Lessing to Whitehorn, January 24, 1945.

88 **How was . . . stop her:** Lessing to Whitehorn, March 21–27, 1945.

88 **"Do you think":** Lessing to MacDonald, May 3, 1945. Alice Neel had a similar argument with Communism. While she was painting the social critic Harold Cruse in 1950, he confessed to her that he still enjoyed some classical music that the Party considered "reactionary." Alice answered, "What the heck. Go ahead and like Debussy." Nemser, *Art Talk*, 128.

88 **"When people":** Lessing to Whitehorn, April 4, 1945.

88 **"I have the curse":** Lessing to Whitehorn, June 24, 1947.

89 **Doris described to John:** Lessing to Whitehorn, March 21–27, 1945.

90 **"an affectionate":** Lessing to Whitehorn, April 11, 1947.

90 **In early 1946:** Lessing to MacDonald, February 20, 1946.

90 **"One of these":** Lessing to MacDonald, July 28, 1945.

90 **"I can't think":** Ibid.

91 **"practicality":** Lessing, *Under My Skin*, 347.

91 **"with a newfangled":** Lessing to MacDonald, February 18, 1946.

91 **"Now I can":** Lessing to Whitehorn, February 1, 1946.

91 **"sensual delight":** Lessing to Whitehorn, September 24, 1946.

92 **In the heat of:** Lessing to Whitehorn, August 7, 1947.

92 **"Why leave":** Lessing, *Under My Skin*, 347.

92 **"second-raters . . . worth it":** Ibid., 256.

92 **"That's what . . . steak":** Lessing to Whitehorn, August 7, 1947.

92 **"only between":** Lessing, *The Sweetest Dream* (New York: Flamingo, 2001), 128.

93 **"was developing":** Lessing, *African Laughter* (New York: HarperCollins, 1992), 84.

94 **"While I was seeing":** Lessing, *Walking in the Shade*, 16.

94 **"shotgun sound":** Diski, "When Doris Lessing Rescued Me," *Guardian*, April 12, 2014.

94 **She taught herself:** Lessing, "The Art of Fiction No. 102," interview by Thomas Frick, *Paris Review*, no. 106 (Spring 1988).

94 **"the flat, dull":** Lessing, *Walking in the Shade*, 102.

94 **"the control and discipline":** Lessing, *Golden Notebook*, 319.

94 **"the most":** Lessing, *Walking in the Shade*, 23.

95 **"being told off":** Diski, *In Gratitude*, 196.

95 **"open, straightforward":** Lessing, *Under My Skin*, 255.

95 **"Silk breeches":** Lessing to Whitehorn, September 29, 1947.

95 **"day-in, day-out":** Lessing, *Walking in the Shade*, 155.

96 **"an irritable need":** Ibid., 156.

96 **"Peter had been":** Ibid., 286.

96 **"chilly grey":** Ibid., 223–24.

97 **"I'm not your mother":** quoted in Feigel, *Free Woman*, 178.

98 **"getting on with it":** Diski, "When Doris Lessing Rescued Me."

98 **responsible for a teenager:** Doris did take responsibility in some ways. Shortly after Jenny came, she made an appointment for her to be fitted for a diaphragm. But when Jenny said she was fifteen, the gynecologist chased her out of her office, shouting: "You're underage. What is that woman doing sending you here? Doesn't she know it's against the law to have sex at your age, let alone for me to provide contraception?" Diski, *In Gratitude*, 57.

98 **"shattering. . . . masterpiece of manipulation":** Diski, interview by Chris Wallace, *Inter-*

view, podcast 2015-3, March 18, 2015, https://www.interviewmagazine.com/culture/jenny-diski-podcast (removed from website as of July 22, 2021).

99 **"independent, determined":** Chloe Diski, afterword to Jenny Diski, *In Gratitude*, 261.

99 **"He had never":** Lessing, *Walking in the Shade*, 247.

99 **"I understand why":** Lessing, *Under My Skin*, 402.

99 **unbearable tension:** Klein, *Doris Lessing*, 75–76, summarizing a letter from Lessing to her friend and editor Robert Gottlieb.

99 **"It was never":** Diski, *In Gratitude*, 198.

100 **One interviewer:** Lessing, interview with Bibeb (pseud. Elisabeth Maria Lampe-Soutberg), Dutch journalist, *Vrij Nederland*, November 18, 1978, in *Bibeb met . . .: Interviews* (Amsterdam: Van Gennep, 1980).

100 **"shuffled . . . double act":** Peter Stanford, "Doris Lessing: A Mother Much Misunderstood," *Telegraph*, November 22, 2013.

100 **"was locked":** Drabble, *The Pure Gold Baby* (Edinburgh, UK: Canongate, 2013), 161.

101 **"drank and wept":** Lessing, *Under My Skin*, 410.

THE UNAVAILABLE MUSE

This chapter would not have been possible without Rosemary Sullivan's biography of Smart, *By Heart*, Christopher Barker's account of his parents' marriage and his childhood, *The Arms of the Infinite*, and Kim Echlin's excellent *Elizabeth Smart: A Fugue Essay on Women and Creativity*. I'm grateful to Georgina Barker for her comments and perspective.

103 **I must marry":** quoted in Barker, *The Arms of the Infinite*.

103 **"How can I":** quoted in Echlin, *Elizabeth Smart*, 28.

103 **"keeping covered":** Smart, *Autobiographies*, 157.

103 **"mooning about":** Ibid., 143.

104 **"beginning of that":** quoted in Echlin, *Elizabeth Smart*, 77.

104 **"I am going to be":** Ibid., 23.

104 **"have to repudiate":** Echlin, *Elizabeth Smart*, 210.

105 **"I am suddenly":** Smart, *By Grand Central Station I Sat Down and Wept*, 44.

105 **"What you think":** Ibid., 78.

105 **"like the fated":** Ibid., 188.

105 **"Pain, pain":** Ibid., 114.

106 **"to face the murderous":** Smart, *Autobiographies*, 170.

106 **"Nothing will ever":** Smart, journal, June 2–July 4, 1944, in Davey, *Mother Reader*, 13.

106 **"in case . . . helpless":** Smart to Didy Asquith, in Echlin, *Elizabeth Smart*, 104.

106 **"The void is":** Rich, "Women and Honor: Some Notes on Lying" (1975), in *On Lies, Secrets, and Silence*, 191.

107 **"Her fulfillment":** Barker, *The Dead Seagull* (London: MacGibbon & Kee, 1950), 33.

107 **"I see no beauty":** Smart to Barker, September 27, 1946, https://lettersofnote.com/2015/10/20/i-see-no-beauty-in-lopsided-true-love/.

107 **"arch-angelic . . . again":** Smart to Didy Asquith, in Echlin, *Elizabeth Smart*, 136.

108 **"freezes the rebel":** Anne Quéma, review of Echlin, *Elizabeth Smart. University of Toronto Quarterly* 76, no. 1 (Winter 2007): 579.

108 **"brilliancy pills":** Sullivan, *By Heart*, 290.

108   **"give, sympathize"**: Smart, *The Assumption of the Rogues & Rascals*, 76.

109   **"Love. Children"**: Smart, *Autobiographies*, 148.

109   **"it simply"**: Fay Weldon, *Mantrapped* (New York: Grove Press, 2004), 30.

109   **"women talking"**: *Queen*, February 24, 1965, in Sullivan, *By Heart*, 294.

110   **"the untenable position"**: Smart, *The Assumption of the Rogues & Rascals*, 77.

110   **afraid to enter**: Echlin, *Elizabeth Smart*, 210.

110   **"self-inflicted . . . should hope"**: Sage, "Death of the Author," 247.

BOOKS VERSUS BABIES

111   **"To think"**: Gail Weiss, "Mothers/Intellectuals: Alterities of a Dual Identity," in *Refiguring the Ordinary* (Bloomington: Indiana University Press, 2008), 189.

111   **"You were supposed"**: Sage, *Bad Blood*, 232.

112   **"It is very doubtful"**: Gerald Massey, quoted in Elaine Showalter, *A Literature of Their Own: British Women Novelists from Brontë to Lessing* (Princeton, NJ: Princeton University Press, 1977), 76. The comic version of men's views on this question is represented by Miss Prism, the lady novelist in Wilde's *The Importance of Being Earnest*, who opens the play's confusion of identities by accidentally replacing a baby with the manuscript of her three-volume novel. In her case the baby isn't hers and she doesn't seem to regret its loss.

112   **"Freud appeals"**: Philip Rieff, *Freud: The Mind of the Moralist* (New York: Anchor, 1961), 191–92.

112   **"Where do I want"**: Sontag, *Reborn*, 306, 9/15/62.

113   **"The mind-body problem"**: Byatt, "Soul Searching," *Guardian*, February 14, 2004.

113   **"Both in their personal"**: Showalter, *A Jury of Her Peers*, 392.

113   **"When I was"**: "An Interview with Adrienne Rich" (1971), in *Poetry* (New York: W. W. Norton, 1973).

113   **"If you're a woman"**: Janet Sternburg, *The Writer on Her Work* (London: Virago, 1992), 152.

114   **"Black women seem"**: Showalter, *A Jury of Her Peers*, 449.

114   **"[In] the Black"**: interview with Margaret Kaminski (1975), in Hall, *Conversations with Audre Lorde*, 3.

114   **"What has been . . . housework"**: Alexis De Veaux, "Creating Soul Food: June Jordan," *Essence*, April 1981, 82.

114   **"I couldn't possibly"**: Collins, *Notes from a Black Woman's Diary*, 69.

115   **"All of my"**: Boris Kachka, "Who Is the Author of Toni Morrison?," *New York*, April 27, 2012.

115   **"the same . . . mad"**: Fay Weldon, *Mantrapped* (New York: Grove Press, 2004), 123–24.

115   **"driven to"**: Walker, "In Search of Our Mothers' Gardens," in *In Search of Our Mothers' Gardens*, 233.

115   **"Writing depends"**: Abel, "The Baby, the Book, and the Bathwater," *Paris Review* (blog), January 31, 2018.

116   **"Everyone was"**: Sarah Manguso, "Writing Postpartum: A Conversation between Kate Zambreno and Sarah Manguso," *Paris Review* (blog), April 24, 2019.

116   **"One day"**: Erdrich, *The Blue Jay's Dance*, 148.

116   **"Imagining"**: Smiley, "Can Mothers Think?," in *The True Subject: Writers on Life and Craft*, ed. Jane Smiley and Kurt Brown (Minneapolis, MN: Graywolf, 1993).

116   **"Art is supposed"**: Nicole Rudick, "Talking to Justine Kurland," *Vice*, July 21, 2010. Kur-

land is a photographer whose series *Of Woman Born* portrays nude women and children in majestic landscapes.

117 **"'Mothering' is a"**: Gumbs, "m/other ourselves," in Gumbs et al., *Revolutionary Mothering*, 23.

117 **"I remember when"**: Isaac Chotiner, "Zadie Smith on Male Critics, Appropriation, and What Interests Her Novelistically about Trump," *Slate*, November 16, 2016.

117 **"I'm of that"**: Emma Brockes, "Interview: Margaret Atwood," *Guardian*, August 24, 2013.

118 **"He told me"**: Di Prima, *Recollections of My Life As a Woman*, 164.

118 **"[Having children]"**: Le Guin, interview with JP, October 2011.

URSULA K. LE GUIN

This chapter is based in part on my interviews with Ursula K. Le Guin. She and I wrote, talked on the phone, and met in person over a period of ten years, from 2007 to 2017, after she invited me to become her biographer. Unless otherwise noted, all quotes come from our interviews and correspondence. I owe a deep debt of gratitude to Linda Long for her ongoing assistance with the Le Guin papers at the University of Oregon.

121 **"Art is two things"**: Patricia Hills, *Alice Neel*, 183.

122 **"inventive spark"**: Le Guin, "The Art of Fiction No. 221," interview by John Wray, *Paris Review*, no. 206 (Fall 2013), 72.

123 **"the loneliest"**: Le Guin, "My Island" (1996), in *The Wave in the Mind*, 24.

123 **"Don't bother . . . around you"**: Le Guin, "Life in the Wider Household of Being," interview by Erika Milo, West by Northwest, November 21, 2003 (site discontinued).

123 **"We were a"**: Le Guin, "Indian Uncles" (2001), in *The Wave in the Mind*, 17.

125 **"an exile"**: Le Guin, "My Libraries" (1997), in *The Wave in the Mind*, 21.

126 **"a little frightening"**: Jean Taylor Kroeber, interview with JP, November, 2010.

126 **"we were there"**: Michael Cunningham, "Ursula K. Le Guin Talks to Michael Cunningham about Genres, Gender, and Broadening Fiction," *Electric Literature*, August 7, 2014.

126 **"never saw a"**: Rich, "Taking Women Students Seriously" (1978), in *On Lies, Secrets, and Silence*, 238.

127 **"forlorn and loveless"**: Le Guin to Virginia Kidd, August 9, 1976. (Courtesy of the Virginia Kidd Agency.)

128 **"sacrificing your training:"**: Le Guin, "The Princess" (1982), in *Dancing at the Edge of the World*, 76.

129 **"opening of . . . mine"**: Le Guin, journal, March 22, 1957. (Courtesy of the Le Guin estate.)

129 **"small and stony"**: Le Guin, introduction to *The Unreal and the Real: Selected Stories* (Easthampton, MA: Small Beer Press, 2012), 1:iii.

130 **"awfully snooty"**: Charles A. Le Guin to his parents, October 24, 1953, University of Oregon (UO), with the permission of Charles Le Guin.

131 **"set me to thinking"**: Ursula Kroeber to Charles Le Guin, November 17, 1953, UO.

131 **"laughing . . . balance"**: Kroeber to Le Guin, November 11, 1953, UO.

132 **"the real work"**: Rich, *Of Woman Born*, 7.

133 **"never would have . . . self-sufficiency"**: Le Guin to James Tiptree Jr., February 25, 1975, UO.

134 **"a good prose"**: Anne N. Barrett to Le Guin, October 17, 1958, UO.

135   **"wasn't socially"**: Le Guin, interview with Laurie Watson McGillivray, *Front Lines*, newsletter of Food Front Cooperative Grocery, Portland, OR, vol. 5, no. 1 (January/February 1994): 1. (Courtesy of Tony Wolk.)

135   **"the pleasures"**: Le Guin, "The Fisherwoman's Daughter," in *Dancing at the Edge of the World*, 233.

136   **"Why does it"**: Le Guin, journal, undated entry. (Courtesy of the Le Guin estate.)

138   **"Caroline (17)"**: Le Guin to Tiptree, January 2, 1977, UO.

138   **"blinking remotely"**: Le Guin to Tiptree, November 30, 1974, UO.

140   **"my consciousness"**: Le Guin to Virginia Kidd, May 24, 1971. (Courtesy of the Virginia Kidd Agency.)

140   **"I walk a rather"**: Le Guin to Kidd, April 28, 1972.

140   **"loose ends quality"**: Le Guin to Eleanor Cameron, May 14, 1971, UO.

140   **"Oh woe, oh damn"**: Le Guin to Cameron, March 17, 1971, UO.

141   **"The degree to which"**: Le Guin, interview with Hélène Escudié, 2002, in *Conversations with Ursula K. Le Guin*, ed. Carl Freedman (Jackson: University Press of Mississippi, 2008), 161.

141   **"Goodbye for now"**: Le Guin to Tiptree, May 8, 1974, UO.

142   **"All my children"**: Le Guin to Kidd, May 21, 1974.

143   **"Now that I"**: Le Guin to Cameron, January 18, 1971, UO.

143   **"work . . . everything"**: Le Guin, "Fisherwoman's Daughter," 226.

143   **"like she had ridden"**: Harlan Ellison, interview with JP, August 2006.

143   **write from her own experience:** When Le Guin attempted to write an autobiography in the 1980s, she gave up after five pages in frustration at not getting the tone right. She felt she was "rounding things off and tying them up, when they should be raw and wet and transmitting lightning from one side to the other." (Courtesy of the Le Guin estate.)

144   **"pregnancy is barbaric"**: Shulamith Firestone, *The Dialectic of Sex* (New York: Bantam, 1971), 198. In her 2020 book *Full Surrogacy Now*, Sophie Lewis reopens the case for communal responsibility for child-rearing, including an awareness of gestation as work that should be engaged in freely and fairly compensated. Le Guin experimented with communal child-raising in some of her science-fictional societies, but not in depth, and she often depicted it through the eyes of characters who themselves preferred family life.

144   **"Motherhood"**: DuPlessis, "Washing Blood," *Toward a Feminist Theory of Motherhood: Feminist Studies* 4, no. 2 (June 1978): 8.

144   **"a child-free . . . space"**: Le Guin, "Fisherwoman's Daughter," 226–27.

144   **"the paradigm"**: Le Guin, "December 5, 1992," in *Khatru 3 & 4, Symposium: Women in Science Fiction*, ed. Jeffrey D. Smith, Baltimore, November 1975. Reprinted, with additional material edited by Jeanne Gomoll, SF3, 1993, 116.

144   **"There is no doubt"**: Le Guin to Kidd, January 30, 1977. (Courtesy of the Virginia Kidd Agency.)

145   **"feel like a foreigner"**: Le Guin, "Earthsea Revisioned" (1992), in *The Books of Earthsea: The Complete Illustrated Edition* (New York: Saga Press, 2018), 983–84.

145   **"I think if I"**: *Worlds of Ursula K. Le Guin*, directed by Arwen Curry, 2018.

145   **"the dark hard place"**: Le Guin, "December 5, 1992," 115.

145   **"the Hero"**: Le Guin, "Fisherwoman's Daughter," 229.

145   **"from outside . . . people"**: Le Guin, afterword (2012) to *Tehanu*, in *The Books of Earthsea: The Complete Illustrated Edition* (New York: Saga Press, 2018), 549.

000 **"We live in":** Le Guin, "Freedom" (2014), in *Words Are My Matter* (Easthampton, MA: Small Beer Press, 2016), 114.

147 **"completely different":** Le Guin, introduction to *The Hainish Novels and Stories* (New York: Library of America, 2017), 2:xiv.

147 **"The difficulty of trying":** Le Guin, "Fisherwoman's Daughter," 226.

147 **"that she and":** Ibid., 236.

GHOSTS

Details from the life of Gwendolyn Brooks come from Angela Jackson, *A Surprised Queenhood in the New Black Sun*, and from Brooks's memoir *Report from Part One*. Elaine Showalter's *A Jury of Her Peers* was helpful to me in thinking about creative lives in 1950s America, and Mary Helen Washington, in *Invented Lives: Narratives of Black Women 1860–1960*, helped me understand Brooks's *Maud Martha*. Shirley Jackson has had two fine biographers, Judy Oppenheimer and Ruth Franklin.

149 **"In the face of":** Erdrich, *The Blue Jay's Dance*, 4.

149 **"There I was":** quoted in Deborah Wye, *Louise Bourgeois: An Unfolding Portrait* (New York Museum of Modern Art, 2017), 15.

149 **"lost her equilibrium":** Robert Storr, *Intimate Geometries: The Art and Life of Louise Bourgeois* (New York: Monacelli Press, 2016), 284.

149 **"housewife . . . world":** Ibid., 294.

150 **"I had the feeling":** Munro, *Originals*, 156.

151 **"of being someone else":** Ruth Franklin, *Shirley Jackson: A Rather Haunted Life* (New York: Liveright, 2016), 63.

151 **"steamroller":** Judy Oppenheimer, *Private Demons: The Life of Shirley Jackson* (New York: Fawcett Columbine, 1989), 106.

152 **"Writer":** Jackson, *Life among the Savages* (New York: Penguin, 2015; first published 1953), 65–66.

153 **"grayed in":** Brooks, "kitchenette building" (1954), in *Essential Gwendolyn Brooks*, 1.

153 **"a small wood frame":** Don L. Lee/Haki Madhubuti, quoted in Jackson, *A Surprised Queenhood*, 99.

154 **"Sex in":** Brooks, *Maud Martha*, 68.

154 **"hearing that part":** Ibid., 99.

154 **"to jerk . . . voice":** Ibid., 175–76.

154 **"a spunky . . . speak":** Washington, *Invented Lives: Narratives of Black Women 1860–1960*, 387.

155 **African American mother-writers:** In her 2019 essay "Black Maternal Aesthetics," Jennifer C. Nash writes that poets Claudia Rankine and Emily Bernard depict "black maternity as haunted, with death constituting the unseen but always-felt backdrop of the quotidian." Wanting Black motherhood to be more than "a kind of metaphorical ground zero for black death, a kind of *ur*-text of black death," Nash looks to aestheticized pregnancy photographs of Serena Williams and Beyoncé Knowles for a vision that "emphasizes abundance, visibility, and even spirituality as black maternal ethics."

155 **"Marriage is a hard":** Jackson, *Surprised Queenhood*, 142.

155 **"Words do wonderful things":** Washington, *Invented Lives*, 433.

155 **"So long as":** Oppenheimer, *Private Demons*, 211.

156 **"I don't want my mother":** Ibid., 240.

156 **"I have failed as"**: Wye, *Louise Bourgeois*, 18.

156 **"If I am"**: Bourgeois, journal, ca. 1960, quoted in *Louise Bourgeois*, ed. Frances Morris (New York: Rizzoli, 2008), 20.

156 **"prov[ing] over and over"**: Mary Gabriel, *Ninth Street Women* (Boston: Little, Brown, 2018), 524.

157 **"At the dinner table"**: quoted in Morris, *Louise Bourgeois*, 102.

LATE SUCCESS

Here I am indebted to Hermione Lee's *Penelope Fitzgerald: A Life.*

161 **"Don't mind it . . . tormented"**: Fitzgerald, *The Bookshop* (London: Fourth Estate, 2014; first published 1978), 81.

161 **"It sometimes"**: Ibid., 134.

162 **"Desmond always thought"**: Lee, *Penelope Fitzgerald*, 234.

162 **"I have tried dyeing"**: Ibid., 187.

162 **"confident only in"**: Terence Dooley, in *So I Have Thought of You: The Letters of Penelope Fitzgerald*, ed. Dooley (London: Fourth Estate, 2008), Scribd.

162 **"geniuses are not"**: Lee, *Penelope Fitzgerald*, 190.

162 **"Helping other people"**: Fitzgerald, *Human Voices* (London: Fourth Estate, 2014; first published 1980), 149.

162 **"to amuse [him]"**: Lee, *Penelope Fitzgerald*, 231.

163 **"As sharp as a knife"**: Ibid., 319.

AUDRE LORDE

I was fortunate in being able to draw on Alexis De Veaux's biography of Lorde, *Warrior Poet*, as well as Alexis Pauline Gumbs's doctoral dissertation, *"We Can Learn to Mother Ourselves": The Queer Survival of Black Feminism 1968–1996*, a terrific work of scholarship and critical imagination. Rodger Streitmatter's essay on Lorde and Clayton in *Outlaw Marriages* gave me insight into Frances Clayton's perspective, as did Clare Coss's "Frances Clayton: Remembering Our Friend and Chosen Family." I'm very grateful to archivists Holly Smith and Kassandra Ware, at the Spelman College Archives, who helped me and my husband, Jan, find our way in the Audre Lorde Papers.

165 **"Mother is"**: Gumbs, "Forget Hallmark," *Aster(ix)*, May 10, 2015.

165 **"The white fathers"**: Lorde, "Poetry Is Not a Luxury" (1977), in *Sister Outsider*, 38.

165 **felt the baby**: Lorde, "Now That I Am Forever With Child" (1976), in *Collected Poems*, 173.

166 **"wrapped in"**: Lorde, essay draft, journal 1969–70, Audre Lorde Papers, Spelman College Archives.

166 **"Something in my body"**: Lorde, "To Marie, in Flight," in *The Collected Poems of Audre Lorde*, 145.

166 **"conducted her life"**: Lorde-Rollins, interview with Aishah Shahidah Simmons, *Feminist Wire*, February 25, 2014.

166 **"a long and sometimes"**: Lorde, "Turning the Beat Around: Lesbian Parenting 1986," in *I Am Your Sister*, 77.

167 **"where queer means"**: Gumbs, *"We Can Learn to Mother Ourselves,"* 75–76.

167 **"As a Black lesbian"**: Lorde, "Learning from the 60s" (1982), in *Sister Outsider*, 137.

167 **"I bore you"**: Lorde, "Now That I Am Forever With Child" (1976), in *Collected Poems*, 173.

167 **"dazzling"**: De Veaux, *Warrior Poet*, 62, quoting Blanche Wiesen Cook.

167 **"without peer"**: Lorde, *Zami*, 223.

168 **"I would recite . . . serve"**: "An Interview: Audre Lorde and Adrienne Rich" (1979), in Lorde, *Sister Outsider*, 82.

169 **immigration forms**: Lorde, petition for naturalization, July 16, 1926. "New York, U.S., Naturalization Records, 1882–1944," Ancestry.com.

169 **"secret poetry"**: Lorde, *Zami*, 32.

169 **"You're a Lorde"**: "Audre Lorde and Adrienne Rich," 91.

169 **"the evenness"**: Lorde, *Zami*, 24.

169 **"a wild . . . into things"**: Phyllis Lorde Blackwell, interview with Sue Edwards, "Bremerton Woman Recounts Growing Up in Civil Rights Era," *Kitsap Sun* (Bremerton, WA), July 6, 2003.

169 **The people you love most**: Patricia Hill Collins writes, "Black daughters raised by mothers grappling with hostile environments have to confront their feelings about the difference between the idealized versions of maternal love extant in popular culture and the strict, assertive mothers so central to their lives." Collins, "The Meaning of Motherhood in Black Culture and Mother-Daughter Relationships," in Bell-Scott, *Double Stitch: Black Women Write about Mothers & Daughters*, 55.

170 **"as if her"**: Lorde, *Zami*, 101.

170 **"She had had to"**: Ibid., 58. The painter Faith Ringgold, born in Harlem in 1929, recalled it in her childhood as a mixed neighborhood, but one where "prejudice was all-pervasive, a permanent limitation on the lives of Black people. . . . From time to time, some kid would blurt out, 'You ain' no better than me,' but this was hard to prove in the Thirties." Ringgold, *We Flew over the Bridge*, 23.

170 **"You don't"**: Ibid., 61.

170 **"I was ALWAYS"**: Lorde to Bernice (possibly Goodman, her therapist and friend in the 1970s), dated "6/27." Box 15 f01, Lorde Papers.

171 **"If I didn't define"**: Lorde, "Learning from the 60s" (1982), in *Sister Outsider*, 137.

171 **"wrote obscure"**: Lorde, *Zami*, 82.

171 **"fierce"**: Di Prima, *Recollections of My Life as a Woman*, 73.

171 **"step by step . . . levels"**: "Audre Lorde and Adrienne Rich," 83–84.

172 **A reader of science fiction**: In January 1953, *Seventeen* magazine published eighteen-year-old Audre's books column describing herself as a science fiction "addict" and recommending the work of Ray Bradbury and L. Sprague de Camp, among others. The unpublished story "The Revolt of the Light Year" is in the Lorde Papers, Box 26 f113.

172 **"I loved her so"**: Lorde, journal, March 17, 1951, Lorde Papers.

173 **"a period of war . . . enough of either"**: Lorde, interview with Nina Winter (1976), in Hall, *Conversations with Audre Lorde*, 12–13.

173 **"misunderstandings . . . relationship"**: Lorde, journal, September 9, 1951, Lorde Papers.

173 **pregnant, presumably by him**: De Veaux, *Warrior Poet*, 37.

173 **"knowing I could"**: Lorde, *Zami*, 108.

173 **"of myself upon"**: De Veaux, *Warrior Poet*, 38.

174 **"Even more than"**: Lorde, *Zami*, 111.

174 **"get mixed up"**: Lorde to Bernice, "6/27," Box 15 f01, Lorde Papers.

174 **"gorgeously fat"**: Lorde, *Zami*, 136.

174 **"was like coming home"**: Ibid., 139.

174 **"how to love"**: Ibid., 209.

175 **"We have some"**: Lorde, interview with Blanche Wiesen Cook, "Women and the World in the 1980s: August 20, 1982, Audre Lorde," Pacifica Radio, https://www.youtube.com/watch?v=R4rDL-xZ8N0.

175 **"vows of love"**: Lorde, *Zami*, 201. In her memoir Lorde called Marion "Muriel."

175 **"Each one of us"**: Ibid., 209–10.

175 **"I feel like"**: Lorde, journal, January 21, 1958, Lorde Papers.

175 **"the safety game"**: Lorde, journal, Lorde Papers.

175 **"often loved"**: De Veaux, *Warrior Poet*, 68.

176 **"The only way to be"**: Lorde to Bernice, "6/27," Box 15 f01, Lorde Papers.

176 **"When in"**: Lorde, "Deotha," in *"I Teach Myself in Outline": Notes, Journals, Syllabi, and an Excerpt from* Deotha.

176 **The married woman . . . one other man**: De Veaux, *Warrior Poet*, 67–69.

176 **"foppish" and "insincere"**: undated letter from "M.," Box 6 f146, Lorde Papers.

176 **"We were celebrating"**: Cook, interview with JP, August 2020.

176 **"the farthest-out . . . middle"**: Lorde, *Zami*, 15.

177 **"With the heat . . . rainbows"**: Lorde, essay draft, journal 1969–70, Lorde Papers.

177 **"poetic excitement"**: De Veaux, *Warrior Poet*, 81.

178 **"easier to deal"**: Lorde, "My Words Will Be There" (1984), in *I Am Your Sister*, 160–61.

178 **When the adoption**: Gumbs, "m/other ourselves: a Black queer feminist genealogy for radical mothering," in Gumbs et al., *Revolutionary Mothering*, 27.

179 **"I know . . . empowering"**: Lorde, interview with Nina Winter, in Hall, *Conversations with Audre Lorde*, 12.

180 **"pain and fury"**: "Audre Lorde and Adrienne Rich," 90.

181 **"Why did this"**: Lorde, essay draft, Box 17 f80, Lorde Papers.

181 **"precious"**: Lorde, "Deotha."

181 **"I think"**: Lorde, interview with Karla Jay (1983), in Hall, *Conversations with Audre Lorde*, 112.

181 **shy and "inarticulate"**: Lorde, interview with Blanche Wiesen Cook, August 20, 1982.

181 **"It was very"**: "Audre Lorde and Adrienne Rich," 89.

182 **South Carolina State**: In her journal for May 1970, Audre criticized the selective outrage of those who protested the Kent State Massacre but not Orangeburg.

182 **"walk out"**: "Audre Lorde and Adrienne Rich," 90.

182 **"right to examine"**: Ibid.

182 **"the consciousness . . . me"**: Lorde, interview with Blanche Wiesen Cook, August 20, 1982.

183 **"food, jokes"**: Rich to Lorde, November 22, 1979, Box 4 f106, Lorde Papers. Quoted with permission.

183 **"I'm not the"**: Coss, "Frances Clayton: Remembering Our Friend and Chosen Family," 190.

184 **"life is"**: Lorde, "My Words Will Be There," in *I Am Your Sister*, 161.

184 **"she regrouped"**: Cook, personal communication.

184 **"the most chaotic"**: Lorde, "Turning the Beat Around," 76.

185 **"the daily"**: Ibid.

185 **"Nothing would stop her"**: Cook, interview with JP.

185 **"You think just"**: Lorde, "Turning the Beat Around," 78.

185 **"hypocrites"**: Elizabeth Lorde-Rollins, "Meeting Audre Lorde," *Advocate*, February 25, 2016.

185   **"Raising two children"**: Lorde, "Turning the Beat Around," 76.

185   **"If I remember"**: Lorde, journal, September 20, 1973, Lorde Papers.

186   **"When I was"**: Lorde-Rollins, "Meeting Audre Lorde."

186   **"I think that"**: Lorde-Rollins, interview with Aishah Shahidah Simmons, *Feminist Wire*, February 25, 2014.

188   **joys of her life:** Streitmatter, *Outlaw Marriages*, 167.

188   **"toweringly angry"**: Lorde-Rollins, interview with JP, November 2017.

188   **"She cuddled"**: Lorde-Rollins, "Meeting Audre Lorde."

188   **"a monster . . . caring"**: Rich, *Of Woman Born*, 2.

188   **"Every . . . secret"**: Lorde, "Eye to Eye: Black Women, Hatred, and Anger" (1983), in *Sister Outsider*, 145.

188   **"It was not"**: Lorde, "Turning the Beat Around," 76.

189   **"on murderous"**: Lorde, "A Woman/Dirge for Wasted Children" (1976), in *Collected Poems*, 285.

189   **"The master's tools"**: Lorde, "The Master's Tools Will Never Dismantle the Master's House" (1979), in *Sister Outsider*, 111. Specifically, Audre had been asked to be on a "diversity panel" at an academic conference on feminism, where she was one of only two Black women presenting papers. She was reminding those present that this was an oppressive situation.

190   **"intensity . . . lose"**: Gloria Wekker, *White Innocence: Paradoxes of Colonialism and Race* (Durham, NC: Duke University Press, 2016), 112.

190   **"Later, when we"**: Jackie Kay, "Audre Lorde Was a Poetic Innovator—and Great Fun," *Guardian*, October 13, 2008.

190   **"a multiple" . . . choose:** Jackie Kay, "Landmark: Audre Lorde," interview with Shahidha Bari, *Free Thinking*, BBC Radio 3, April 30, 2019, https://www.bbc.co.uk/sounds/play/m0004my0.

190   **"devoured"**: Pratibha Parmar, "Personal Is Political: Audre Lorde: Sister Insider," *Feminist Wire*, February 18, 2014.

191   **"You really are"**: Thompson to Lorde, January 17, 1978, Box 7.1 f175, Lorde Papers. Quoted with permission.

191   **" 'No?' she said"**: Kay, "Feminist, Lesbian, Warrior, Poet," *New Statesman*, September 30, 2017.

192   **"Each woman"**: Lorde, *The Cancer Journals: Special Edition* (San Francisco: Aunt Lute, 1997), 7.

192   **"like the [bumble]bee"**: Lorde, "Nov 19, 1979," *Cancer Journals*, 11.

192   **"You're going"**: Lorde-Rollins, "Meeting Audre Lorde."

192   **"mix of"**: Ibid.

192   **"poetry was"**: Ibid.

192   **"why we weren't"**: Lorde-Rollins, interview with Simmons, 2014.

192   **"Talent does"**: Lorde-Rollins, interview with JP, quoting Edward Bulwer-Lytton.

193   **"I have come . . . yours"**: Lorde, "The Transformation of Silence into Language and Action" (1977), in *Sister Outsider*, 41–43.

193   **"So it is better"**: Lorde, *Collected Poems*, 256.

193   **"Implicit in"**: Lorde, interview with Blanche Wiesen Cook, 1982.

NOT BEING ALL THERE

This chapter draws on the two volumes of Sontag's diaries, *Reborn* and *As Consciousness Is Harnessed to Flesh*, and of course Benjamin Moser's *Sontag*.

195 **"One of the great"**: Carter, "The Life of Katherine Mansfield," in *Shaking a Leg*, 505.

195 **"[Adults] possess"**: Jordan, "The Creative Spirit: Children's Literature," in Gumbs et al., *Revolutionary Mothering*.

196 **"somewhere along"**: Jonathan Cott, *Susan Sontag: The Complete Rolling Stone Interview* (New Haven, CT: Yale University Press, 2013), 109.

196 **"I will be popular"**: Sontag, *As Consciousness Is Harnessed to Flesh*, 114, 9/6/65.

196 **"I feel that I"**: Sontag, *Reborn*, 11, 12/25/48.

197 **"Work's your only"**: Radclyffe Hall, *The Well of Loneliness* (London: Virago, 1983; first published 1928), 343.

197 **"My desire to write"**: Sontag, *Reborn*, 221, 12/24/59.

197 **"because no one"**: Joan Acocella, "The Hunger Artist" (2000), in *Twenty-Eight Artists and Two Saints* (New York: Pantheon, 2007), 450.

197 **"I marry Philip"**: Sontag, *Reborn*, 62, 1/3/51.

198 **An unwanted pregnancy**: In a teenage journal entry, Susan accused Mildred of hating sexuality and added, "Your horror is ugly and unclean—You and the memory of your mother's buckle-like contraception lying on the table—your mother dying on a clean hospital bed—dying, in your mind, of Sex" (Moser, *Sontag*, 75). Sarah Jacobson, Mildred's mother, was said to have died of food poisoning. But her death report shows a different, vaguely worded cause—"intestinal obstruction probably following post-operative adhesions"—and mentions a blood transfusion that evidently came too late. That Susan's grandmother died from an unsafe abortion seems not out of the question.

198 **"I would have"**: Sontag, *Consciousness*, 286, 8/10/67.

198 **"That's one of"**: Acocella, "The Hunger Artist," 450.

198 **"It never occurred"**: Sontag, *Consciousness*, 25, 5/5/64.

198 **"the center"**: Moser, *Sontag*, 146.

199 **"concentrated in"**: Ibid., 116.

199 **"I hardly ever dream"**: Sontag, *Reborn*, 179, 1/6/58.

199 **"Wrote a letter"**: Ibid., 152, 9/17/57.

199 **"I stood at . . . hand"**: Ibid., 74, 1/21/53.

200 **"I'd rather . . . best friend"**: Nunez, *Sempre Susan*, 98–99.

200 **"P and I"**: Sontag, *Reborn*, 243, 2/19/60.

200 **"If only I get"**: Ibid., 128, 1/15/57.

201 **"the tired binary"**: Nelson, *Argonauts*, 94, quoting Susan Fraiman, *Cool Men and the Second Sex* (New York: Columbia University Press, 2003).

201 **"In any case"**: Carl Rollyson and Lisa Paddock, *Susan Sontag: The Making of an Icon* (New York: W. W. Norton, 2000), 44.

201 **"I didn't feel like"**: Sontag, "The Letter Scene," *New Yorker*, August 18, 1986.

201 **"sense that things"**: Sontag, *Reborn*, 175, 1/4/58.

201 **"I can't give myself"**: Ibid., 300, 3/3/62.

201 **"good to be home"**: Ibid., 183, 1/12/58.

202 **"Like smoke . . . first act"**: quoted in David Rieff, *Swimming in a Sea of Death* (New York: Simon & Schuster, 2008), 142.

202 **"eating, homework"**: Sontag, *Reborn*, 217, 9/59.

202 **"little boy"**: Sontag, *In America* (New York: Farrar Straus and Giroux, 2000), 24–25.

202 **"given up on"**: Sontag, *Consciousness*, 216.

202 **"I've experienced"**: Ibid., 227, 8/10/67.

203   **"When did I"**: Ibid., 214–15, 8/9/67.

204   **"safety, refuge"**: Ibid., 276, 2/17/70.

204   **"someone I can"**: Ibid., 297–98, 4/26/70.

205   **"darkest rage"**: Nunez, *Sempre Susan*, 117.

205   **"It is easier"**: Lorde, "Eye to Eye: Black Women, Hatred, and Anger" (1983), in *Sister Outsider*, 153.

205   **"Why did . . . started to cry"**: Nunez, *Sempre Susan*, 115–16.

205   **make love:** Hilary Holladay, *The Power of Adrienne Rich* (New York: Nan A. Talese, 2020), 269.

206   **"If I can keep"**: Le Guin, *Steering the Craft* (Portland, OR: Eighth Mountain Press, 1998), 149.

206   **"It feels true"**: Sontag, "Singleness" (1995), in *Where the Stress Falls* (London: Jonathan Cape, 2002), 259.

206   **"her first . . . not loved"**: Moser, *Sontag*, 479–80.

207   **"She went through"**: Van Gelder, personal communication, June 2020.

207   **"Which one is"**: Moser, *Sontag*, 651.

207   **"humanity"**: quoted in Jeanette Winterson, "Patricia Highsmith, Hiding in Plain Sight," *New York Times*, December 20, 2009.

208   **"Most of all"**: Lorde, "The Transformation of Silence into Language and Action," in *Sister Outsider*, 42.

ALICE WALKER

This chapter could not have been written without *Alice Walker*, Evelyn C. White's excellent biography.

211   **"I have looked"**: Lorde, journal, November 7, 1972, in De Veaux, *Warrior Poet*, 127.

211   **"What kind of love"**: Rich, "Motherhood: The Contemporary Emergency and the Quantum Leap" (1978), in *On Lies, Secrets, and Silence*, 263.

211   **"When everything"**: Dr. Carol Cooper, personal communication.

212   **"I found it"**: Walker, interview with Justine Toms and Michael Toms, 1996, in *The World Has Changed*, ed. Rudolph P. Byrd, 167.

212   **"that didn't sound"**: Walker, "A Writer Because of, Not in Spite of, Her Children" (1976), in *In Search of Our Mothers' Gardens*, 66.

212   **"She does not"**: Alexis De Veaux, "Alice Walker," *Essence*, September 1989, 57.

213   **"could charm"**: White, *Alice Walker*, 40.

213   **"made of some"**: Ibid., 319.

213   **"dared not complain"**: Walker, *The Way Forward Is with a Broken Heart*, 28.

214   **"You just need"**: Walker, interview with Margo Jefferson (2005), in Walker, *The World Has Changed*, 240.

214   **"I used to"**: De Veaux, "Alice Walker," 58.

214   **"rarely saw"**: Walker, "Looking to the Side, and Back" (1979), in *In Search*, 314.

215   **"She . . . holds my face"**: "Beauty" (1983), in *In Search*, 392–93.

215   **In response, over a thousand:** "Finding Aid for University of Georgia Integration Materials 1938–1965," Hargrett Rare Book & Manuscript Library, University of Georgia Libraries, www.libs.uga.edu/hargrett/archives/integration/integration1.html. In September 1962, when James Meredith attempted to integrate the University of Mississippi, three thousand white students and others rioted, killing two, a French journalist and a white bystander.

216 **"staid . . . dust":** Edelman, "Who Mentored Marian Wright Edelman," in *The Person Who Changed My Life: Prominent Americans Recall Their Mentors*, ed. Matilda Raffa Cuomo (Secaucus, NJ: Carol, 1999), https://sites.sph.harvard.edu/wmy/marian-wright-edelman/.

217 **"Perhaps this was":** Walker, "Saying Goodbye to My Friend Howard Zinn," *Boston Globe*, January 31, 2010.

217 **"limitation on":** Walker, "What Nurtured My Outrage, Really?" in *Howard Zinn's Southern Diary: Sit-ins, Civil Rights, and Black Women's Student Activism*, ed. Robert Cohen (Athens: University of Georgia Press, 2018).

217 **"I shall write":** White, *Alice Walker*, 80.

218 **"The whole town":** Ibid., 82.

218 **"freedom to":** Walker, "Duties of the Black Revolutionary Artist" (1970), in *In Search*, 130.

218 **Her eldest sister . . . marriage:** White, *Alice Walker*, 114–15.

218 **"it was":** Ibid., 112.

219 **"all the marks":** Walker, "The Abortion," in *Complete Stories* (London: Women's Press, 1994), 193.

219 **"I have fought":** Walker, "The Civil Rights Movement: What Good Was It?" (1967), in *In Search*, 125.

220 **"I was smitten":** White, *Alice Walker*, 144.

220 **"the biggest glow":** Walker, *Way Forward*, 16.

220 **interracial marriage:** A few months later, on June 12, 1967, in *Loving v. Virginia*, the Supreme Court invalidated interracial-marriage bans in sixteen states. Georgia's law was repealed in 1972, Mississippi's not until 1987.

220 **Mel's mother said:** White, *Alice Walker*, 156.

220 **"The first two":** Walker, "Recording the Seasons" (1976), in *In Search*, 224.

220 **Margaret Walker:** The author of the acclaimed poetry collection *For My People* (1942), Walker (no relation) was herself trying to write while teaching full-time and raising four children. Between her first book and her second, the historical novel *Jubilee* (1966), was a twenty-four-year silence. She once said, "People ask me how I find time to write with a family and a teaching job. I don't." Olsen, *Silences*, 209.

221 **"as if the last":** White, *Alice Walker*, 165.

221 **"I did not":** Walker, "Coretta King: Revisited" (1971), in *in Search*, 148.

221 **"When I didn't":** Walker, "*One* Child of One's Own: A Meaningful Digression within the Work(s)" (1979), in *In Search*, 369.

222 **"I feared being":** Ibid., 363.

222 **When she was . . . sole:** White, *Alice Walker*, 172.

223 **"The first":** Walker, *Grange Copeland*, 101.

223 **"her big belly":** Ibid., 147.

223 **"thaw the numbness":** Ibid., 233.

224 **"screaming in":** Rebecca Walker, *Black, White, and Jewish: Autobiography of a Shifting Self*, 12.

224 **"chilly and abrupt":** Walker, *Way Forward*, 34.

224 **"an old acquaintance":** Ibid., 34.

224 **"Curled around":** Walker, "One Child," 369.

224 **"I loved":** *Alice Walker: Beauty in Truth*, directed by Pratibha Parmar, 2013.

224 **"to slay":** Walker, *Way Forward*, 28.

225 **"solitary confinement":** Ibid., 36.

225 **"More than I"**: Ibid., 28.

225 **"the old conflict"**: Ibid.

225 **"badly arranged"**: Walker, "One Child," 362.

226 **The title of the essay:** Fellow writers have themselves pushed back against Walker's one-child manifesto. Among others, Zadie Smith, Jane Smiley, Aimee Phan, and Ayelet Waldman have argued that support is the issue, not number of children. Smith observes that the fundamental limit to maternal autonomy is "time, which is the same problem whether you are a writer, factory worker, or nurse." Alison Flood, "Zadie Smith Criticises . . . Author Who Says More Than One Child Limits Career," *Guardian*, June 13, 2013.

226 **"For me, there has"**: Walker, "One Child," 362.

226 **"We are together"**: Ibid., 382.

227 **"I never knew"**: Walker, "Looking to the Side, and Back" (1979), in *In Search*, 318.

227 **"often felt like"**: Lorde, "Learning from the 60s" (1982), in *Sister Outsider*, 137.

227 **"putting down"**: White, *Alice Walker*, 194.

227 **Giovanni wounded Alice:** Ibid., 198.

227 **"I had a huge . . . ordinary dress"**: Ibid., 200.

228 **"no person is"**: Walker, "A Talk: Convocation 1972," in *In Search*, 36.

228 **Change doesn't take time:** paraphrasing Mary Kay Blakely, *American Mom: Motherhood, Politics, and Humble Pie* (New York: Pocket, 1995), 6.

228 **"worn out"**: Walker, interview with Evelyn C. White, in *Way Forward*.

228 **"I would not"**: Lessing, *Under My Skin*, 265.

228 **"I know, however"**: White, *Alice Walker*, 218.

229 **"It was as if"**: Ibid., 270.

229 **"refusing . . . go unheard"**: Rich, National Book Award Acceptance Speech, National Book Foundation, https://www.nationalbook.org/nbaacceptspeech_arich_74.html#.WUMX09xLfIU (removed from site as of July 24, 2021).

229 **"To this day"**: Walker, "Audre's Voice," in Audre Lorde, *I Am Your Sister*, 238.

230 **"how many of us"**: Morrison, "A Knowing So Deep" (1985), in *What Moves at the Margin*, ed. Carolyn C. Denard (Jackson: University Press of Mississippi, 2008), 31–33.

230 **"Caring for myself"**: Lorde, *A Burst of Light*, 130.

231 **"shatter"**: Walker, *Meridian*, 51.

231 **"the horror . . . meant"**: Ibid., 97.

231 **"worthy of this"**: Ibid., 91.

231 **"Burn 'em out"**: Ibid., 115.

231 **"Her side?"**: Ibid., 139–40.

232 **"the respect she owed"**: Ibid., 200.

232 **"Frankly, I"**: White, *Alice Walker*, 278.

233 **"There should be"**: Rebecca Walker, *Black, White, and Jewish*, 64.

233 **"I felt proud"**: White, *Alice Walker*, 296.

233 **more like siblings:** Walker, *Black, White, and Jewish*, 231.

233 **"I feel strong"**: Ibid., 231.

233 **"as inconsistently"**: Parker, *Mother Love, Mother Hate: The Power of Maternal Ambivalence*, 244.

233 **"I put pressure"**: De Veaux, "Alice Walker," 122.

233 **"Our intention . . . love"**: White, *Alice Walker*, 296.

234 **"fragmented"**: Ibid.

234   **"blocking"**: Mel Leventhal, in *Alice Walker: Beauty in Truth*.

234   **"My parents"**: Walker, *Black, White, and Jewish*, 4–5.

235   **"Rebecca gave"**: Walker, "Writing *The Color Purple*" (1982), in *In Search*, 359.

235   **"It is . . . point"**: White, *Alice Walker*, 350.

235   **"with her beauty"**: Walker, *The Same River Twice: Honoring the Difficult* (New York: Scribner, 1996), 156.

236   **"drew battle lines"**: De Veaux, "Alice Walker," 58.

236   **"It was said"**: Walker, *Same River Twice*, 22.

236   **"the strong one"**: Ibid., 30.

236   **"complicated . . . starve"**: Ibid., 27.

237   **"amazing"**: Le Guin, review in *San Francisco Review of Books*, quoted in White, *Alice Walker*, 447.

237   **"Can I survive"**: Rebecca Walker, *Baby Love*, 5–6.

237   **"the first club"**: Walker, *Baby Love*, 94.

237   **"The idea of my"**: Sharon Krum, "'Can I Survive Having a Baby? Will I Lose Myself . . . ?'," *Guardian*, May 26, 2007.

237   **"final and dramatic"**: Walker, *Baby Love*, 6.

237   **"joined me to . . . *now*"**: Walker, "One Child," 369.

THE BABY ON THE WRITING DESK

239   **"A change in"**: Lessing, *A Small Personal Voice: Essays, Reviews, Interviews* (New York: Vintage, 1975), 115.

239   **"To destroy"**: Rich, *Of Woman Born*, 286.

239   **"We don't feed"**: Sage, *Bad Blood*, 264.

239   **"caught up in"**: Ibid., 269.

239   **"fueled my conviction"**: Ibid.

240   **"It was a lot . . . fight back"**: Ibid., 265–66.

240   **"I truly would"**: Byatt, "The Art of Fiction No. 168," interview by Philip Hensher, *Paris Review*, no. 159 (Fall 2001).

240   **"not to get stuck"**: Marianne Brace, "That Thinking Feeling," *Guardian*, June 9, 1996.

240   **"The first baby . . . at once"**: Byatt, interview with JP, November 2016.

241   **"a writer"**: Walker, *In Search of Our Mothers' Gardens*, 66.

242   **"After he died"**: Byatt, "The July Ghost," in *Sugar and Other Stories* (New York: Penguin, 1988), 47.

243   **"very much in [my]"**: Emine Saner, "Lorna Sage, My Mum," *Guardian*, October 8, 2010.

ANGELA CARTER

Edmund Gordon's biography, *The Invention of Angela Carter*, was invaluable. Quotes from Angela Carter's journals and correspondence are from the Angela Carter Papers, British Library Manuscript Collections.

245   **"All times"**: Le Guin, foreword (2001) to *Tales from Earthsea*. *The Books of Earthsea: The Complete Illustrated Edition* (New York: Saga Press, 2018), 558.

245 **"in the . . . own version"**: Sage, "Death of the Author," 236.

246 **"an accident"**: Carter, interview by Paul Bailey, *Third Ear*, BBC Radio 4, June 25, 1991, www.bbc.co.uk/archive/third-ear--angela-carter/zr4s7nb.

246 **one journalist . . . "common noun"**: Marc Chavannes, "Heimwee naar optimisme," *NRC Handelsblad* (Rotterdam), November 1, 1985.

246 **"The beauty of children"**: Carter, journal, November 7, 1985, Add. MS 88899/1/98.

247 **goats . . . sex:** "Stealing Is Bad Karma," BBC broadcast, February 13, 1970, BBC Written Archives Centre.

247 **"the saleslady"**: Carter to Pearce, September 23, 1980, Add. MS 88899/3/3.

247 **"You know I am"**: Carter to Pearce, n.d., September 1980, Add. MS 88899/3/3.

247 **"I am often"**: Carter to Pearce, October 22, 1980, Add. MS 88899/3/3.

248 **"was charged with"**: Moody, "Writers and Mentors," *Atlantic*, August 2005.

248 **"she could say"**: Coover, interview with JP, December 2011.

249 **"of course . . . hurried into it"**: Carter to Pearce, October 31, 1980, Add. MS 88899/3/3.

249 **"I will be a"**: Carter to Pearce, November 2, 1980, Add. MS 88899/3/3.

249 **"He came to help"**: Carter to Adcock, April 1976. (Courtesy of Fleur Adcock.)

249 **"caretaker"**: Carter to Susannah Clapp, October 16, 1980. (Courtesy of Susannah Clapp.)

249 **"From that time"**: Coover, interview with JP.

249 **"rootless"**: Sage, "Death of the Author," 240.

250 **"the wonderful"**: Carter, "The Mother Lode" (1976), in *Shaking a Leg*, 2.

250 **"predictable . . . proper"**: Carter, "Living in London—X," *London Magazine*, March 1971, 53.

250 **"the dream-time"**: Carter, "The Mother Lode," in *Shaking a Leg*, 14.

251 **"Age cannot wither"**: Ibid., 10.

251 **"watching the flora"**: Adcock, journal, May 27, 1973. (Courtesy of Fleur Adcock.)

251 **"women girlified"**: "Death of the Author," 238.

251 **"The fact that"**: Sage, "The Savage Sideshow," *New Review*, July 1977, 54.

251 **overprotective:** The unexplained gap of eleven years between Angela and her older brother suggests that Olive may have had trouble conceiving or lost a pregnancy, or more than one. If so, that might explain her feelings. Despite Angela's feud with Olive, she also felt valued by her mother. Thinking of a rose in a pot that her mother once gave her, Angela wrote that though she hadn't seen its worth at the time, it became a treasured memory. "I did not realize this rose tree was not a present for my tenth birthday, but for my grown self . . . a present like part of herself she did not know about that she could still give away to me." Carter, "The Mother Lode," in *Shaking a Leg*, 14–15.

252 **"I thought they . . . myself"**: Carter, "Sugar Daddy" (1983), in *Shaking a Leg*, 22.

252 **"a more or less conscious":** Carter, "Trouser Protest" (1975), in *Shaking a Leg*, 114.

252 **"Oh good, here comes"**: Edmund Gordon, *The Invention of Angela Carter*, 58.

252 **"like a cross"**: Ibid., 40.

253 **"kissing for . . . at hand"**: Ibid., 46.

253 **"one of my typical"**: Ibid., 48.

254 **menstruation:** Carter, "The Company of Wolves" (1979), in *Burning Your Boats*, 215.

254 **"If only"**: Gordon, *Invention*, 92.

254 **"To have lots"**: Carter, journal, March 5, 1963, Add. MS 88899/1/88.

254 **"like barely congealed"**: Carter, journal, October 30, 1961, Add. MS 88899/1/87.

255 **"an element"**: Carter, "Notes from the Front Line (1983), in *Shaking a Leg*, 38.

255 **"an odd mixture":** Gordon, *Invention*, 99.

255 **"I was always":** Carter, "Flesh and the Mirror" (1974), in *Burning Your Boats*, 69.

256 **"My lovely monster":** Carter, journal, November 5, 1961, Add. MS 88899/1/87.

256 **"Women's instinct":** Lessing, *Under My Skin*, 237.

256 **"desire . . . attention":** Carter, journal, n.d., Fall 1986, Add. MS 88899/1/98.

256 **"massive infantile . . . go home":** Carter, journal, November 12, 1961, Add. MS 88899/1/87.

256 **"Oh dear . . . me":** Gordon, *Invention*, 59.

257 **"As I try & grow":** Ibid., 116.

257 **"prim . . . kindness":** Carter, "Tokyo, Directed by Fellini," *The Nation*, January 25, 1971, 115.

258 **"the great":** Gordon, *Invention*, 139.

258 **never got over:** When I wrote to Paul Carter in 2011, asking to interview him, he responded with the email equivalent of slamming the door in my face, nor would he speak to Edmund Gordon, Carter's biographer. He died in 2012, apparently unreconciled to the last with Angela's memory.

258 **"Home is where":** Carter, "Living in London—X," 55.

258 **"interesting Freudian . . . me":** Gordon, *Invention*, 144.

259 **"Sustained by passion":** Ibid., 153.

259 **"so thin":** Carter, "Tokyo, Directed by Fellini," 116.

259 **"living in":** Carter, "A Souvenir of Japan" (1974), in *Burning Your Boats*, 31.

259 **"a painful":** Carter, "Notes from the Front Line" (1983), in *Shaking a Leg*, 39.

259 **"I had never . . . Glumdalclitch":** Carter, "A Souvenir of Japan," 31. Glumdalclitch is the Brobdingnagian child who cares for Gulliver in *Gulliver's Travels*, and who is "not above forty feet high, being little for her age."

259 **"our flesh":** Carter, *Sadeian Woman*, 9.

260 **"my own heroine":** Carter, "Flesh and the Mirror" (1974), in *Burning Your Boats*, 68.

260 **"created him":** Ibid., 72.

260 **"She knew she was":** Carter, "The Company of Wolves" (1979), in *Burning Your Boats*, 219.

261 **She stayed . . . disapprove:** Gordon, *Invention*, 193–94. Mansu Kō was the same age that Angela had been when she started dating twenty-seven-year-old Paul.

261 **"It really means":** Ibid., 207.

261 **"one of the few":** Ibid., 210.

262 **throwing a typewriter:** Ibid., 213–14.

262 **"ravaging":** Ibid., 268.

262 **"the loneliness":** Ibid., 216.

262 **"she relished":** Coover, interview with JP.

263 **"All the mythic . . . life":** Carter, *Sadeian Woman*, 5.

263 **"his appetite":** Carter, "The Tiger's Bride" (1979), in *Burning Your Boats*, 168.

264 **"extraordinary . . . true mystery":** Carter, journal, July 1974, Add. MS 88899/1/95.

265 **"When I recovered":** Carter, journal, n.d., 1974, Add. MS 88899/1/95.

265 **"It never occurred":** Adcock, interview with JP, July 2011.

265 **"style of appearing . . . go":** Downton, interview with JP, December 2011.

266 **"One has to work":** Carter, journal, n.d., 1974, Add. MS 88899/1/95.

266 **"whiff of sour . . . lost him":** Carter, journal, March–April 1982, Add. MS 88899/1/97.

266 **"It's uterine":** Adcock, interview with JP.

266 **"peeked round":** Downton, interview with JP.

267   **"A bit . . . undignified":** Carter, "Notes from a Maternity Ward" (1983), in *Shaking a Leg*, 29.

267   **"She pressed down . . . insides":** Sage, "Death of the Author," 252.

267   **"If she delivers":** Carter, "Notes from a Maternity Ward," 29.

268   **"more like that of":** Gordon, *Invention*, 343.

268   **"post-partural . . . event":** Carter, "Notes from a Maternity Ward," 31.

268   **"More like bondage":** Ibid., 30.

268   **"find *nothing*":** Clapp, *A Card from Angela Carter*, 90.

269   **"What do you . . . equal":** Adcock, interview with JP.

269   **"It seemed . . . did":** Weldon, interview with JP, February 2009.

269   **"Most women feel":** Atwood to JP, October 7, 2013. Judging by Atwood's novels such as *The Handmaid's Tale*, written after her daughter was born in 1976, for her it was a temporary condition, though in Atwood's 1988 novel *Cat's Eye* the narrator observes, "Because I am a mother, I am capable of being shocked; as I never was when I was not one." *Cat's Eye* (New York: Bantam, 1989), 333.

269   **"intense miserable":** Gordon, *Invention*, 360.

270   **"a journal of my":** Carter, journal, n.d., 1988, Add. MS 88899/1/98.

270   **Lessing, who helpfully:** Salman Rushdie, *Joseph Anton* (New York: Random House, 2012), 213.

270   **swearing:** Clapp, *A Card from Angela Carter*, 72.

270   **"fairy godmother":** Atwood, in Lorna Sage, "Angela Olive Carter," in *British Novelists since 1960*: *Third Series*, ed. Merritt Moseley (Detroit, MI: Gale Group), 1999.

270   **"a wolf in":** Ibid.

270   **"Mother is":** Carter, *Wise Children*, 223.

271   **"Truthfully, these glorious":** Ibid., 227.

TIME AND THE STORY

I'm grateful to Midori Snyder and Maria Tatar for their help in thinking about fairy tales and motherhood. My thoughts on time were inspired by (and in the case of *kairos* and *chronos*, borrowed from) *Enduring Time*, by Lisa Baraitser, in which she looks at relationships between time and care.

274   **"It's precisely":** Jones, *How I Became Hettie Jones*, 149.

274   **"small selfishnesses . . . to say":** Claire Dederer, "What Do We Do with the Art of Monstrous Men?," *Paris Review* (blog), November 20, 2017.

277   **"half-blind impostor self":** Steiber, "Brother and Sister: A Matter of Seeing," Journal of Mythic Arts, 2007, https://endicottstudio.typepad.com/articleslist/brother-and-sister-a-matter-of-seeing-by-ellen-steiber.html.

277   **"The Armless Maiden":** See Midori Snyder, "The Armless Maiden and the Hero's Journey," In the Labyrinth, n.d., midorisnyder.com/essays/the-armless-maiden-and-the-heros-journey.html.

Bibliography

Allara, Pamela. *Pictures of People: Alice Neel's Portrait Gallery*. Hanover, NH: Brandeis University Press, 1998.

Als, Hilton. *Alice Neel: Uptown*. [New York]: David Zwirner Books, 2017.

Baraitser, Lisa. *Enduring Time*. London: Bloomsbury Academic, 2017.

———. *Maternal Encounters: The Ethics of Interruption*. London: Routledge, 2009.

Barker, Christopher. *The Arms of the Infinite*. Waterloo, ON: Wilfrid Laurier University Press, 2010.

Bell-Scott, Patricia, Beverly Guy-Sheftall, Jacqueline Jones Royster, Janet Sims-Wood, Miriam DeCosta-Willis, and Lucie Fultz, eds. *Double Stitch: Black Women Write about Mothers and Daughters*. Boston: Beacon, 1991.

Brooks, Gwendolyn. *The Essential Gwendolyn Brooks*. Edited by Elizabeth Alexander. New York: Library of America, 2005.

———. *Maud Martha*. 1953. Chicago: Third World Press, 1993.

———. *Report from Part One*. Detroit: Broadside, 1972.

Calder, Jenni. *The Burning Glass: The Life of Naomi Mitchison*. Dingwall, Scotland: Sandstone Press, 2019.

Carter, Angela. *Burning Your Boats: The Collected Short Stories*. New York: Henry Holt, 1995.

———. *The Sadeian Woman: An Exercise in Cultural History*. London: Virago, 1979.

———. *Shaking a Leg: Collected Journalism and Writings*. New York: Penguin, 1998.

———. *Wise Children*. Boston: Little, Brown, 1991.

Cavarero, Adriana. *Relating Narratives: Storytelling and Selfhood*. Translated by Paul A. Kottman. London: Routledge, 2000.

Clapp, Susannah. *A Card from Angela Carter*. London: Bloomsbury, 2012.

Collins, Kathleen. *Notes from a Black Woman's Diary: Selected Works*. Edited by Nina Lorez Collins. New York: Ecco, 2019.

Collins, Patricia Hill. *Black Feminist Thought*. New York: Routledge, 2000.

Coss, Clare. "Frances Clayton: Remembering Our Friend and Chosen Family." *Sinister Wisdom* 122, Fall 2021.

Curry, Arwen, dir. *The Worlds of Ursula K. Le Guin*. 2018.

Cusk, Rachel. *A Life's Work: On Becoming a Mother*. London: Fourth Estate, 2001.

Davey, Moyra, ed. *The Mother Reader: Essential Writings on Motherhood*. New York: Seven Stories, 2001.

De Veaux, Alexis. *Warrior Poet: A Biography of Audre Lorde*. New York: W. W. Norton. 2004.

di Prima, Diane. *Recollections of My Life as a Woman*. New York: Viking, 2001.

Diski, Jenny. *In Gratitude*. London: Bloomsbury, 2016.

———. *Skating to Antarctica*. London: Granta Books, 1998.

Echlin, Kim. *Elizabeth Smart: A Fugue Essay on Women and Creativity.* Toronto: Women's Press, 2004.

Enright, Anne. *Making Babies.* New York: W. W. Norton, 2012.

Erdrich, Louise. *The Blue Jay's Dance: A Birth Year.* London: Flamingo, 1996.

Feigel, Lara. *Free Woman: Life, Liberation and Doris Lessing.* London: Bloomsbury, 2018.

Fowler, Karen Joy. "The Motherhood Statement." In *The Science of Herself*, 27–34. Oakland, CA: PM Press, 2013.

Gordon, Edmund. *The Invention of Angela Carter.* London: Chatto & Windus, 2016.

Gumbs, Alexis Pauline. *"We Can Learn to Mother Ourselves": The Queer Survival of Black Femi-nism, 1968–1996.* PhD diss, Duke University, 2010; see https://dukespace.lib.duke.edu/dspace/handle/10161/2398.

Gumbs, Alexis Pauline, China Martens, and Mai'a Williams, eds. *Revolutionary Mothering: Love on the Front Lines.* Oakland, CA: PM Press, 2016.

Hall, Joan Wylie. *Conversations with Audre Lorde.* Jackson: University Press of Mississippi, 2004.

Hall, Lesley A. *Naomi Mitchison: A Profile of Her Life and Work.* Seattle: Aqueduct Press, 2007.

Hills, Patricia. *Alice Neel.* New York: Abrams, 1983.

Hirsch, Marianne. *The Mother-Daughter Plot: Narrative, Psychoanalysis, Feminism.* Bloomington: Indiana University Press, 1989.

Hoban, Phoebe. *Alice Neel: The Art of Not Sitting Pretty.* New York: St. Martin's, 2010.

Jackson, Angela. *A Surprised Queenhood in the New Black Sun: The Life and Legacy of Gwendolyn Brooks.* Boston: Beacon, 2017.

Jones, Hettie. *How I Became Hettie Jones.* New York: Dutton, 1990.

Klein, Carole. *Doris Lessing: A Biography.* London: Duckworth, 2000.

Kristeva, Julia. "Stabat Mater." Translated by Arthur Goldhammer. *Poetics Today* 6, no. 1/2 (1985): 133–52.

Lee, Hermione. *Penelope Fitzgerald: A Life.* New York: Knopf, 2014.

Le Guin, Ursula K. *Dancing at the Edge of the World.* New York: Harper Perennial, 1990.

———. *The Wave in the Mind: Talks and Essays on the Writer, the Reader, and the Imagination.* Boston: Shambhala, 2004.

Lessing, Doris. *Alfred and Emily.* London, Harper Perennial, 2009.

———. *The Golden Notebook.* 1962. New York: Harper Perennial, 1994.

———. *A Proper Marriage.* 1954. Frogmore, UK: Panther, 1966.

———. *Under My Skin: Volume One of My Autobiography, to 1949.* New York: HarperCollins, 1994.

———. *Walking in the Shade: Volume Two of My Autobiography, 1949 to 1962.* New York: Harper Perennial, 1998.

Lorde, Audre. *A Burst of Light: Essays.* 1988. Mineola, NY: Ixia, 2017.

———. *The Collected Poems of Audre Lorde.* New York: W. W. Norton, 1997.

———. *I Am Your Sister: Collected and Unpublished Writings.* Edited by Rudolph P. Byrd, Johnetta Betsch Cole, and Beverly Guy-Sheftall. New York: Oxford, 2009.

———. *"I Teach Myself in Outline": Notes, Journals, Syllabi, and an Excerpt from* Deotha. Edited by Miriam Atkin and Iemanjá Brown. CUNY Center for the Humanities, *Lost & Found* series 7, no. 1 (Fall 2017), Manifold.

———. *Sister Outsider: Essays and Speeches.* 1984. Berkeley, CA: Crossing Press, 2007.

———. *Zami: A New Spelling of My Name.* Berkeley, CA: Crossing Press, 1982.

Manguso, Sarah. *Ongoingness.* 2015. London: Picador, 2018.

Mitchison, Naomi. *You May Well Ask: A Memoir 1920–1940.* 1979. London: Flamingo, 1986.

Moser, Benjamin. *Sontag: Her Life and Work.* New York: Ecco, 2019.

Munro, Eleanor. *Originals: American Women Artists.* New York: Simon and Schuster, 1979.

Nash, Jennifer C. "Black Maternal Aesthetics." *Theory & Event* 22, no. 3 (July 2019): 551–75.

Neel, Andrew, dir. *Alice Neel.* 2007.

Nelson, Maggie. *The Argonauts.* Minneapolis: Graywolf, 2015.

Nemser, Cindy. *Art Talk: Conversations with 12 Women Artists.* New York: Scribner, 1975.

Nunez, Sigrid. *Sempre Susan: A Memoir of Susan Sontag.* New York: Atlas, 2011.

Parker, Rozsika. *Mother Love, Mother Hate: The Power of Maternal Ambivalence.* New York: Basic Books, 1996.

Parmar, Pratibha, dir. *Alice Walker: Beauty in Truth.* Kali Films, 2013.

Rich, Adrienne. *Of Woman Born: Motherhood as Experience and Institution.* New York: Bantam, 1977.

———. *On Lies, Secrets, and Silence: Selected Prose.* New York: W. W. Norton, 1979.

Ringgold, Faith. *We Flew over the Bridge: The Memoirs of Faith Ringgold.* Boston: Bulfinch, 1995.

Ruhl, Sarah. *100 Essays I Don't Have Time to Write.* New York: Farrar, Straus & Giroux, 2014.

Sage, Lorna. *Bad Blood.* London: Fourth Estate, 2000.

———. "Death of the Author." *Granta* 41 (Autumn 1992): 235–54.

———. *Doris Lessing.* London: Methuen, 1983.

Showalter, Elaine. *A Jury of Her Peers: American Women Writers from Anne Bradstreet to Annie Proulx.* New York: Vintage, 2010.

Smart, Elizabeth. *The Assumption of the Rogues & Rascals.* London: Panther, 1980.

———. *Autobiographies.* Edited by Christina Burridge. Vancouver, BC: Tanks, 1987.

———. *By Grand Central Station I Sat Down and Wept.* 1945. London: Granada, 1966.

Solomon, Andrew. "Transition to Motherhood: The Acquisition of Maternal Identity and Its Role in a Mother's Attachment." PhD diss., Jesus College, Oxford, 2013. Courtesy of the author.

Sontag, Susan. *As Consciousness Is Harnessed to Flesh: Journals and Notebooks 1964–1980.* Edited by David Rieff. New York: Farrar, Straus & Giroux, 2012.

———. *Reborn: Journals and Notebooks 1947–1963.* Edited by David Rieff. New York: Farrar, Straus & Giroux, 2008.

Streitmatter, Rodger. *Outlaw Marriages: The Hidden Histories of Fifteen Extraordinary Same-Sex Couples.* Boston: Beacon, 2012.

Sullivan, Rosemary. *By Heart: Elizabeth Smart, A Life.* London: Lime Tree, 1991.

Walker, Alice. *Her Blue Body Everything We Know: Earthling Poems 1965–1990 Complete.* London: Women's Press, 1991.

———. *In Search of Our Mothers' Gardens.* London: Women's Press, 1984.

———. *Meridian.* New York: Pocket, 1977.

———. "*One* Child of One's Own: A Meaningful Digression within the Work(s)." (1979). In *In Search of Our Mothers' Gardens,* 361–83. London: Women's Press, 1984.

———. *The Same River Twice: Honoring the Difficult.* New York: Scribner, 1996.

———. *The Third Life of Grange Copeland.* 1970. London: Women's Press, 1985.

———. *The Way Forward Is with a Broken Heart.* New York: Ballantine, 2001.

———. *The World Has Changed: Conversations with Alice Walker.* Edited by Rudolph P. Byrd. New York: New Press, 2010.

Walker, Rebecca. *Baby Love: Choosing Motherhood after a Lifetime of Ambivalence.* New York: Riverhead, 2007.

———. *Black, White & Jewish: Autobiography of a Shifting Self.* New York: Riverhead, 2001.

Washington, Mary Helen. *Invented Lives: Narratives of Black Women 1860–1960.* London: Virago, 1989.

White, Evelyn C. *Alice Walker: A Life.* New York: W. W. Norton, 2004.

Text Credits

Illustration Credits

26 Courtesy The Estate of Alice Neel and David Zwirner. © The Estate of Alice Neel. Photo by Sam Brody.

72 Doris Lessing Archive, British Archive for Contemporary Writing (BACW), University of East Anglia.

102 Courtesy of Georgina Barker.

120 Courtesy of the Le Guin Estate.

164 Courtesy of Clare Coss and Blanche Wiesen Cook.

194 Photo by Bill Meurer/NY Daily News via Getty Images.

210 Photo by DwightCarter.com.

244 Photo by Liam White / Alamy Stock Photo.